DREAMING THE COUNCIL WAYS

DREAMING
THE COUNCIL
WAYS

True Native Teachings from the Red Lodge

OHKY SIMINE FOREST

SAMUEL WEISER, INC.
YORK BEACH, MAINE

First published in 2000 by
Samuel Weiser, Inc.
Box 612
York Beach, Maine 03910-0612
www.weiserbooks.com

Library of Congress Cataloging-in-Publication Data

Forest, Ohky Simine.
    Dreaming the council ways : true native teachings from the
red lodge / Ohky Simine Forest.
        p. cm.
    Includes bibliographical references and index.
    ISBN 0-57863-132-7 (pbk. : alk. paper)
    1. Spiritual life. 2. Indians—Religion—Miscellanea. I. Title.
BL624.F662 2000
299'.7—dc21   99-058151
                                          CIP

EB
Cover and text design by Kathryn Sky-Peck
Typeset in 10/13 Berthold Garamond
Cover and interior art by Ohky Simine Forest

PRINTED IN THE UNITED STATES OF AMERICA

06 05 04 03 02 01 00
7 6 5 4 3 2 1

To a Rainbow Warrior,
Star Brother of the Red People,
who, in the most impacting Dream of my Life,
has planted the seed of his pressing signal,
compelling me to pull all these words together.

CONTENTS

PART ONE
THE SACRED QUEST OF THE TRUE HUMANS

ILLUSTRATIONS

ACKNOWLEDGMENTS

I would like to give my deepest gratitude to all the people who always appeared at the right time and at each of the important steps of the creation of my book. Without them, this birthing would have been truly difficult. My wholehearted thanks to:

Brian Arthur, Irish economist. His valuable insights on my first draft in English allowed me to re-write important parts in such a way that a western mind could more easily bridge with the teachings of this Red Lodge;

Benjamin Yeomans. He appeared out of the blue sky, traveling to Chiapas in search of his spirit. He happened to stay a few months with us, just the time needed for him to pre-edit my manuscript in English. As English is not my maternal language, he helped me with the corrections of many sentences;

Jan Willem de Wetering, author of spiritual detective books and *The Empty Mirror*. He generously offered to help find a publisher from his far corner of the U.S. To access the American world of publishers was a most difficult task for me;

Jose Stevens, author of shamanic studies. His reputation made the name of Samuel Weiser a wonderful reality in my life;

The great companion of my life, Eliberto M. Jimenez, Maya artist and medicine healer. His devoted attentiveness, his most spiritual listening during the writing phase, and his eye and hand during the elaboration of my illustrations were always beside me;

My Wolf father, Louis F. Forest, a retired textbook editor. His dedicated presence, his grounded experience, and at times, his words of wise patience helped me stay on the wolf track, especially during the last cycle, understanding the unknown and exacting phase of the editors' final work.

To all these "Angels" sent to me by the Powers, may the Great Spirit always bless their paths.

And to the Meadowsweet Council of Maine, I wish to give my heartfelt gratitude for their spiritual support and well-sounded drumming.

INTRODUCTION

~~~~

A Moon in each breast was given by the Gods to the women mothers so they may feed their Dreams to the True Men and True Women. In them come the history and the memory, without them death and forgetfulness will appear. She is the Earth, our great Mother of two breasts, so men and women can learn to dream. Learning to dream, they learn to grow tall, to become dignified and they learn to fight. For this, when the True Men and the True Women say, "We will learn to dream," they say to others and to themselves, "We will fight."[1]

I can only initiate this book by acknowledging my mysterious journey, the path that led me to my sacred vision. I can only embark on this voyage with you along these pages, as days blowing and whispering the strong wind of the past, by recalling and rediscovering my Red path. Here I am, sitting in my round medicine center, with a fire burning in the middle, looking over the enigmatic mist rising from the skirt of the ancient, extinguished volcano that inspired the final journey to this book. I am writing from the mountains of Chiapas, Mexico, where I have been living since 1985. My pen here is my talking stick. Please receive my talk as my truth and my integrity—as my life.

These pages—old birch bark relating ancient memories; these words—tiny signs of mystery beyond myself. My voice is the voice of those who have shed blood to preserve their infinite knowledge in the time of the great conquests. This is the reminiscence of their journey, a journey that became mine, a pilgrimage to retrace their remembrance. My Mohawk ancestors are calling through my blood. They are guiding me through the resonance of these words. I am the voice of my ancestors and, with their permission, I will speak of their love for

---

[1] Marcos, "The History of Dreams," *Tiempo* (San Cristobal de las Casas, Chiapas, Mexico), 2 January 1996, p. 5.

life. I will voice the dreams with which they have imbued my nights. It seems eons ago that they impregnated me with the seed of their devotion and their knowledge. I became pregnant with this book in March 1996, with the powerful compulsion to write it down at last, in reverence for their vision. This long gestation is now over. It is time to deliver their wondrous wisdom and impart their message.

Although in this life I was "born" twice, this journey originated the day I came out of my mother's womb and entered this universe of sense and matter. On that day, everyone was celebrating Canadian Thanksgiving, the first Sunday of Indian Summer of that year, October 13th. It was a bright, sunny, and warm day after weeks of rain in this Great North of my forefathers. Nevertheless, the path to take full responsibility for the sacred purpose with which I was "imprinted" at birth was revealed to me when I died and was reborn one morning in 1985. It was then that I awakened to a clear inner knowledge of this sacred vision, which was apparently unveiled in my conscience in this little interval of time between death and return to Life. That morning I left behind what was, by then, an old wandering skin. I knew exactly, for the first time, for what reason I had come here. Since then, I have done nothing but quest for the warrioress that lives in my chest. Born to a new reality two years before the Harmonic Convergence (August 1987), I knew the path before me. That very morning led me to Mexico and guided me to the profundity of this vision. There, I met my Maya companion who stood waiting for me at the corner of my life. Together now, we unravel both ends of the sacred staff of our mutual vision.

At this point, you might ask me: "But what is your vision?" For the occidental mind, a vision must be something definite, systematic, and rational—something you can describe in a single paragraph or a brief outline. For us, for those who carry the Red heart, a sacred vision is that of which we are created—our original spirit flesh. A vision manifests as fire and thunderclaps in our being, revealing the existence of a superior power. A sacred vision is mysterious in essence, unknowable to the mind at first, unattainable by the reason, but, nevertheless, authentically infinite and real for the soul. It is a striking flash of essence made true in spirit, with sounds, colors, and signs from the external world reflecting the Great Spirit's design for us. Being and becoming one fragment of the great lost dream of the universe, a vision expands in ways that are often amazing, yet not surprising for the eyes that witness it. A vision unfolds unexpectedly, at times, as we "kill our vision" into this reality to make it come true.

This book is my genuine canoe to illustrate this sacred vision. This gratifying voyage was initiated the day I opened my tiny eyes to see this world of inconceivable mystery. What I glimpsed then will forever be impressed upon my perception of the world.

When I was a very young baby a fireball struck a huge centenary oak by our house in the dead of the night. My mother was watching the scene with me in her arms. We looked together through the window at the mightiest electric storm she had ever seen. She told me later that her intention had been for me to watch this tremendous storm so I would not grow fearful of lightning. A sacred fireball falling from the sky flashed with great power, cleaving the ancient oak in two. One half fell on our roof, the other half stood straight. I do not remember this consciously for I was just a baby, but during my entire childhood, I dreamed this scene at least once a week. This went on for ten years, until I finally asked my mother what the significance of this obsessive dream was.

In my adolescence, after many attempts to psychoanalyze this impressive happening in my early life, I just gave up. Later, the answer came from one of my medicine teachers. I learned then that fireballs are not simple current manifestations of the lightning. I was told that the thunder beings had appointed me to meet with them in this lifetime. From this shaman's perspective, the tree falling on our roof was a signal that someone chosen by the Great Powers was in this house. The Mongol medicine shaman, whom I met in my adolescence, was the first teacher to take me under his wing, to guide me. Very significantly, his name meant "power of thunder" in his own native language. The day I met Power of Thunder, we both knew that the meeting was significant. It was my "day of fate." That rendezvous had been prearranged a long time ago, somewhere in the mysterious plane in which we live. It became clear that what had led me to this meeting to align my true consciousness and spirit had been preordained from this first significant happening in my infancy and, probably, even from before birth.

In my childhood, I was sent to a French Canadian catholic school. This was a torment for me at times. I knew I was so distinct from the other students. Although outwardly I often was the leader of my classes, I was unable to adapt inwardly. It was apparently also difficult for the white girls to understand me. By nature, we natives are a quiet people. We have a great need to retreat into ourselves, a need for times of silence. I wished simply to be accepted the way I was. This was not always possible. I observed the ways in which some little girls competed with each other. Many of their pretenses and their cheating unfortunately came from the culture of their parents. I was often bored and reacted or acted so differently from my class-mates, constantly seeking to help those who were less talented, poor-er, or downtrodden. I grew up with an inner knowing that I would never be able to adapt to the Western world. My heart was different. But as the years went by, I became immersed in the predominant white culture. In my teens, I fell into the trap of denial that many col-ored people have experienced. I felt shame for the color of my skin, wishing to be born blond and a man. It would have made life so much simpler!

In the midst of this terrible refusal to accept who I was, however, there were ancient voices that would not leave me in peace. In those days of my adolescence, I dreamed almost every week of ancient drums thundering and resonating in my ears. They awakened me, sweating, from these dreams. I was discovering then that there was something greater out there in the great mystery, something that whis-pered so loudly in my ears that I was becoming deaf and dead, spiral-ing outward from my true roots. My ancestors were urging to me not to forget, and inspiring me to recall. It is then that I was unlocked into trusting that my path was guided by powerful forces beyond me—the ancient drumming of my ancestors. I knew that they had made pow-erful ceremonies in the last centuries, so that the next seven genera-tions, their children would never forget, even in times of great confu-sion. And, admittedly, I was confused.

At this point, the painful but rewarding journey to my hidden roots began, mostly as an instinctual journey. The spirits were always arranging for me to meet the people who would instruct me, and give me at every step, the spiritual food for which my restless soul cried out. The universe was definitively training me.

During this time, many of the initiations and teachings in this book were given to me by medicine healers of various traditions. Some I received on the physical plane, others in dreams. All were confirmed by great signs or by my spiritual teachers, who were primarily of the Bird Tribe entity. And, one day, after years of preparation, my medicine guides sent me out to fulfill my path. Then, alone, I died and, alone, I was reborn.

In these long nights of my youth, my ancestors were crying into my blood and bones. Although they are still crying for a hundred years of desecration of Etonoha, the Earth mother, they are also rejoicing as they witness the changes of these times and their return. Now, they request that I share the seeds of their dreams with you. For I know I am they. I was there when they flourished tall on this great continent. I truly remember. Their spirit is back. They wish to help Indian and Western people to heal. They have no shame, no anger, only an infinite love. These are the times. Because the White people are to be healed, to be shaken free, they are not our enemies. Their race may agonize spiritually, suffering because of their ancestors' imbalances. Ourselves, we have suffered from the terrible ignorance they have imposed on Mother Earth. But now, we are emerging again.

The deep misunderstanding toward natives from which I have so often suffered in my very core has inspired me to reaffirm the "Indian blood" within me. It has been a great motivating force to dedicate my life to helping natives and the White people, bridging this abysmal breach between two opposite ways of being. Our ancient ways of being come from the Earth. They are the very core of her teaching. The soft, yet powerful, sacred voices of my forefathers and foremothers speak of the ancient ways of the Council, how they have been lost and forsaken by the predominant cultures.

I cannot stay silent. My blood is ignited by their presence, by the Mohawk inheritance that I received predominantly from my father, as well as from the mixed blood of my mother, whose parents were French and Mohawk. I carry this powerful Mohawk warrior blood from both sides. This has not let me live in peace within the values of the Western world. I got lost there. At one point, my paternal grandmother broke her oath, denying her hereditary title of Mother's Chief of the Wolf Clan at Oka, Quebec (Kanasetake). She went away, lost all entitlement to her land and to her Indian rights. When I was young, I knew that I was from a lineage of chiefs, but didn't know exactly what it really meant. At one point in my intense seeking, I went back to the Iroquois traditional long house of Kahnawake (Caughnawaga), where

I was accepted into the Wolf clan of the Great League of Peace (Haudenosaunee), as part of them. It was imperative that I heal the lineage of seven mothers before me, who were crying for this woman who had broken the vow of chiefs by being ashamed of her native ways and heritage. I knew I had to renew this lost link for myself, for my father, and for these mothers.

Although, in these pages, I may discuss matriarchal societies and ancient Council ways at length, I do not represent in any way the Great Peace League of Iroquois Nations. I do not pretend to carry a title of clan chiefs or to be entrusted to talk directly for the Iroquois Confederacy. The experience of being accepted at the traditional long house before my canoe carried me to the Maya region will always be in my heart, and I will treasure this for the rest of my life. I know that the great binding law of peace of the Iroquois Confederacy (Gai Eneshah Go' Nah) is living innately through me. This is the greatest model for life—for all people to support themselves in harmony with the universe. I know that, in my blood, flourishes the great tree of peace, the ancient memory of the most perfect and oldest living participatory democracy practiced in community. This model goes beyond a simple idea of Utopia. In fact, it has been kept alive by the Iroquois people for over 800 years.

When I play the drum in my dreams, or walk, or teach, the Medicine Wheel ways come through me so powerfully, so immensely beyond any sense of myself, that I just cannot deny them a place within. I can only move with this spirit.

In 1988, an important spiritual book was published—*Return of the Bird Tribes*, by Ken Carey.[2] This book, which has impacted many people, was an accurate channeling announcing the return of a group of spiritual guides who have incarnated over the last centuries. These spiritual teachers came often among natives. They have also appeared as well-known spiritual beings throughout humanity's history: as White Buffalo Woman among American Indian tribes, as Kukulcan, the plumed serpent, among the Mayas, as Deganawidah, the great peace maker, among the Iroquois people, and as the Christ himself. These past incarnations of Bird Tribe souls always came with the clear

---

[2] Ken Carey, *Return of the Bird Tribes* (San Francisco: HarperSanFrancisco, 1991).

intent and mission to create true seeds of change among humans by bringing back the Medicine Wheel ways in one form or another. The Bird Tribe teachings also show a way to become the true humans, the real *Ongwhe Onwhe*. My book not only confirms their return, it shares their ancient and actual spiritual teachings, as told by my own medicine teachers, who are also living incarnations of the Bird Tribe entity as they revealed these to me.

Ongwhe Onwhe are Mohawk words that refer to the "true humans," the people true to reality. In the Maya Tzotzil language, the same concept is expressed as *Nichimal Vinik*, the flowering man, or the flowered people. This is the true vision that sustains every page of the teachings from my Bird Tribe guides who have inspired this path. This vast and awesome vision of becoming a true human will unfold with your learning through my words. It will lead you to understand every step on the spiritual journey to meet your inner warrior and to grow into an authentic *Ongwhe Onwhe*. I hope that my invitation will be received by many of you.

In the sharing of this journey, I have no more to say about me personally. I will leave room for these voices of ancient visions to come through me, hoping to be a perfect and humble vessel for the emergence of their power and beauty. My talk is me and I am their talk. This book is theirs. I am consumed by the task of bringing back their messages, emanating now from the sacred Earth. As a warrioress of life and death, I am, and will always be, in constant spiritual resistance against ignorance, striving to bring back the great laws of the Earth.

I can only sincerely hope that this book will be a path that the reader can walk with me. My original intent in writing this book is to reach reality and you—a reality beyond the separation and division that pervades the world today.

In these pages, filled with words of ancient ashes being rekindled to life, I am only a pathfinder in this vast hunting territory of spirit. I can only take you by the hand as your humble guide and show you how to hunt and share what our Red vision means, its awesome purpose. I can only guide you through the preeminent dangers and ambushes in this spiritual quest, to a place where the good game named spirit is. I can only tell you what a good spiritual stalker may or may not do. Whether or not you become a good vision hunter depends on you. I can only invite you to discover your own trails through my words, through my sharing of this ancient wisdom of ages, and to dream these words circling in this book.

I do not know if this should be called an introduction. In spirit, there is no such thing—nor any beginning, nor any end—only an infinite circular movement, which is the purpose of my talk. You must break the linear concept of time and stop seeing life in a dividing rational way. You cannot say that a circle starts here or there. Likewise, my circular way of writing and thinking reflects a song, a deep, ancient native chant that has its roots in the ancient medicine wheel.

In reality, the dance of this book does not commence here, but was initiated on a certain 13th of October, the day of my spiritual birth, and even earlier, in the spiraling silence of times. Each of the thirteen chapters presented here depicts my very path unfolding. They are dedicated to the thirteen Maya Upperworlds, to the Great Council of Thirteen Fires of the Iroquois Confederacy, to the thirteen medicine centers within—all teachings presented in this book. I will attempt to convey to you a synthesis of various ancient shamanic practices from three important ancient cultures into which I was initiated: the Maya, the Central Mongolian, and the Canadian Indian.

In my apprenticeship in these three physically distant cultures, I encountered many stunning reappearing spiritual teachings—similarities in their conception of the cosmos that translated into their arts of ancient healing and spirituality. I found some important parallel and cyclical universal teachings and prophecies that urge us to align truly to our human tree and showing us that we must see the mirrors within to reach beyond the self.

PART ONE

THE
SACRED QUEST
OF THE
TRUE HUMANS

"Before talking of holy things, we prepare ourselves by offerings . . . one will fill his pipe and hand it to the other who will light it and offer it to the sky and earth. . . . they will smoke together . . . . Then will they be ready to talk."

—Mato-Kuwapi, or Chased-By-Bears,
a Santee-Yanktonai Sioux

1
POWER

THE RED LODGE
BEYOND THE VEILS

Whenever you truly birth into the Red Lodge of my ancestors, you will discover a vision that one day will grow to be yours. It is a vision of the universe birthing and drumming in your heart, pounding steadily with your every thought and every movement of your soul. The Red Lodge is welcoming you to touch this incredible vision of life, encouraging you to walk the passage to merit this unforgetful glimpse of beauty. You, whoever you are, whatever the color of your skin. The true Red Lodge will always be a Rainbow Lodge in essence. You are all children of the Great Spirit and have received your own inherent gifts and these are the times to meet within the rainbow bridge of all the hoops of nations.

To meet on the rainbow pathway together, it is essential to understand what the ways of the Red Lodge are and the proper state of mind vitally needed to board this narrow canoe toward the true spirit. To encounter the teachings within the Red Lodge, you must first be conceived in the respective lodge of the color of your skin, to recognize and assume it in your flesh. On my path, I have felt, if not suffered, many misunderstandings toward our native blood. Therefore, I find it absolutely necessary, before we engage together in the road of this book, to express some of the pitfalls and the states of mind of which anyone interested in the Red ways must be aware. Many Western people are attracted to a journey into the Red Lodge. Many find themselves at home with native ways, for these teachings are rooted within universal and natural laws, grounded in a true understanding of spirit. The Red ways are not identified with dogma and theology, or with doctrines or religious practices that may only numb your fears. True native teaching from the three Americas is much more than a religion. It is a way of living, of being. It is a quest for true consciousness beyond any particular religious or philosophical system, a journey to your true self by the self, to the great vision of the real man and the true woman. In reality, the Red Lodge bestows the true seeker with a universal map on the canoe to spirit, and it is you who do the traveling, in nakedness and in truth.

These are the times foretold in native prophecies, when the first people of this continent will share their ways and encourage people to undertake the journey toward healing their own race. Assisting in the growth of the White Lodge is a powerful healing for natives after over

500 years of great silence. In the long night of our isolation, the European ancestors didn't want to hear our wisdom. They rejected our invitation to smoke the peace pipe with us and sit at the Wheel of Nations. Despite this, our talk has not changed, for the true Red Lodge will always be a lodge of inclusiveness.

Now more than ever, people of all colors are entering the Red Lodge with a genuine, yet often naïve, desire to uncover their spirit, to discover something purer and closer to their nature. Regrettably, many enter our Red Lodge with a distorted view of the world, inculcated by modern and post-modern society. Many are not aware of this. Hopefully, they are here to learn, as I am.

I have often shared my perception of the Western mind, in an attempt to help natives and non-natives reflect and, hopefully, to elucidate the controversy that surrounds these questions. Before starting this reflection, however, there are some distinctions to be considered about my use of the expression, the Western mind. The term, the Western mind, as I use it refers to a mind-set, to a pattern of mind translated into a way of being. It is not a racist attribution on my part. If I were a racist, I would not be pursuing the vision I was given—to humbly assist in healing the light skins, among others, and to share a way to deepen the Western culture that has adopted superficial and materialistic tendencies and diverged from the great values of a now-distant past.

It is important to understand, in entering into the Red Lodge, that every race and every color of people draws its essence primarily from a particular direction around the wheel (see figure 1, page 6). Also, every race of people is given some inherent lessons that are translated into the meeting and the confrontation of the particular wall of each direction. Generally speaking, Red people draw their essential particularity from the South, representing the blood of Earth and heart of the people. All natives inherently carry the gift of trust in spirit, the gift of feeling and connectedness to the heart of the Earth. If we tune into her, we can hear her solid and steady heartbeat translated as powerful emotions and very deep feelings, qualities belonging to the South. Black (African and Afro-American) people are born naturally in the West, carrying the gift of the Earth as well, driven by her powerful rhythm that they translate into their trance-music and their dances—an innate knowing of Earth's pace, qualities of the West. White people embody the gift of the

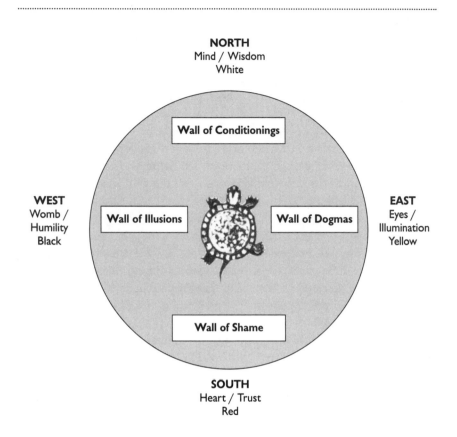

NORTH
Mind / Wisdom
White

WEST
Womb /
Humility
Black

EAST
Eyes /
Illumination
Yellow

Wall of Conditionings

Wall of Illusions

Wall of Dogmas

Wall of Shame

SOUTH
Heart / Trust
Red

Figure 1. Gifts and Walls of the Wheel of People.

North, the power of the great mind. If they cultivate their intelligence well, it is translated into an amazing, ingenious potential. Yellow people are represented in the East, place of the rising Sun, direction of contemplation and inward enlightenment, expressed through their ancient wisdom and meditative practices. Brown people (from India or the Middle East) bear both the gifts of the Red (South) and the Black (West). This does not mean that a Red person cannot be enlightened or a Black person ingenious. It refers rather to the primary gift that each race is naturally given by the cardinal direction.

For non-Indians to learn the teachings of the Red Lodge, therefore, means they must first understand the innate direction of their race. They must be willing to meet the inherent wall of their color, and then move into the light and perspective of Red people. The other prerequisite consists of being opened to perceiving what the Red Lodge is for the natives—for example, our ways of behaving, the spirit we feel is to be held in our Lodge, and so forth.

The first step in meeting us in our Red Lodge is thus to see through your own wall and only then, free from your own cultural conditionings, will you receive more fully and grasp our ancient wisdom. In order for Western cultures to see through the wall of their color, they must discern what is imprisoning them. More than once, I have come in contact with Western men and women, who, though sincere, do not fully understand what it means to participate in and be initiated into the Red wisdom—how to respect and integrate the teachings in a truly deep way. Many sincerely want to heal themselves, while others only seek refuge from something they want to elude in their own culture. What I have discerned more than once is that many have much difficulty grasping that their own mind-set, the way the Western mind thinks, is diametrically opposed to the ways of our collective mind. Often, our mind does not think, but rather "feels" first, allowing us to "see" things and spirits that others cannot. I have also noticed that many have entered the Red Lodge to release their ancestral guilt toward natives, an old blame being brought to the surface, felt deep within, about the pain their White forefathers inflicted upon natives. This is good to feel. It is a step toward a healing of the inherent wall of the White race.

In the incredible times in which we live, there are so many people of mixed blood. Most modern countries are so cosmopolitan that we cannot divide the world in two anymore. This was the reality of many natives in their youth, but not today. Yet still today, the daily reality of most natives includes a dominant White world with the Indian segregated from it. Within the social reality of the White Lodge, the Red people are discriminated against. Equal opportunities are not granted to them on many levels. On the other hand, the marginal conditions on the reservations have contributed, to a certain degree, to providing the opportunity for many natives to preserve their ancient spirituality as it was before the conquest.

Deplorably, we never divided the world in two in this way. It was divided for us. To us, the Western world always claimed to be superior, claimed its ways were better. Unfortunately, natives were thought of as a finished people, a dying people, part of what was called the Termination Time, even as recently as twenty or twenty-five years ago. Once considered a finished people, "unassimilable elements," the natives were then seen as harmless and good. (This can still be seen today in the potential of massive genocide that hangs over the 20,000 heads of Maya Zapatistas in Chiapas, Mexico). During the wars of the last centuries in the Americas, it was truly impossible to eradicate the first nations, because most tribes were, and are still, living in circles. The circle is a perfect form and is unbreakable. In the northern regions, by drawing squares called reservations around the hoop circles of the Red people, by isolating this proud race and forbidding the Indians to pray openly to their spirits, to talk their tongue, to hunt, to fish and even to plant corn, the White forefathers didn't know they were ensuring the preservation of much native knowledge and many native teachings. Inside these imposed fences, our teachings were kept intact in the obscure night of the Red old people in North America, more so than in the case of the other groups of natives made slaves and conquered by the Spaniards further south. When everything else was restricted, the only thing left for natives was the Red spirit, which couldn't be annihilated, for it was not tangible to the conquerors.

Because of these regrettable ruptures in native history, many spirits were apparently broken and many took refuge in alcohol on the most affected reservations. Fortunately, many reservations are now recovering from this illness. The reasons for native drinking differ greatly from those of other people. Indians drink to appease a deeper spiritual anguish, a remote remembrance of their ancestors crying into their bones. They don't drink with social and selfish intent, or to have fun at a party, or because a girlfriend has left, or for superficial reasons.

Many natives have grown up being ashamed of who they are. This remains a tangible reality within the Red Lodge. Because, we are so aware of power, lamentably, many natives came to understand that "power" was owned by those who ruled them, and no longer by the old traditions. Partly due to this, we became a "reserved people," despite our continued inner and outer revolts. By not being seen as we are, we suffered many injustices, and were forced into a corner called death. The Red nations, the original people, were the only ones in various places in the United States, until the 1980s, who were not allowed to play their drums or to exercise freedom of religion (this is still the case for the Native American church and their peyote ceremony). Until the 1980s, in some states, natives could go to jail for playing and chanting with their spirit drum. Yet all immigrants in this country were granted freedom of religion from the beginning of the century!

Before, everything belonged to the Red people, and our ancestors were ready to share with discernment and justice. The Iroquois people say, half laughing, that first the White people came and stole their land, then their rivers, then their women, and a few centuries ago, their constitution. At last they even stole the sky of the Iroquois and filled it with planes and elevated highways.

When you lean on the sacred Mother and bring your ear closer to her, you will hear the natives whispering in unison: We, the first nations, original people of this land, of the three Americas, we are back after this long nightmare and we wish to speak of our dignity and tell our truth, the one that the White forefathers have not heard. We may have been despised and forgotten, but we are here and have not sur-rendered. Now we are back, for our dead have always been alive. They are buried in this very Earth, they are everywhere around you in this great continent of Star Turtle. They are whispering now in your ears and awakening you.

Some old European values that were based on arrogance and fear of God, led to a culture of conquest, domination, slavery, and exploitation by those in positions of power. Some of these old values unfortunately have now led to an imperialistic Western way of being that has dominantly contributed to humanity's suicide and the extinction of all natural resources of the great Earth. Regrettably, the common people of many races, often brainwashed by the media, have adopted many of these destructive ways, because of the ignorance of not knowing a better way or through fear of the imposed system.

Because of these values, Western culture's totem of money has become the antithesis to spirit. In reality, for us, money is nothing more than a tool for trade among the people. It can become a spiritu-al tool, like any other object, if considered truly sacred. Whether we talk of exchanging corn, cacao, a blanket, a pair of moccasins, a piece of paper, or a plastic card that allows you to charge items, a trade must always be considered sacred. What counts in a native trade is not what we get, but the relation to spirit created with the person with whom you trade. The material value determined by the modern society is not important in such a trade. What becomes meaningful in the trade is this true value, not a relative price put on an object, determined by a mind locked up in materialism, caught in the fear of being cheated. It does not matter if we trade a pencil worth one dollar for a watch worth fifty, as long as each one has their heart fully in the trade. This is what counts in native trade. To blame the money system itself, however, is shortsighted. We must fight against the grasping tendencies that the Western mind-set has attached to the dollar sign—the mentality of always missing, the idea that in the name of money and competition, you can step upon your brother or betray a sacred friendship, or even kill someone. This mentality has grown to be the sickness and the plague of humanity.

This is not to imply that, in essence, the White people of the North are a greedy race. I am surely not saying this. Fortunately, there are good and spirited people everywhere on this great Earth, incarnated in every color of people, seeking health for humankind. But the entity of death and destruction infiltrated its way into the Caucasian race long ago. Once, this great White people stood powerful, rooted, and dignified. Regrettably, however, they lost touch with the Earth and her reality many centuries ago, losing their ancient ways that had been very similar to ours in many ways. This has created disastrous consequences for Westerners (and the natives they colonized). To the great distress of many people of all races, this evil has adopted the color "white" (probably to appear more pure!) and forced its own race to adopt this mind-set. Over time, it has reached many other cultures and races, in this way creating new kinds of people propagating this mentality and disease all over the planet.

Many light-skinned people are tired of hearing about old racial issues, and I can understand this, for I feel the same. I wish it were not still necessary to make these distinctions. My talk is surely not new, but the dichotomy between the intellectual acknowledgment of these ideas and their application in mindful behavior is often prevalent in many Westerners. It is therefore imperative to talk once more, hoping to reach the hearts and minds of those who are deaf to our truth. Some spiritual people have suggested to me that it is time to transcend any speech about races and reach the universality of the family of humans.

We are poised at the edge of a new era, and we are all humans first. We should, they say, enlarge our perception to consider everyone a part of a global humanity and drop speeches about races. I agree with this, as well. But for us, for people of color, this often appears to be disconnected talk, a senseless reflection with no roots.

"Those who do not know history are condemned to repeat it."[1] Many may reply that they know history, but their knowing may only remain an intellectual affirmation, as they continue to repeat old patterns in unconscious and insensitive ways in the little gestures of life. To be truly known, history must be experienced in our deep core in order that we may transcend it. There is no other way to reach a posthistoric civilization (as urged by some spiritual channelers). Of course, we are all humans, that is clear. But we can only transcend our human conditions and the reality we live by first assuming, in flesh and body, our inheritance, our conditions of life, and what is prescribed inherently in the culture we carry. If we say to a South African who has been struggling for years for the basic right of citizenship, or to the Zapatistas who have sent their call of *Ya Basta* to the world (meaning "enough" of death by hunger and disease in the post-historic dawn), if we say to them that we, humanity, must transcend any speech about racial issues, then our talk may appear terribly biased to these people and may even be taken as an offensive lack of common sense. It may suggest a definite insensitivity to their subreality. For Westerners, with their great gift of mind, developing a just awareness of how they express themselves must be weighted from all perspectives. For a colored person, the fight for survival will always be a battle first connected to the color of his or her skin, a battle seeking true avenues of change where possible. In the midst of their Western security and the "holy comfort" (to which we all want access), many privileged people may be unaware of this.

It may be an old theme, this theme of racial issues. But, as we are at the dawn of a new golden order, much of the pseudo-spiritual language of the New Agers still tries to transcend anything that is too painful, anything too earthly, anything that has to do with real social problems or wars, anything that has to do with our dealing directly with the human mud and meeting the true shadows of the world. Because

---

[1] George Santayana, *The Life of Reason*, vol. 1 (New York: Dover Publications, 1983).

true spirit must be the perfect balance of light and dark. It is easy to adopt a perception of spirituality disguised as supposed cosmic enlightenment. This often suggests unrootedness and disconnection from any real center of discernment or true cognition of spirit on Earth.

Many New Agers (often well-meaning, but seriously misguided) claim they have no need for any teachers, that everything is in books. They feel more at home taking bits and pieces from various ancient and modern spiritual practices. I am sorry for this mentality, as these people may never learn to confront themselves, and risk living endlessly in an illusion of spirituality. They may never know the joy of learning the true path to our spirit with a real guide, the joy of overcoming the obstacles involved in a true spiritual test. We are all so basically human, we just love to lie to ourselves and believe what we want. We can only become one with the path and uncover the true self after much hardship. Only a true teacher can point out the shadows we refuse to see. Only a true guide will impede us from escaping when we become bored with the teachings, for it is at this exact moment that we will really awaken and grow with the universal truth, ultimately maturing into our inner teacher after years of hard work. This indispensable merging into spirit cannot happen when someone is constantly shopping for books and workshops, moving from one spiritual tradition to another, and, with the first sign of boredom or discouragement, escaping to more exciting propositions. This state of constant spiritual arousal is contrary to true centering. Many New Age people exalt themselves in collecting teachings and connecting with stars, while only copying and imitating with no true depth the very ancient teachings from this Earth. The star knowledge in ancient teachings always has a counterpart; a star meditation inspires a pathway toward grounding and birthing us into the Earth. Educating the spirit does not mean you must stay ignorant of other spiritual traditions and never read. On the contrary. However, to reach the void, the infinity of self, it is imperative that your mind be free of encumbrance, be in a perfect state of emptiness and openness, a state that intellectual accumulation and false spiritual elation may hinder.

Despite all of this, what characterizes the New Age movement reflects something true as well. The New Age comes as a definite wave of awakening. People are awakening to new spiritual realities that their own people and lineage had lost centuries before. As children learning to be in this new world of spirit, they may juggle, emulating for a while, wishing to seek and find answers for a missing dimension in their lives. By mixing traditions and often confusing what is what in the spirit domain, however, they are playing with fire. In fact, some New Age followers may make the terrible mistake of dabbling in things for which they have not been prepared, things that should be learned strictly under the competence of an expert eye of a true priest or shaman. Unfortunately, many do not realize the dangers of being guided by half-trained shamans who are no different from the New Agers, holding only bits and pieces of wisdom. Of course, seeking roots that their race has lost is not wrong. It is a truly healthy pursuit. It is essential, however, to bear these pitfalls in mind in order not to be lost in endless wandering and shopping around.

THE LANGUAGE OF SPIRIT

The ancient native teachings have come to us, sprung from an unbroken ancient lineage. They carry the power, wisdom, and introspection of wise people who, for thousands of years, improved upon them and evolved with the teachings and the careful observation of the path to life and death. My ancestors shed blood protecting and preserving these teachings at all cost, cherishing them for thousands of years with all their souls. They were often killed for refusing to forsake these teachings and menaced by conquering men of greed. For this immense suffering that we carry in our blood, the natives who held on to their traditions have earned the right to say they are the keepers of these sacred teachings. Their immense loyalty to Mother Earth has given the Red people a sacred mission, instilled in their blood, to protect and care for her very ancient ways in these Americas.

The spiritual background that most Western people received from their parents, a background that comes from a false Christian Puritanism and a scientific-materialist mind, proclaimed that Mother Earth was dead matter. A simple example of how this is well expressed in English, is found in the term "a dirt road." Sacred Earth, called dirt, is here associated with all ideas of being unclean. Many Westerners come from a heritage that mutilated all symbols of birth tied to blood and the Earth, seeing them as dirty. Westerners are the most aseptic people on this planet. Their practices often express a compulsive, aseptic mentality that implies a need for something more than basic, vital cleanliness, the need to kill all microbes at any price, thus killing life, reflecting a strange fear of reality.

In another perspective, their heritage has often severed them irremediably from the true meaning of the blood of Christ that they drink every Sunday. In this way, the essence of the Earth (sex, woman, and her sacred blood) became foreign (and evil) to them. And since the Earth is foreign, so are all her children. Blinded by greed and hungry for power, many Westerners have forgotten why their Christ shed his Blood—for all Earth's children. By virtue of this, Christian institutions have only recognized the elevation toward sky and God, as opposed to the horizontal native perspective of the Medicine Wheel ways.

For two generations now, many people have rejected the spiritual background of their parents, often seeing the hypocrisy, disconnectedness, and apparent lack of true spirit. Even if they seek the Red Lodge with a deep intense desire to learn the Native Ways, many may still bear within a deeply ingrained idea of a fearful and punishing God of guilt, false humility, and judging attitudes that make them deny their true selves and doubt reality. Despite their good and sincere intentions to learn, they may not realize how this was transmitted as a wrong and often harmful notion of good and bad from generation to generation. These people may not be fully aware that these fears are still in them, somewhere deep down. Many may wish to break away from this, but, having been indoctrinated for so long with this detrimental habit of mind, they cannot achieve this easily. Only with a deep inward capacity for truth can we unveil what has kept the White people away from true spirituality for such a long time.

Natives from North to South, in their original way of being, have no sense of guilt. I must say that the Western sense of guilt, appearing as a contracted fear, is totally unknown to me. The same can be said for remorse, which naturally follows guilt. Not that we natives do not care for others. On the contrary, we care so much that we abhor any fear of the self that creates guilt. Not fearing our own selves, we are free to love other selves. There is a difference between recognizing a mistake in a constructive way and allowing an internalized guilt to kill any clarity of judgment or mental sanity. It took me a long time to understand that most Western actions and reactions are based on guilt, remorse, and fear of self, impeding a discovery of the profound realm of the never-ending power of true feeling and the legitimate freedom of a soaring spirit.

When I sit and meditate, a powerful thread surfaces from my ancestors that carries a great love for Earth from one generation to another—a love so true, so immense, and so real that it does not belong strictly to Red people, but to all children of Earth. However, the White heritage has sadly broken away from its roots, from this sacred healing to which all people should commit their lives. The light skins must regain the humility to recognize the sickness inherent in their race—a sickness passed down by their forefathers for the most part—and embrace the healing of their lineage of seven mothers and seven fathers to restore the balance of the great Earth. Unfortunately, however hard it may be to say, the White race, throughout history, has brought ignorance, enslavement, extermination, rape, devastation, and blasphemy to all the originals of this planet. Death has been its legacy for so many centuries, permitting separation and division among the people. For this, the White race has lost its spirit in a very long cycle. I am sure that most people of color would welcome the transmutation, changing this adverse impression we carry in our memories. For the White people, this can also be acknowledged and healed in the Red Lodge.

Because of this, a person of the White race must walk this sacred Earth with more humility than a colored person. True humility in our ways means not feeling diminished. Authentic humility means surrendering and merging our thoughts and entering into Earth. These are not times when the White people should walk proud on this planet, not until they heal, along with us, all the imbalances their forefathers have inflicted on *Etonoha*, the Earth mother.

These are times for us, for all natives, to walk proud to heal our wall of shame. We have no reason to feel shame. We have always heard the Earth mother, somewhere in our deepest dreams, even when we were lost. For this, many natives are not understood. We usually have a hard time getting people to understand us as we are. We are regarded with a sense of wonder and fear, with an aura of mysticism. Because we were a powerful and beautiful people, we are a myth to many, and we often are not understood as we really are. This is our reality. This has also brought many internal confusions to the Indians, who are under the influence of the dark, infiltrating, and overwhelming shadow of

Western societies that covers many native communities. This has created a situation in which some natives fight against other natives, their own brothers and sisters. Unfortunately, all three native Americas are contaminated with this to a certain degree, but one simply cannot ask a people so long oppressed and isolated to awake and be perfect.

Even though we are naturally a very direct people, many natives carry over 500 years of legitimate, unexpressed rage as a powerful wall. This is the very first wound of the Americas, inflicted at the time of the meeting of the European and native races. This first wound is symbolized in one of the biggest historical mistakes: all native nations of America were erroneously called "Indians" (from India). Because of this, we have not been seen for who we are, not heard for who we are. We have been mistaken for another people. As long as this wound is not healed, as long as the responsibility to correct this monumental error is eluded, the three Americas will never find full sanity and balance. This is the very first wound, the wound now waiting to be amended.

This is our Red wall now, this is the healing for Indians—to meet at last with the White people with patience, tolerance, and forgiveness. Native anger may become an awakener to those who have suffered injustice and rejection. It cannot be a song to follow throughout life, for it is an essentially reactive emotion. Many zealous natives wage a militant battle against any natives who have the deep desire to heal the sacred Earth from the old out-dated Western mind, against those of us who love all children with the compassion of Mother Earth, regardless of their color, against those of us who wish to share with the White people the wonders of her knowledge and take steps toward mutual acceptance. On one hand, I know various "Apples" (those who are Red outside and White inside) as well as many real-hearted Indians with no native "numbers." It is time now, as before, for all natives to recognize each other for their spirit, not for their "reservation numbers."

Most prevalent today, are the natives who are angry with the White people for their unconscious behavior when entering the teachings of the Red Lodge. It is a justifiable form of anger, resulting from the lack of respect shown by many Whites. But patience and openness must be our teacher. Because our wall is a source of deep sadness steeped in our memory cells, in our DNA, it must be our transcendence to learn to walk tall against the Red wall of shame and rage.

The ancient Medicine Wheel teachings show that there are four inherent walls, each specific to a race. Every race must move through them and the wall that is faced is not necessarily the inherent direction a race may represent. These veils demand to be faced, learned, and transcended by every one of us. For the Red people, the wall of past and shame in the South appears as a dark hole within, where hope is often buried deep in the shadows and night of our hearts. Now, we are healing our veil and our Red heart returns to the light to share in the Rainbow Lodge of all nations. Ultimately, Earth teachings do not belong to one race, but rather to all children, for they are from the sacred heart of the Earth. They are given to anyone who will hear her truth in the soul and spirit, who will truly make the commitment to look at this predominant Western mind-set and heal it. The Red vision, also mine, does not belong to anyone in particular, but conveys the dream of the Earth revealing herself to all her children.

In these times, the Black people, the Africans and Afro-Americans, share the same wall of shame as the native American, while the Eastern people must meet their wall in the East. This wall is called the wall of religion or dogma, often translating into their religious system as an obsession for illumination or as a bloody fanaticism that we have observed, for example, in India in the last decades, bringing terrible clashes between opposing religious beliefs.

Ultimately, the White people have two walls to penetrate: the western wall of arrogance, self-importance, and illusions, and, afterward, once the lesson is learned, the northern wall of conditioning and lack of true wisdom. The passage for Western cultures in the tunnel of Earth is already happening. As many realize, the American (material) dream is vain and ungrounded. This illusion of the West is crumbling apart. The imperial nation of the great "democracy" of the United States is undergoing a death passage, for its democracy is often counterfeit, corrupt, and unreal.

I can only hope that my words create a bridge toward you to warmly invite you into our lodge to heal these wounds. If you accept the invitation to birth into the Red Lodge, I would suggest, as a first requisite, that you truly put yourself in native moccasins. We have done the reverse, entering more than our share of times into the modern Western lodge, forced to understand the White wall in order to survive. But tell me how many have experienced the Red wall in their very core?

In the rainbow meeting of all people, those who refuse to wear other moccasins are quick to judge others and situations and are caught in self-pretense. I have seen many who will go far out of their way to prove that they are right, all the time resisting an understanding of a foreign vision of the world, only seeking to recreate their limited world wherever they go around the globe. They may go so far as to proclaim their intent to save all other people who have not their comfort and culture. This is a mind contrary to simple *trust*. This total emptiness is reflected in the grasping materialism that impedes our momentous rendezvous at the Rainbow Lodge.

The mirror of the Red Lodge reflects that many Westerners are afraid of their minds. They are afraid to look at themselves, to take responsibility to break their chains, the very walls of their people. Most of you are already aware of what the concept of power is in this society and the harm it has produced for so long, and still does within many. This simple word, power, contains two perceptions of the world that are opposed forever—two irreconcilable ways of being, unless a deep examination is achieved.

Power, in the Western society, exists in many forms: wealth, investments and capital, material acquisitions, advanced scholarly degrees, high-paying jobs in prestigious corporations, advantageous marriages based more on social status than love, security and the comforts of the material world, profitable deals, package vacations, Hollywood's fame, Rambo's muscles, violence and machine guns, false pride, arrogance, and anything based on the mind. Anything that makes life easy becomes a symbol of power. An easy life is seen as a sign of power—for example, working less for more money. Power for such a society is expressed in the Star Wars movies, computer technology, a sexy lover, war between the sexes, or a brand new car with a sexy blond in it. Power for Western societies is represented by all sorts of external things. Identification with these things gives a false sense of greatness that entraps everyone. Finally and most tragically, power for the scientific "club" has been, and still is, a drive for supremacy over nature.

In contrast, power for the Red people is more than a concept. It is a knowing. It is our very life itself. It is to fight for our veracity, for the truth beyond spirit. It is circular power, the capacity to meet ourselves with honesty, to walk with our fears, to fight face to face with our illusions and defeat them forever, to hear the *language of spirit*, to talk and to touch the heart of the people, to love the Earth in an infinite, unconditional way. Power for us is the ability to recognize our own mistakes with great humor. Real power is respect for the dead, for the elders. It is to consider ourselves a sacred temple in which the Spirit can live. It is to practice detachment, for we will not bring anything with us into the Happy Hunting Ground. Power is our sacred vision, and fighting a long life to make it come true. For this, power is to grow very, very old. Power for us is to follow the signs of fate with no cowardice, with intensity, to trust entirely in the universe, to think of our people before ourselves, to hold our sacred arrows, to be our own chief, not fearing pain. Our highest sense of power is to give our lives for our brothers, for our sisters, to shed blood in true honesty. The great power around us and in us is the strength of a river, the beauty of Earth, the laugh of a child, the force of the wind. Power is rooted in us by the Moon, and the true source of inspiration and sacred dream she sustains within us. The power to touch and be touched is the greatest manifestation of bounty we may feel, the gift to learn to become true men and true women, *Ongwhe Onwhe*, the real people.

In my quest as a woman, I have encountered many Western women who long to reverse the principles of the Western mind-set within themselves, seeking a more real purpose in their lives. But many women still fear claiming their "power" in the most spiritual sense. They reject the Western model of woman, an often male-imposed ideal that depicts a grown woman as a teen model. Men often treat us as little girls, shutting us down intellectually and not allowing us to have strong voices in the society. They may show a condescending smile of acquiescence when a woman talks, but they never allow her to be truly who she is. As a result, a woman may fall into the trap of adopting the man's projections onto her feminine self-image. As a result also, many women oppress their sisters, women of color, denying them the freedom, rights, and understanding that they themselves have been denied.

If women could only see, in their intense seeking, how many still hold the out-dated, patriarchal mind-set of fear that manipulates their minds and hearts, harming them, keeping them from opening to inner understanding, asking them to give up their original Earth strength. This harmful patriarchal mind-set still tells women that men will be their conscience on many levels of their lives, that men will guide women and be everything for them. In their inner sense of being lost, women agree to this. This is their defeat.

I can only urge men and women who have adopted this mind-set of fear to look at this rampant sickness that lurks all around them and make a choice. Many know already that this mind-set of fear in their mind and soul is imprisoning them, blocking them from true freedom and love. Because real freedom is only given fully to those who love the Earth in their deepest soul, to those who are truly willing to embrace responsibility for the Earth and to shed blood for her.

Shed blood for Earth and you will be free. Loving Earth and shedding blood for her will give you wings, a deep sense of sacred purpose. She dreams within us, she dreams the sacred vision with you. Below all of your veils, the true self of the true man and the true woman is found in all its purity.

To shed blood in the Red Lodge, for both men and women, is not a literal act, but it is not simply a metaphor either. It is not to grip a knife, cut yourself, and spill blood onto Earth and be done. That would be too easy. To shed blood is a deep commitment of a lifetime, a reaching far beyond yourself, always fighting for her love, protecting her by all means, being willing to sacrifice yourself, if needed, to live her intensity, her beauty, to change the world, to foster spiritual revolutions—and to do all this with a true sense of balance. Fanatic extremism only leads to more separation and destruction and is contrary to her sacred designs. To shed blood is to give of your soul in a gesture of perfect commitment. Then the great Earth will give you the power, the strength, the understanding, and the infinite love to move mountains, to be aligned and to help align the world with her.

It is interesting to observe that, in the human body, the medicine center of *power* is located in the throat behind the tongue and refers to the spiritual capacity of speaking one's own truth. The natural gift of power is also to recognize and allow the higher forces of spirit within one's self, giving us perfect inner guidance to meet the great universal truth in our lives.

Entering the Red Lodge does not, therefore, imply that you become an Indian. We are not living a fantasy here. It means to expose and embrace yourself as you are, with all that you are, independent of the color of your skin, to be disposed to hear, to unveil to truth, to learn true courage, and to deepen your sense of spirit. You will not become a true universal and spiritual warrior if you cannot see first the wall of your own race, embrace it, and heal it forever. You will never discover your essence. You may strive arduously. You may even fool yourself into believing you are enlightened, but you will still be caught in your ego and the wall of confusions, drying up like dead trees, untouched and filled with resistance.

Some people have, at times, expressed themselves to me in this way: "I have a hard time thinking I am part of the White race even though they are my people, I do not feel as they do. My personal spirit animal feels more 'individualistic' to me and, for this, I feel alone. I have a hard time being group-related." I can understand this very well, but still, these words reflect what is already predominantly at the base of the Western culture: individualism. Language is powerful and expresses a vision of the world. As natives, we would not say, "Our spirit animal is individualistic." This is a Western concept. We would say, "My spirit animal is a more solitary one." We do not consider ourselves as individuals; we know we all are related.

People of the modern world, especially in cities, are trained to be so individualistic that they cannot be group-related. They have lost their sense of brotherhood and sisterhood and this is contrary to our ways. Most of these "individualistic" people cannot stop talking about themselves, and they do not really talk *with* each other, but *at* each other. This is why so many end up seeking a psychotherapist.

"Individualistic" means there is *no trust*, and this lack of inner connection creates people who think of themselves as separate entities. I have noticed, in my work, how some Western people are quick to be offended. Sadly, many are living full of resentment, shutting off their true feelings, becoming cold-hearted. They think this is how they can retain power and keep from getting hurt. But this is a false protection; this is no real shield. Their judgmental attitudes create divisions and small-scale wars in their daily lives. In brief, one of the preponderant differences between natives and non-natives is seen in situations that would, for us, be cause for kindly laughter, but that often become painful dramas for people raised in the Western world. In contrast, what we perceive as a matter of extreme importance and seriousness is not taken seriously at all by Westerners. For example, Westerners may harshly scold their children about what we would consider to be a superficial matter—something that would be a motive for laughter to us. In this regard, it appears to us that White folks exaggerate diminutive details, forgetting to grasp the larger perspective. We laugh over things that Westerners take as deadly serious. On the other hand, on crucial issues, when it is time to speak our truth with great veracity and integrity, I have often observed that many Westerners are so bound by fear that they withdraw instead of expressing their true feelings, preferring not to take the matter seriously. Our ways of seeing life seem diametrically opposed. Another example of this resides in our understanding of privacy. This holds a significant value to us as a peculiar way of keeping secret, but it is seen differently in Western minds. For us, secrets hold the power we gain from our ceremonies and our medicine ways. A secret for the Western mind refers to something kept hidden because of its value, good or bad. For a native, it is not what is kept secret that holds such a precious value (be it an object or a sentiment). It is privacy itself that retains the greater meaning and power. Even a simple word such as "honesty" also expresses two views. Honesty, in our sense, is to manifest our true feelings. It goes beyond whether someone is telling the truth with all the correct facts. Personal information is not important for a native—age, height, weight, income, marital status, or personal history. Definition of the self in this way (often appearing empty to us) is not important. It has nothing to do with honesty, because we deeply know that, at every moment, we naturally change. We do not attempt to try to understand ourselves through external standards. A native will never tell you the exact facts of an event, for example, but rather what is most meaningful in terms of spirit, even if this means mixing up the continuity of events.

Everything is based on silence in our world. This is why, when we are called to talk our truth, the truth of what we feel and think, we can do so with great accuracy in relation to our true sentiments. We never lie or become of twisted tongue. Visions are what we received for our time of reverence to silence and solitude, visions expressed in songs and gestures of life. And this is power. A native essentially thinks in terms of wholeness, not in terms of individuality. Therefore, analyzing thoughts in the way a Western mind does is one of the things that a native would never take seriously. For us, when you know what you truly feel, there is no doubt, nothing to analyze. For us, the world is perfect as it is. There is nothing to doubt, not even ourselves. We know harmony in most situations, even in the hardest ones, for we do not fear death. We recognize the poetry behind all the winds of life. Because we recognize the perfection of the universe, we have absolutely no understanding of *progress* in the Western sense. We consider every living thing as already completed, perfect, and part of us, not as separate entities. The native mind sees essentially what is alike, what is held in common, always in circles. The Western mind, on the other hand, always sees what is different and what is missing, always linear.

Therefore, when Western people get cold in the frozen wall of their North, dehumanized as automatons, rendered insensitive to the nature of their lives, there is no way for us to communicate with them in a full way. Unfortunately, they cut apart the entire universe, often judging all that is around them from a self-important perspective. This leaves no place for true understanding of the mind. If you notice yourself one day in this sterile space, regardless of your color, I can only urge you to reach out, to transform this poison. Try to understand to what degree you may be caught in this destructive way of being, how it may be dominating and controlling you, even in the most hidden corners of your being.

In spirit as well, contradictions do not exist for us. One moment it is required to be as stubborn as a sacred buffalo, and the next, as fluid as the eagle. This may appear contradictory to the Western mind. Beyond all our walls, however, spirit flows spontaneously, in the everlasting rhythm of life. When we move in spirit, we proceed with the moment, knowing what is hoped for, not following what people expect of us, but what the universe tells us. In this inner place, there are no confusions, no doubts created by the mind complicating our existence.

I have also observed that many Western people join in the Red Lodge with a true sense of respect and reverence. This is good. This is a deep healing for us, one that always makes me shed some tears of purification, my ancestor's tears rolling through my veins. For many, however, there subsists the danger of entering in our lodge with the take-and-take mentality, lacking the proper behavior, even when their apparent intentions are sincere. A resolute and full heart—looking beyond yourself to laugh at your ego—is what is required in the Red Lodge. Deplorably, some attempt to shape these teachings to suit their present, modern life. Others unconsciously take only that which they crave. Others expect that they can simply trade for these teachings or even "buy" spirituality, thinking it will be theirs without ever making any substantial commitment. Fortunately, it doesn't operate this way. Spirit will force anyone to be an open vessel, or will otherwise restrict them to spiritual abatement. Manipulating sacred teachings unconsciously, sorting and collecting only the knowledge that pleases them is the most dangerous pitfall that all spiritual novices may face. A good antidote to these pitfalls is to constantly ask yourself what you are giving of your life in exchange for these wondrous teachings and for the blood of native ancestors, those who were killed for this wondrous knowledge we have received and that you will experience in this book.

The Medicine Wheel teachings encompass a way of life, a twenty-four-hour-a-day consciousness for the rest of our lives. Sitting in a Medicine Wheel for fifteen minutes every morning will not make you spiritually "okay." This is a big illusion, because the integration of the teachings is not an intellectual knowing, nor related to the amount of time you practice, but to how you take the waves of life in the worst circumstances, and how you manifest mindfulness in every moment. Spiritual achievement is not what you may have achieved or think you have achieved, but the love you hold while you express life in all its forms.

Seeking empowerment strictly for yourself is a selfish quest. However, merging with Earth will give you a natural empowerment that is subtle, quiet, almost invisible, and will make you move mountains before you realize it. Many are obsessed by their need for spiritual empowerment. It is the new attraction in vogue right now. What are we pursuing, an individualistic empowerment with a spiritual flavor or the true health of our spirit? True empowerment can only be reached through acts of losing any ordinary sense of self. It is only given in the realm of the great sacred dream to those who are worthy. This sacred dream from Earth is within each one of us. After shedding blood, as I explained, and after reaching a point of no return, after not owning your life anymore in the ordinary sense, only then can you truly exist in impersonality, and breathe in spirit, no longer concerned with the "me," yet more human than ever.

Real consciousness is an inner pressure that keeps you from living in self-satisfaction. It holds your heart down to Earth so you do not forget, so you can listen to the great vastness of Earth with your amazed soul.

THE RED HAND

Many people have forgotten how to listen. They have forgotten how to truly fight. This is why the spirit of the Western society is gone. Many fight over meaningless things. In turn, what they gain is a meaningless, dead, and unspirited life. After all their actions and their meaningless fights, they have no energy left to seek and aim for what could be truly rewarding—the conquest of ego and the true sacred vision. Be honest, be ready to give of yourself with no resistance. When you always think you lose something, when your eyes only see what is missing and not what is full in the moment, you suffer from the sickness of hungry behavior. This is a wall to meet spirit. You must meet with your people's wall first to allow yourself to battle its absurdity. You must reach for your most loyal friend, your very spirit. See its shadows, cultivate the trust needed to be an empty vessel, for without this, your "medicine" will never move you—only your fears and resistance. Be ready to die for what you have chosen and you will have shed blood. Feel the shame of your ancestors and you will sense the native wall, the red cloud of shame imposed on us, beyond the veils. Regardless of your color, the shame you may experience of our wall is the first step toward the true sacred healing needed to occur in the Americas to heal the first wound before the others. You will hear its wisdom and its truth.

Once this is accomplished, I will offer you my Red hand, inviting you to sit with me in the sacred Red Lodge of a warm winter teepee, with a steady fire burning, to hear an ancient council of chiefs within, dreaming of the Sun and Moon, and to meet at the circle of mind that sees what is alike. With me, you will agree with the eloquent talk of Tadodaho, Chief Leon Shenandoah of the Iroquois Nations: "We must recognize our enemies, the forces of darkness that now march across all lands of the Four Sacred Directions, throwing the shadow of Death and destruction even in the seventh generation to come . . . we must stand together, the four sacred colors of humankind, as the one family that we are in the interest of peace . . .to be one Body, one Heart and one Mind. . . ."[2]

---

[2] Words spoken by Tadodaho, Chief Leon Shenandoah at the 40th anniversary celebration of the UN, published in *Akwesasne Notes*, New Series (Jack Wardell, "Demonizing the Big Glass," Fall 95, vol. 1, pp. 118–120).

Then, and only then, the Red and the White Lodges will reconcile themselves forever, fully, as truest twins on this cosmopolitan Turtle continent and this must inevitably occur before all the colors of lodges will meet in the rainbow circle of mind. It should have happened from the beginning of our destiny together as two people. For us, it is to redeem what was not even 500 years ago and to share our Red gifts. For all other people, it is to put on our moccasins and walk in a soft, silent, and sacred respectful way on the sacred flesh of the Earth we have loved for thousands of years. We have been waiting for you all this time.

When the sacred White race understands the significance of shedding their blood in spirit, when their hearts and voices are one, rising deep from the sacred ground, then we, the family of man and woman, will navigate along on two parallel canoes, down the same stream of life together. And we, the family of humans, will purify our spirits in a gigantic planetary metamorphosis, in a major Earth menstruation, in a world-wide Moon-Time ceremony, all together, for the coming faces, for the future generations of humanity. Meanwhile, we are waiting for you.

~~~

Sometimes in the old Maya temples, in the dead cities, you can find stamped in the inner walls a Red Hand that is quite stunning and freezes your blood instantly. Red is this hand of a man or a woman painted on the lime wall of polished stone, a hand of a standing person who had wished to leave his thousand-year-old mark forever. When entering the temple, alone with yourself, you walk slowly, and suddenly she appears, this Hand in the dark mysterious cave from the depth of time, permeated with majesty. Is it a war sign? A strange enigma? Someone killed by an enemy? A seal of conquest from a warrior?

Old natives may know but they don't talk. They know it is not a human hand. It is the Hand of some God, the Hand of a whole people, and wherever you will find these red palms, there is nothing else speaking than these hands. Alive and forever, they talk without voice. You can hear them, but no one understands them except the Indian. They talk only to those who can understand. They appear only to those who can see them. The stained Blood is not superficial on the wall, it has impregnated the lime, and has been absorbed by the very wall itself. These Hands manifest that it was the time to hide the secret knowledge in the clandestine caves, when the time of light was gone, when the Indians were threatened, at the time of the Conquest. Since then, everything has changed, but the Red Hands still persist, unerasable after an eternity that no one can recount.

Brothers, sons of sons of the Red people, those who will reach the day drawing near, those who will be reborn with eyes to see and ears to hear and the light inside of you to understand, Brothers and Sisters, you who have come back from the deepest of time to walk on the Sacred Earth, you hear her mystery and enigma. You who recall, you will explain to the people who are blind and deaf to the Great Wisdom that we cannot stay silent, for the Red Hand is whispering in the shadows of our dreams.[3]

---

[3] Inspired by Antonio Mediz Bolio, *Tierra del Faisan y del venado* [The Land of the Pheasant and the Deer] (Merida, Yucatan, Mexico: Produccion Editorial Dante, S.A., 1989), pp. 143–146.

2
WILL

THE SPIRIT ANIMAL
BEHIND THE SOUL

Now that you have birthed forth into the Red Lodge of Earth, I wish to share with you the most ancient knowledge of the Americas, the Spirit Animal teachings. This knowledge may be more than 30,000 years old, its obscure origins lying somewhere in the lost ages when Indians walked this great continent. As you awake into this ancient lodge, the first stepping stone you meet is the transformation through the spirit animal, also called power animal, guardian spirit animal, *tona* animal, and *nahual* animal, depending on the native tradition. The teachings shared here are found widely among the Inuit people, the natives of Canada and the United States, and the Maya, as well as the people of Siberia and Mongolia. They were spread long ago throughout these continents and among these people.

THE PRESENCE OF
THE POWER ANIMAL

There has been much written on the spiritual meaning of native symbology and the medicine of each spirit animal. So far, however, I have not come upon any cohesive literature describing the intensive practices, as well as the integration of the power animal that is involved in the lifelong work to encounter such a spirit companion. Power animals have gained much popularity over the last ten years, reflecting the developing spiritual awareness of many people who sense this other existence within them as a powerful way to understand their deepest souls. Consequently, I find it essential here to provide some clarity around the inner involvement that the spirit animal teachings entail, by sharing some of the oral traditions given to me, as well as my personal observations from my childhood, when my direct experience of power animals began.

Mysterious and profoundly sacred, the power animal opens gateways to domains beyond normal conceptual consciousness, providing you with a new sense of being. The realization that we all carry with us a spiritual power animal that sustains our physical body in every instant of our lives, is the first level of awareness you must acquire. The ancient teachings instruct us that, without the animal spirit, whether we are conscious or not of its presence, we would be dead. Therefore, our deepest soul and the spirit essence of our animal breathe together, identical in nature, one and indivisible. The spirit animal is attached to our body from birth and is a shadow behind us, following us as another consciousness. Besides being a powerful guardian of our physical body, it guides us toward aligning properly with our path and our higher evolution.

The two means of guidance that the power animal provides you are protection and direction. Without these two guiding tools, which are absolutely essential to human survival independent of the Power Animal teachings, no one would be capable of decent fulfillment in a life purpose. The protection of your animal ensures health to your physical body, resisting against death, illnesses, and any negative energies that may enter into your medicine field (aura) or your dreams. The spirit animal assists you in the unfolding of your innate gifts as a human, your inner capacity to create and serve your community in whatever way you have chosen for this lifetime. Your inherent gifts are in all ways similar to the animal's gifts and knowing them helps determine the way you can unfold your life's purpose within your community. As an example, a turtle person will always create strong and solid foundations for the community, while a hawk person will be more inclined to create bridges of communication and ideas within his or her group.

Your power animal and your soul (or spirit) are directly linked. So, as you integrate your spirit animal on a daily basis, discovering how to be it, witnessing the world through its eyes, you may eventually master your true self and sustain your path with a powerful will to live. This is the significance of the word "power" in the term power animal. With conscious work, the spirit animal eventually develops our *will center*, located at the kidneys, where the dream body enters. We must be careful here not to confuse true will with willfulness, for the two are entirely opposed. Willfulness always wants to hurry and worry, coercing the intuition into doing what it wants. Willfulness is usually associated with the needs of the ego, while the true will is an inner power center that is attuned to higher understanding, helping to reach great awareness beyond personal concerns. True will is necessary to health and life in general, for without it, we would be extremely passive. Yet spiritual will must be tempered with fluidity.

Once your animal essence and your soul are at last identified, a sense of absolute self-confidence will pervade you, granting you the courage to meet your challenges as a warrior-apprentice of life. Because knowledge is power, knowing yourself is the first step toward inner power and natural authority.

In order to reach the realm of your animal in all its expansiveness, it is of utmost importance that you constantly purify your self as a way to keep clear the channels to the spirit animal. In our native ways, the persistent purification that I referred to consists of meditating to calm the mind, of practicing mindfulness and right action at all times, of fasting and doing sweat lodges with an entitled leader, performing prayer ceremonies, attuning to the greater harmony in nature, as well as embarking on inner journeys to communicate with the spirit animal. On the other hand, the daily and often strenuous integration of your guardian confers many rewards, for it will always stand as your best friend and ally, helping you to find your truth and realizing great deeds.

For all of us, the journey with our personal spirit animal begins in our mother's womb. The spirit animal is around the pregnant mother to protect her and the child against any dangers or harms. Generally, when the soul incarnation of the child arrives with strength, the animal's protection will be strongly energetic around the mother. The previous incarnations of the soul and the lessons learned (or not) determine the capacity to make clear choices with regard to your mother's womb, your new family, and the challenges in your new life. Usually, younger souls, inadequately developed, fight to come back quickly into a woman's womb, making inept choices for their new existence, while older souls wait and receive greater preparation in the realms between life and death before being reborn.

Unfortunately, most younger souls are consumed by painful, violent, and fearful emotions during the dying process. This contributes to their choice of difficult lives. At birth, most incarnating souls slip into a trance state, forgetting their previous lives.

Independent of the level and aptitude of the soul, however, the spirit animal is always selected in the passage between life and death, both essences recognizing each other. It is at birth, with the first breath of the baby, that the spirit animal attaches itself to the body and protects it. Most native medicine people own the awareness that, during the first months of life, an infant's soul floats loose over and around the small body, not fully anchored, still bound to the dream world from which it comes.

Performing a native baptism for the newborn energetically secures the spirit guardian to the body. A native baptism consists of offering the baby to the four directions, and under a shaman's guidance, calling the four winds to blow in the baby's crown center, mind, heart, and womb. The four winds represent the four hills or four seasons of life: infancy, adolescence, maturity, and old age. Blowing the soul, along with the guardian animal, powerfully encourages the incarnation of the soul, definitively sealing the space between the body and the spirit animal, so the child does not grow vulnerable to accidents, illnesses, and loss of soul.

During the very first days of life, the newborn is immersed in the dream state and we often can observe that an infant animal is present in addition to the spirit animal. This infant animal will guide the child's soul on the road into this life, from the dream realms into the awareness of this reality. It is common to find such an infant animal dominating even more than the guardian animal itself, for the infant animal is better adapted to the baby's emotional life. The spirit animal's medicine is the chief one, protecting both the soul and this infant animal. Without the softer ways of the infant animal, the power animal may create too heavy a presence for such a defenseless newborn. As an illustration, a child may have chosen the protection of a large elk as the main spirit animal for his life, but this commanding medicine will be very hard for such a small baby to handle. Hence, the infant animal smoothes the way, becoming a more suitable ally in this delicate and vital transition to life. Animals such as a frog, lizard, butterfly, docile snake, small water turtle, little bear, dragonfly, or fawn more easily aid the small child in adjusting to the spaciousness of the emotional world in which he is now submerged. Usually, this baby animal will sojourn with the child up to age 3, depending on the rate of development and soul awakening of the child. At this age, the main power animal fully embraces the space around the child's body and the infant animal will leave permanently.

It is interesting to see that, later, during childhood, many young sense their real animal guardian or even dream of it, independent of their cultural conditionings, feeling intuitively a stronger affinity to one animal in particular. To encourage a child to understand and identify with their own spirit animal is one of the most wonderful and beneficial spirit-tools we may give them, to help them grow fearless and bring clarity to their own path.

The old Maya teachings and practices, still alive in various regions of the Maya land, transmit to us the knowledge that every person finds themselves under the guardianship of a spirit animal through a special pact between the animal and the self made at birth. At age 7, this pact is renewed, once the child develops reason. Since the Conquest, the Maya often refer to the spirit animals as angels, a necessary ruse to hide their knowledge from the Spaniards. This animal spirit "angel" holds the native name of *tona*, or *chanul*, in the Tzoltzil dialect. They also believe, as do the northern cultures, that, when a person dies, his or her animal also dies to the physical realm and the spirits fly as one to the lowerworld regions, to the land of the dead. All the *chanules* live inside a colossal sacred mountain, called *Bankilal Mukta Vitz*, or Great Mountain Brother. In this mountain, there is one *chanul* for each Maya. All the spirit animals of the Maya are fed by the ancestral gods.

The soul or spirit of a person is known as *chulel*. Considered the vital force of specific character traits, the soul is recognized by the *chanul* and, upon agreement, they share the same fate for this life. Each time a child is born, a *chanul* is also born in the sacred mountain and, because spirit has many dimensions, it can exist here with the person and dwell there in the mountain at the same time.

Most northern native cultures have also maintained the knowledge of the power animal's shifts that frequently take place during adolescence. Before birth, an opportunity is given in the astral levels to accomplish the chosen challenges with the same animal, from childhood through adulthood, or with another. This decision varies widely from one soul to the next. The soul may prefer to remain with the same spirit animal or shift to a new power animal, one more suited to the task of achieving the adult's purposes. The shift of animals during the teenage years always produces a difficult and perplexing time for the young person. Some shifts are more drastic than others. For example, shifts from a four-legged creature, such as a bear cub, to a big bird, such as an eagle, may create a tremendous crisis. A less dramatic transfer would be from a frog, as a child, to a water turtle, as an adult. Both these animals already have much kinship in their medicine characteristics. However, any mutation into another animal will create some turmoil to a certain extent.

It is important to understand that, in all power animal transfers, the child animal is no longer appropriate to the inner growth needed at this point. This identity crisis often manifests in rebellion and inner confusion for the adolescent, who is deeply struggling to grasp his or her new essence and release the old one. A crucial sacred rite of passage is the traditional Vision Quest at the beginning of puberty. This is actually a small death experience. It ensures the proper alignment for receiving the new spirit animal and it serves to open the young person to find the vision and the life's purpose according to the great universe's dream.

Traditionally, preparation for a young warrior's Vision Quest is imparted by the medicine chiefs. When the young man or young woman returns to the camp after the four days and four nights of fasting and tested endurance, he or she is given a new sacred name by the medicine people in accordance with the new animal and the visions received. Depending on the tradition, the sacred Indian name is often kept secret, its meaning never entirely revealed. This often represents the new animal. Of course, we cannot name ourselves, as this is totally contrary to the essence of the tradition. The significance of a sacred name also contains our life vision, our purpose, and it must be given by the universe, and confirmed by medicine people who can pierce our essence much better than we can ourselves.

Adolescents must be properly guided during this major crisis and transfer of essence. To be precise, it is not the soul that abandons the body with the spirit animal. It is the animal who leaves, allowing a new one to emerge in its place. For the soul that remains, this substitution appears as a transformational turn of life, helping it to discover other aspects of its essence. This shift is by arrangement, determined before birth between the soul, the child-animal spirit, and the adult-animal spirit.

Whether or not you choose to change animals during adolescence, the power animal accompanying you during your adulthood usually remains with you for various lifetimes, although there are no set rules. The medicine of some spirit animals, such as wolf, cougar, eagle, crow, or bear, are so vast that many lifetimes are required to unravel all the medicine aspects and lessons that each particular medicine encompasses. Nevertheless, there are instances when an animal with simpler medicine visits for only one lifetime, depending on the life purpose and the lessons learned.

Another reason why the guardian animal may stay with you only for one lifespan, resides in the self-pretense of your ego and its apparent resistance to the teachings and guidance you are granted by your *tona* animal. Of course, most people have no awareness of their spirit animal, and, though not fully developed spiritually, they still may lead a good life. The animal remains with them, granting physical protection. On the contrary, when people live behind the masks of ambition, self-pride, and arrogance, eluding their true work on this great Earth, trying to be what they are not and denying their own simple gifts, the power animal begins to depart slowly in the face of this internal split. This is when real communication is impeded on an essential level.

To learn to meet their essence is a sacred duty for all humans. This is the purpose of the *Ongwhe Onwhe*. If you do not live in line with your soul, as is the case for many people entangled in their ego, the spirit animal may abandon you. This leaves you entirely unprotected from the dangers of accidents, depressions, and suicidal feelings, as well as from physical and spiritual death. This rejection from the spirit animal therefore creates another sort of inner crisis. In a traditional culture, to remedy this deplorable circumstance, a shaman may be called to retrieve the guardian companion of this ill or extremely depressed person, for the complete healing of the body and soul. If the healing is successful, a new animal may enter into the medicine field, the one that has departed often not wishing to come back.

The direction that the power animal provides is your life guidance. When you undertake your spiritual path, you may wait and expect unattainable results due to a lack of clarity and purpose. But you need to open the internal gates of your ego and let your animal merge within you. This requires much perseverance and patience, knowing when to wait, when to be detached, and remaining fluid.

Your spirit animal is the perfect mirror for your ego, reflecting the level of awareness of your spirit. The power animal forces you to examine all aspects of your identity—imbalances, doubts, and fears. For this reason, you must be prepared to withstand many blows, since the preoccupation and anguish of your ego often may tire your guardian animal and may be reflected back onto you as external adversities.

It is necessary to understand that the power you may receive from your animal will not suddenly remove your fears. To be fearless is not to get rid of fear or to numb yourself to it, but to experience your fears even more strongly. This will help you to avoid hiding in falsity, by letting you embrace your fears and overcome them once and for all.

In all cases, this exchange of energy between soul and power animal must be understood as a trade, in much the same spirit as the native trade I discussed previously. In its realm, the spirit animal has not developed intellectual mind energy as humans have, though it is surely not deprived of acute cosmic intelligence. In the exchange for mutual evolution, it obtains some of your mind's energy, which you probably have in excess, while it gives you back the instinctual and intuitive power, powers often relinquished by humans. This allows you to connect more fully with your inner centers and gain a proper balance. In agreeing to this barter, you allow the animal to incarnate further in your human form. It compensates by becoming your full ally. This communion and fellowship of diving thoroughly into your essence with your best friend is a lifelong journey. At death, your soul will merge with your spirit animal and they will leave together for other trails, in other worlds, before rebirth.

The power animal lives in your back, attached to the dream body as a shadow behind you. The dream body spreads from above your head to the base of your spine and is also called the medicine field. When natives dance with headdresses or skins on their heads as an emblem of their animals, it serves to strengthen the connection with the animal spirit. The dream body itself enters your body through the kidneys and is attached to your navel. So your dream body can expand above, around and beyond you, enabling the power animal to induce the vivid dream of its presence easily for most receptive people. At first, as you start a conscious integration, you may feel the eyes of your own animal placed on top of your head. This gives the peculiar impression that, at times, you are looking through two pairs of eyes. This continuous process of integration is deeply fulfilling, as you come to know the magic and the power of the animal medicine as your own.

One day, after much conscious effort to bring your animal closer, you may find yourself seeing with the eyes of your spirit guardian, but this time through your own eyes. As if by enchantment, the spirit animal is witnessing the world through the window of your eyes. This is a meaningful time for your sacred team, but you must continue further integration, for many content themselves with this achievement or desist at this point. Next you must deepen the connection with your animal, reaching down to your other inner centers—your voice or throat center, your heart, stomach, womb center, arms and hands, legs and feet—until you entirely become your spirit animal, or, better said, until your animal seizes your full being, embracing your whole body in a perfect synergy and unity of essences.

This is also the native purpose of dancing our spirit animal, to change and shape-shift into its form. As previously mentioned, the power animal is not named lightly. The more we integrate it and release resistance, giving away our selfish ego, the more the animal grows powerfully within us. It grants us strength, health, clarity, and fulfilling opportunities of life. But, of course, the animal's power cannot be exploited for selfish purposes, for it will leave or destroy its owner. To avoid this, you must never forget that your animal has the gift of perfect discernment and intuition, endowed by the intelligent realm in which it lives. You cannot for one instant lie to your spirit animal.

In integrating the animal in all the inner centers of your being, you will uncover your true self, and acknowledge your chief within. You will become your own animal. You have probably seen pictures of Indian chiefs from the last century, or you may have met a native who really looked like his or her animal. Being so close to nature for so many generations, natives have often developed the facial traits of their power animals. Therefore, after many years of integration with your spirit animal, one day you may realize to your amazement that even your features, your appearance, have been transformed, as well as your attitudes of being. You are more than ever yourself, without reserve, fear or shyness, and with a greater sense of control.

In my practice of helping people attune to their animal, I have often found that some people may look physically like one animal, while the way they relate to and perceive the world indicates another. It can be quite tricky. Someone may look as frail as a deer, but his or her essence constantly seeks the expansion and space of a bird, such as a falcon, while someone else may have the dominant appearance of a buffalo, but truly have the tender heart of a sea turtle. This is why, in our traditional way, we seek the guidance of medicine people to corroborate our findings.

One of the greatest accomplishments of the spirit power animal is to make you unafraid to enter more wholly into this reality. The spirit animal alone guides you in the tonal realm. This is why the Mayas call these spirits the *tona* animals. The tonal realm is the plane in which we live. It includes the first level of consciousness or the awareness of this reality. By providing you with protection as well as direction in this vast world of the tonal, your spirit animal assists in opening gates before you, sending you the lessons that insure your true growth. The animal provides eternal guidance at every moment, if you learn to hear its message. You may then learn to enlarge your perception, and to discern the difference between your way of perceiving and that of your animal. Through your own eyes, lessons may appear as overwhelming and awful obstacles, but in the spirit animal's eyes, they often appear as the most incredible opportunities to grow, challenges of the highest beauty. In learning to become sensitive to your animal's eyes, you will distinguish which lessons to embrace, as well as the traps to avoid along the path.

Full alignment with the animal's essence takes many years to achieve, especially for the "big" medicines. When I refer to big medicine, I am not creating a hierarchical structure of medicine power. All medicines hold their own gift and all are powerful within their realm. But when the mission is big and there is a need to have strong influence in the world, a person requires a medicine that will know how to handle a vast range of frequencies of power—for instance, the jaguar, the eagle, the bear, or the rattlesnake. However, one medicine is not better than another. Each holds a unique, sacred place of its own. Not to accept your medicine animal, or wishing to obtain one of a bigger distinction, is to deny your self. This is common, but you must not forget that, many times, smaller medicines teach the big ones. For example, a mouse person can teach an emotional whale on precise matters.

In addition, a sense of secrecy is indispensable in holding your medicine animal. Calling everyone on the phone to talk about your new animal as I have seen done, may offend it and the spirit animal may abandon you on the spot! Apprentices of these ways must gather and develop an inward sense of power in order to hold their spirit animals, in order to be worthy of their sacred presence. In integrating your spirit animal, a subtle perception and discernment are indispensable.

Giving the spirit animal too much importance may overpower you, while on the other hand, not allowing it enough space or attention may weaken your protection. It is thus indispensable that your inner barometer be clear at all times to sense these subtleties.

When the balance is established, when you have learned your way with your sacred companion, a sense of who you are prevails. For example, in society, bursting out in anger at someone is frowned upon (especially for a woman) and this fact may cause someone to inwardly suppress their emotion. But anger is a natural, human emotion. To release the valve once in a while (as those with cougar or grizzly totems often must) is healthy. The consequences of this expression will provide a mirror for them and for others. The animal helps defeat these inhibitions of shame and guilt, and forces you into a full acceptance of your self, with no detours. A few shadows of animal natures follow: horses are usually quite skittish and susceptible; eagles are quite direct and often impatient; deer are sensitively nervous and often unsettled; bears are often slow and lazy to a purpose; coyotes are often unconscious. We natives usually display a great sense of humor toward our own shadow sides, as well as toward those of others, often laughing openly in a loving manner at ourselves and at others. This is something not too well-received in the world, due to people's self-importance. To help you embrace your shadows without denial and fear is one of the strongest objectives of your animal, which seeks to help you reach who you fully are, without being bound to what others may think.

FAKE SHAMANISM
OR SACRED INITIATIONS?

I must express an important caveat about some of the workshops given on power animals in the Western world. I have found some of these teachings to be extremely incomplete and not well taught with regard to our ancient ways. Unfortunately, these techniques are among the most popular on the international scene of shamanic interest. One of my major aims in writing this book is to assist people in discerning between what is false and what is true, between fake and real shamans, between good practices and hazardous ones. There is so much shamanic "stuff" out there. Some of it makes my hair stand on end each time I hear stories of people receiving inadequate practices improperly imparted. Just the fact that these ancient practices are announced as power animal "techniques" is a good sign of a lack of true appreciation, divesting these noble traditions of their sacredness. The Spirit Animal teaching is one of the most sacred matters for us and is, by all means, a way of living and of finding our soul. Describing our very soul as a "technique" is, therefore, aberrant and totally out of place. I often meet people who have attended such seminars and workshops, and I always hear the same story. The teaching material of the so-called shamanic practitioners imparting these seminars consists of an "Americanized" or Western technique of power animals and spiritual journeys, probably copied from ancient knowledge, but which has, without a doubt, suffered a process of serious "injury."

Dozens of people who have participated in these workshops have told me that these instructors incite everybody to *journey*, a form of inner meditation with drumbeat, teaching that whatever animal the student finds in visualizing a tunnel, is their power animal. Apparently, no one is verifying any of the participant's findings to ensure that they have the proper animal. Deplorably, sincere and innocent aspirants may believe whatever they hear in these seminars. This is critical to me. I have led numerous private meetings with people in order to "replace" the spirit animal for people who were genuinely convinced they had found the correct guardian animal by themselves.

One of the most serious examples I recall is that of a lady who joined a teaching circle I offered a few years ago. This woman was silent in the circle, and everyone asked me what was wrong with her, as her energy was so heavily "off" and depressing. I was glad when the lady asked to speak privately with me. She then shared that she had participated in one of these "famous" workshops eight years ago and had found a bear in her journeying tunnel. Having been told that the animal they would meet in the tunnel would be their own spirit animal, she adopted the bear she saw as her animal and started a process of intimate identification with it. This error was causing her major problems. I expressed to her that we need not talk more, that the spirit animal I was seeing as she was talking was one of a completely different nature. I told her then that her animal guardian was a red hawk and not a bear. For a long minute she did not say a word, seemingly puzzled. Then her face simply illuminated. She told me she remembered in her adolescence that she had a most striking dream of a red hawk flying directly at her face, looking straight into her eyes. There was no more to say on the subject. A year later, I saw this lady. She was very radiant and her depression had lifted. It is no wonder! How could a hawk needing to fly live happily in a bear's cave for eight years?

I have countless examples similar to this lady's misfortune. To surrender to an erroneous spirit animal as your essence and call its attention to you on a daily basis may bring deranging consequences for the rest of your life, if not amended promptly. This can become quite dangerous.

In traditional ways, the medicine people always point out the animal spirit to you, depending on their own vision or your own visions. Even if you receive a vision of a certain animal, this may not necessarily signify that you have encountered your true spirit animal. Often, an animal may come as a strong sign in your life, but that doesn't mean in any way that this is your own animal. Even when you dream about a particular animal, however lucid the dream, you must confirm your findings with the shaman guide or a competent medicine person. Moreover, the power to determine or "catch" spirit animals for others is not given even to all shamans or medicine people. Traditionally, this capacity belongs to certain shamans gifted in this art. Permission for a future shaman to recognize spirit animals for others is only entrusted to them by the main shaman teacher when the time is ripe. Furthermore, each medicine person possesses his or her own gift or medicine specialty, as we will see in the next chapter, and not everyone is dedicated to the same shamanic occupations.

In addition, some of these practitioners have established what they call "shamanic institutions" that offer instruction in these supposed "techniques." I ask myself, how can people institutionalize shamanic ways? If the spirit animal teachings are a sacred way into life, how can life be institutionalized? Life is a wondrous reality of transient qualities, and there exists no way to retain it in a cage like a bird or in a "building" as a captive. From ancient times, shamanic ways could never be contained in any societal or religious classifications, for they reflect the great ways of Earth and nature.

Furthermore, anyone who lacks the maturity of these ways may experience all sorts of animals in the journey's tunnel. The inexperienced may even encounter the animals of other persons present in the room with them, all trying to undertake their first journey. A beginner is as a child, fresh and open, not always possessing the aptitude to discern what is real. Many animal guides may surface in the tunnel. Your own fears may be disguised as spiders, rabbits, or snakes, reflecting your own psychological complexes. Angry animals may represent your emotional traumas and ravens, among others, may appear if you are pursuing a healing at some level. But these do not signify in any way that you have unearthed your true power spirit animal, the one that will dwell with you for the rest of your life.

In these questionable seminars, a "technique" of Soul Retrieval is also taught. The instructors have people work in pairs, and one of the two partners must journey to find the power animal, as well as their partner's soul in the Underworlds. This is done simultaneously, as the other pairs also attempt to accomplish the exercise in the room. These students, hardly knowing each other, are assisting one another in retrieving their souls. They are not taught to discern the significance of an animal or entity encountered in the tunnel, yet the novices are expected to bring it back and blow it into the body and chest of the partner. For instance, if someone finds an illness in the form of a spider or, by chance, the animal of someone else in the room, whatever animal is found in the journey is then blown into the partner's chest as if it were the power animal of that person. When I hear these stories I do not know if I should laugh or cry!

It is important to understand the magnitude of the emotional damage such "methods" may produce for someone inexperienced in these practices. First, not everyone possesses the natural gift of soul retrieval. It is given to specific types of shamans or healers who indubitably must undergo years of hard training. As I have experienced myself, *true* soul retrieval ceremonies performed by native shamans generally last a few hours, during which the shaman, in a deep trance state, suffers and endures the anguishes of the ill person. Upon his return, he is sweating, considerably exhausted.

Second, not everyone suffers a loss of soul. This practice is the latest vogue, poorly divulged by all sorts of false shamans. Many are led to believe that their souls are lost. Regularly, people ask me in their healing to retrieve their souls, when, in reality, there is nothing wrong with them at that level. These doubtful seminars announce: "Let's have everybody retrieve their souls, now!" Why do people allow an unfamiliar and inexperienced person to blow anything into their chest, their heart center, the seat of their spirit, and one of the most delicate and subtle organs of their emotional lives?

This flimsy emulation of native ways exhibits no respect or discrimination. I can only urge people to be careful. These supposed practices are imparted with the assumption that whatever emotional blockages or past traumas we have suffered have caused a loss of soul. A true native perspective of soul loss would be more discerning and not so generalized. Consistently, all the Maya, Mongolian, and Native American shamans and healers I have met, have taught me that, when someone suffers a complete loss of soul, he or she usually lingers sick in bed, physically depleted as the days go by. They would, therefore, certainly be physically unable to attend any seminars! In the case of a partial loss of soul, the patient is commonly quite emotionally disturbed, seeming far away and totally incapable of functioning properly on a daily basis. I frankly doubt that everyone who attends these seminars finds themselves in such a state.

Of course, all humans have, at some point, suffered a strong trauma, the reality of their emotional blockages and past ordeals. Who has not? But this in no way implies that your soul is kept captive by a spirit, is missing, or must be retrieved. Time reveals itself to be the best healer for these emotional problems. And for this, you must find an appropriate internal path to liberate you from them through the course of your life. But the soul generally remains fixed in the body. Though it may be wounded, it is nonetheless there. Often, life situations may create a catharsis, allowing us to purge past hurts, injuries, or sentimental bruises, in much the same way that our bodies will create an ailment such as a high fever. With the majority of people, it is not retrieval that the soul needs, but to be *freed*. This naturally involves an entirely different type of healing and spiritual practice. So it is important to place your emotional and spiritual life in the hands of competent healers or shamans when you seek guidance to uncover your inner puzzles and understand your illnesses.

The worst and most critical fact is that all sorts of people "graduate" from these seminars after only a few classes, claiming to be shamans, when, in reality, they have no real gift, no true vocation, no veracity, nor any real understanding of these ways. In turn, they may only create more ungroundedness and imbalance within those they instruct or heal. The universe has not chosen everyone to be an enduring shaman, one who must strive along the road to obtain these special ways and develop medicine powers. Even among natives, the medicine people develop their own distinctive field. There are the prayer people, the healers of all sorts, the retrievers, the removers, the blowers, the transformers, the shakers, the shape-shifters, those who pulse, those who perform *limpias,* the seers of the spirit world, the sweat lodge leaders, and the vision makers. In actuality, there are not many true retrievers. This skill is only mastered after many, intensive years of self-healing, through various arduous initiations that corroborate whether someone possesses an authentic spiritual tenacity and vocation.

So it is absolutely essential that ancient Power Animal teachings be taught properly, with sound guidance, to enable true and serious seekers to reach, through animal integration, the true gifts of their essence.

This is primarily because the sacred initiation to meet your power animal will change you forever. The identification must be absolute (though not blind), to continually witness the deepest blaze of yourself enlivening your spirit. This is why a discipline of meditation and purification is absolutely essential in your life.

In meditation, you will observe that your thought process considerably hinders you from glimpsing the vastness within the moment and your very spirit. Therefore, as you meditate to allow your animal within you, you may realize that thoughts are never free. Freedom cannot be in thoughts and mind, for they are unmistakably the cause of much suffering. Thoughts are depicted as clouds—white, gray, or black—passing in the clear blue sky or your spirit. The thoughts (always bound to the grasping of ego) create attachment and suffering. Behind, beyond, and beneath thought is its shadow side: *the world of true feelings*. By acknowledging your true feelings, you will gradually become aware of your dream body, your power animal, and your true spirit. Only taking responsibility for your spirit rewards you with freedom. Only through *listening* can you free yourself and calm your mind from grasping tendencies. Freedom from internal chains, depending on your particular medicine, may take a whole lifetime. Many situations will alter around you as you integrate your power animal, so you must be ready. You may find the need to purify your existence of old, stagnating relationships or sterile occupations. This is because the spirit animal lives in the vital fire of your inner being, waiting for you to discover your own chief, your true self.

The power animal is a direct passage to your spirit and has a secret language waiting to be uncovered by you. At one point in the course of integration, you may hear a special song, for instance, a call to your double. Or your animal's voice may talk to you or through your drum.

The spirit animal is a great responsibility. Many have received it, but left it sitting there, unactivated. Both your animal and your soul must be awakened and your medicine activated. There are hundreds of ways to do this. You can call and project the animal to open doors in the external world, to protect you when in danger, to bring the animal into your body to heal you, or to send your animal to heal someone else. (However, you should never interfere in another's medicine field without consent.)

The potential always exists that, one day, your animal may attack you in the journey time or in dreams, wanting to bite you, surprisingly coming at you with a forceful and aggressive appearance. If your spirit guardian is assumed to be your ally, then why might this occur? In this instance, your animal may have been scared by the contentious tendencies of your ego. By reflecting your internal fears, your inner aggressiveness, or your passivity, it is forewarning you of external or internal danger.

Even after years of integration, many may still erroneously project their own blockages, their obsessions and resistance, onto their spirit animal, mistaking this for their animal medicine. I have seen people despising the company of humans, who have told me that this was their animal medicine. This is an evasive justification. Inner insight must mature to welcome our shadows and not misinterpret the characteristics of our medicine. Moreover, many feign a reverse misconception, falsely assuming that the animal is of a particular nature to excuse their bad habits—for instance, thinking the animal does not like other people, when it is they themselves who refuse to open. Keen observation and a clear mind are of the utmost importance in preventing these internal misinterpretations.

The spirit animal will help you peel and remove your masks, one by one, uncovering yourself in your most dignified nakedness. This is the greatest energetic transformation we can seek, severing ourselves from imprisoning self-images and egoistic self-absorption. Without enough vitality, this moment of quiet alignment between the spirit power and the self can be quite overwhelming and may even disintegrate the seeker. So we must not be afraid of facing our fears. When the seeker feels a tangible disinterest, after years of actively calling the spirit animal, then, at that very moment, the powerful long-awaited *oneness* will emerge from within. No longer will there be an outside existence of another being. At this point, the spirit animal may even appear to have vanished. If the power animal is no longer found in the journeying tunnel, it is by virtue of its full adherence to your soul, your spirit, and your body. This means that now, at last, you are your power animal and your power animal is you, forever.

THE APPEARANCE
OF THE ANIMAL GUIDE

On the day that you realize, after years of intensive intercommunication with your spirit animal, that you are one, then you may observe another animal existence around you. This is what we call the animal guide or the *nahual animal* of the Maya. *Nahual* means secret, occult, and mysterious in the old Mexica language. The term is used to describe *the nahual realm*, another sphere of consciousness beyond the tonal reality. The nahual realm refers primarily to the reality of the dream time and to other subtle, psychic worlds.

The discovery of the nahual can only occur once you fine tune your power animals' connection, aligning your life with your true essence's purpose. The increased activity with your own guardian animal will incite an animal guide to access your medicine field, gradually attaching itself directly to your own power animal. The animal guide does not appear until your spirit animal is in place and well integrated within you. And not all who have received their spirit animal will necessarily have an animal guide appear to them.

The animal of the tonal dwells in the dream body or medicine field, principally attached at the seventh, or crown, center. Eventually it may extend to the whole body, within and without. The nahual guide lives at the star, or eighth center, above the seventh center. You must understand that this second animal guide is *not* your essence and does not merge with you at death, as does your main tonal spirit. The animal guide may facilitate your travel into other realms, may sustain and heighten your psychic awareness, your telepathic and other visionary powers. It may also guide you in out-of-body experiences in the dream time, allowing you to see the invisible, to unmask the unknown. The animal guide is frequently a bird (such as an owl, a raven, an eagle), or a dragonfly, due to their versatility in entering the occult. It may also be a special four-legged animal, such as a lizard, a jaguar, or a bear—all animals that manifest a strong relationship to the dream time.

Intensively calling forth your nahual guide may prove more dangerous than calling your power animal. Unlike the necessary activation of the power animal in tonal practices, giving the animal guide all your energy and focus may cause you to become lost in the appealing immensity of the unknown, depleting and depriving your life's purpose of the force of intent. I have seen people preferring their animal guide, to the detriment of their tonal spirit animal. I remember the case of a woman whose spirit animal was an opossum. She much preferred her crow animal guide. This reflected her own denial of her true essence. If you do not discipline yourself to remain centered with your power animal, daily practice with the animal guide may create tremendous imbalances and a total loss of grounded reality. The nahual guide should be activated only once in a while, in the context of a specific journey requiring its medicine.

In the journey or dream time, you should turn your eyes away from the animal guide, not giving it too much importance. The abstract and seducing power of other realms can easily empty and overpower you. You must constantly remind yourself that the animal guide is primarily there to assist your own power animal by nourishing it with insights of higher visions that will be translated into your life's path. In other words, it is preferable to be more passive toward your nahual guide, unlike practices with the spirit animal. It is favorable to let the animal guide lead the way to the mysterious nahual realm, entering and leaving this other consciousness according to its own will, without too much interference from you. Before anything else, it is the great mystery that perceives us and makes us perceive through our own eyes.

In order to see the mystery behind the soul, you must gather tremendous energy and cultivate a strong will to life. Herein abides the mystery that encircles you. Underneath you is an abyss without end. Once you coalesce with the other side, you cannot revert to old ways of being. Only strong warriors, who have created their lives with strong foundations, may voyage freely in the other regions without losing their sense of balance. For they know deep within that, in reality, there is nowhere to go but inward, nothing to do but to value, at every gait, every fragment of our life here.

3
INTUITION

EMERGENCE INTO
THE CAVERN OF DREAMS

In merging with the spirit animal's presence within your dream body, you will encounter a deeper awareness of the dream reality. This awareness arises as two folds of the same realm: *the awake dreams* and *the sleeping dreams*. The first group, the awake dreams, are revealed in your tonal consciousness, often as intuitive and mental revelations. The second category, the sleeping dreams, is where the double (or dream body) walks in the gateways of the dream world, or nahual, while you sleep. In order to approach your dream body, you must tame its unrestrained existence within yourself. This consists primarily of adopting a daily practical discipline. Here I will try to expose the nature of the dream body through safe practices. Talking about it, however, may only teach you to glimpse its free nature, for mastering it cannot happen by just reading words. So as not to lose ourselves in the immensity of the subject, my talk here will be only an introduction to the dream world from a native perspective.

The dream realm emanates from deep within Earth. Earth herself is incessantly dreaming the entire universe, the Moon and her children (in this instance, us). It is the nature of her deepest consciousness and reality. For humans incarnated on Earth, she provides a great reservoir of energy for our own dreaming, a receptacle for channeling the great cosmic dream of the universe.

The Great Spirit is dreaming the Earth. She, in turn, is dreaming us, all living beings. We, in turn, are dreaming the sacred vision of emergence into the mystery of the Great Spirit. This is how we connect to the great circle of life. It is this dreaming that confers on us our vision of life's purpose. When we allow our being to attune to Earth's consciousness, our human state of wakefulness enlarges into a clear perception of being dreamed, as we are dreaming who dreams us, rising in our inner universal spirit.

Earth is the great feminine shield of our solar system. So also is the dream reality. At night, as we naturally lie down and fall asleep on her lap, she is calling us back into our primal awareness, within her womb, returning us to our very source. This is dreaming. You cannot easily sleep while sitting, for your head will always be falling down, in extreme fatigue, toward the Earth that calls you. As your mind touches and penetrates the Earth, she begins inducing you to dream. Better said, she receives you in her entrails to journey within her center and reality. The native understanding of how the tonal and nahual realms interpenetrate each other is that the dream time (nahual) exists as the true reality and the daily reality (tonal) is actually a dream of endless reflection, as exposed in the following poem.

THE INTEGRITY OF THE DREAM BODY

*Spirit of dreams, invisible being who is whispering in the dark,
   the song of inner fears,
The sound of your true Visions, sacred feeling from your hidden
   Lodge,
Spirit of the dreaming, who awake the double from an eternal
   sleep,
Other Self, emerging and rising at the sharp call of the Nahual,
Ears that discern beyond falsehood, eyes that see behind
   disguises,
To conquer the other side of the Self, to sublimate the everyday
   consciousness
The one that has long forgotten its magical twin named soul.*

*Spirit of the Moon, who reveals what cannot be seen,
Who shines with her silver visage, deeply buried inside the
   cavern of hope,
Dreaming an unknown dwelling Spirit, the shadow of our
   totality,
She is to be revered for the inspiration of her ancient brilliance.
Those who search may remain blind to her beauty,
Impenetrable seducement that persists in you,
Though she manifests the everlasting path toward freedom,
Forever walking with the Moon at your side in a strange world
   of illusion,
With her knowledge of ultimate paradox where she is your
   unique ally.*

*The dream is the reality, this reality is the dream.
The spirit of the unseen cave is behind anything your eyes can
   witness,*

Spirit of mountains, spirit of trees, spirit of the great prism
  underneath the cavern,
At the other side of the Self, where all spaces are recorded in the
  great book of revelation.
At the gateways of this cavern stands the spirit of Dreams,
  ancestral guardian
Who may delude you, who may teach you if you are real to your
  feelings.
To reveal your lies, shame triggering awareness,
To watch selfishness being caught in your own web of ignorance,
To be Self, simply.
Then the power of entering the dream line may permeate its way
  to you,
Through this very tiny door, almost imperceptible, in the back of
  the mind,
So small it cannot be discovered with the eyes of the normal,
This shallow fissure to the threshold where a violent wind may
  receive you,
May chase you forever in an endless circle
Or may invite you to traverse and leap into the abyss of your
  power.

Sacred privilege of the Gods, vertiginous fall in the empty void,
Deserting behind the old Self, forgetting all that you know of you,
Of the mundane world.
The door will seal behind you forever as you descend into the
  interminable abyss,
Where there is no reversal.
Endless seeker, may your heart be never satisfied, may your thirst
  be never satiated,
May you never repose, sinking asleep once more,
Now that you are one, now that the Spirit of Dreams has shown
  you the unseen cavern,
Immense treasure in the subterranean recondite self,
Now that you hear the sacred rise and fall of your ocean within.

Right now, as you read these words, you are dreaming the world of
tonal reality. It is your persistent reason that keeps you from seeing the

dreaming that exists in the now. Every day, you constantly do the same, dreaming and self-reflecting your images into this world. At night, you enter the gateways of a realm so much more real. In the dream time (beyond conceptual time), you can approach all levels of consciousness, where knowledge is absolute and within your reach, if you perceive its concealed secret. What is lived in the dream state is so sharp and so real that your confined and inadequate mind cannot recall all the details of the expansiveness of that reality. In contrast, the only things truly real in this tonal existence are the ephemeral moments of vision in your dream life that you host within, emanating from your dreaming of Earth. The rest, what you sense as reality, is only a dream of the world of sense and feeling.

We all need personal power to fulfill our path. But personal power can only be acquired through real visions, and through their realization on this plane. In order to perceive the flashes of life visions vividly living within, you must have clear access to your dream body, where it lives, the confines of the other realm, the dream time. There is no specific "recipe" for reaching your dream body, except to develop your own spiritual warrior qualities: discernment, courage, persistence, and a strong aptitude for fully aligning your life's daily awareness. For it is here, in this plane, that you will initially generate the secure cognizance of your dream body by honoring the mystery here and confronting yourself with your fears, while at the same time perfecting the memory of each moment. You can hardly become sensitive to your dream body if, in the majority of your daily gestures, you are not fully attentive. Many people cannot even remember all of their actions after the day is done. Developing your memory is, therefore, the first gate to your dream body. At night, before going to sleep, try to remember what you did first thing in the morning. By doing this regularly, you will be forced to pay more attention to your first gestures of the day, therefore bringing with you your dream body for the entire day.

The consciousness of death as a presence in tonal reality is an important element in awakening to the presence of the great mystery around you. The reality is that we live a paradoxical enigma. We must face, in the labyrinth of our being, the key to our solitude. We must confront the internal fears that hinder our path to our dreams, and yet be as innocent and fresh as children in the Sun. This meeting in solitude helps you to reach your true self, to give your death a true meaning. Without it, your life is empty and absurd, without meaning. Knowing your death will help you to appreciate and celebrate in a full way every moment of life. You will live the living dream of being an enlightened human of Earth, passing beyond the illusions of your personality-ego. This is the direct gateway to the most powerful vision of the universe, conferred within the deepest strata of your self, to become the true human, real *Ongwhe Onwhe,* flowering *Nichimal Vinik.*

The nature of the dream body is uniquely naked, living in a world quite similar to the ocean, bathing as a sea nymph in a world of feelings. At times, the tidal flow is hostile and your dreams are agitated. At other times, it is as calm as a mountain lake. All incidents unfold directly in the dream state and all movements are intuitive, as is the link with the source of life, where silence precedes the mystery of the great void. For example, there are no boundaries and physical limitations in the dream reality. You dream of flying and you fly. You learn that you can change a scene at will, if you exercise this power. The spirit world and the dream world are one, and both impregnate the reality in which you live, inviting you to extend to the infinite at all moments, in all spaces.

The dream body is pure feeling and perfect intuition. This is the only way in which you can relate to it. Feelings are not emotions. Each exists distinct from the other. Usually, emotions are created by the selfish waves of your ego, entirely bound to the thought process. For example, emotions create excitement at one moment. At the next, you may cry out in desperation. All of this can occur in less than an hour. Emotions are not grounded, nor is the ego. But true feelings abide in a reality *underneath* the emotional world of surfaces. Feelings penetrate the essence of everything, beyond the world-reflection of your ego, whose emotions often defame the great mystery and inhibit the sensing of its profundity.

It is in the nahual world of the other reality, of dreams, that your inner dreams of Earth (conscious or not) are reviewed and remembered before manifesting into this reality. The dream body reveals your own shadows following you, opening the portal to a deeper perspective of seeing the invisible. Beyond the craziness of each mind, the dream body is eternal and has always existed. It gives perfect cosmic guidance, for it is a perfect witness to both the tonal and the nahual, always detached from any emotional involvement. This is the emotional involvement of the ego, of the grasping mind that confuses us, making us doubt and suffer. The dream body does not suffer. Nor can it be created or developed. It is already there, breathing behind, with a perfect nature. You can only witness and experience it in its most natural and simple state.

I think we all have had vivid dreams that were powerful enough to follow us all day long, keeping us from being entirely present to the moment, making us see every event of the day through the reflection of that particular dream. This happens when the dream reality captures us for a short interval and the dream body is not fully retrieved, but remains enchanted and captive somewhere in the other realm. Increasing the awareness of our dreams is, therefore, nothing to joke about, for we may easily be caught in the seduction of this realm and lose our grip of the tonal. When acting in *this* reality, we should always do so with humor. When dealing with the dream realm, do so with great seriousness. Most people live contrary to this truth. We are too serious and dramatic about the daily events of our world and do not give enough serious attention to dreams.

Many dream explorers who directly experience the dream state without proper preparation may never return. If they do, they may come back insane, having lost their balance within our worldly reality. You should, therefore, never work directly in out-of-the-body experiences without solid spiritual training and a strong physical guide to initiate you. If you are without a guide, it is usually preferable to adopt simple and sequential practices like those exposed here, to reach the awareness of the dream body and experience it in a slow, moderate, and steady manner. First, try simply to remember your dreams in the morning. Then be attentive to your dream body during your daily acts. It is always better to enhance the dream body in your daily awareness, during your various activities, than it is to dive directly and precariously into the dream time while asleep. After all, the balance between your two consciousnesses (mind and intuition) must be mastered in a perfect mutual reliance. This balance is crucial in any spiritual practice. One seeker may be attracted irresistibly to the dream time and constant journeying, while another (a person of reason) may be totally unable to dream anything clearly, even when awake. Both are maladjusted spiritually and are, unfortunately, missing the point of being true humans. One world cannot live without the other. This symbiosis must be weighed in the cosmic scale, in the same way that we humans must found the unity of our two sides: *true reason and true dreaming*.

Natives say that crazy people are touched by the great spirit. This is true. These beings are truly inspired, for they recognize the great divine void and live totally in its intensity. Nevertheless, the true purpose of humans on this planet resides in beholding the mystery and walking the tangible paths on this Earth plane to deliver the dream of the sacred vision. Ultimately, the higher purpose of humanity is to dream together, people and nations birthing together to share their fragment of the bigger picture, of this vast dream and their mutual missions on Earth.

This begins with knowing your dream body. Once you achieve this, you may hear your dream body whispering these words ceaselessly in your newly unveiled ears: There is nowhere to go. There is no beginning and no end. Magic is a windstorm in the middle of your peaceful ocean and, at the same time, an oasis in the middle of your stormy and rough sea. I am all of this, at the same time. As a passenger riding the dream universe, you may fear getting lost forever in my gateways, though only in your own maze of illusions, of your ego. Feel the sacred wind of your inner shadows, blowing in the mirror of the Earth's vision, and you will find wisdom forever. You will be one in Serenity without end.

THE REMINISCENCE OF THE DREAM BODY

When you are constantly self-reflecting, you are too caught up in past and future to notice the presence around you . . . . you are not vibrating fast enough to channel the immense energies of creation because your attention is scattered and you are closed to the one moment where the love that would quicken you exists: the moment where you are.[1]

Humans spend almost half of their lives sleeping and dreaming. Yet the majority have absolutely no awareness of what occurs in this dream reality, or that they even possess a dream body. They remember very little of their activities during the dream time.

---

[1] Ken Carey, *Return of the Bird Tribes* (San Francisco: HarperSanFrancisco, 1991), p. 140.

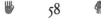

This is a shame. It represents a tremendous loss of power and knowledge entirely available to us if we would only wet our toes in this sacred ocean. Most people merely subsist, carrying on the relentless business of their lives and have very little time to dedicate to their other life. They prefer falling each night, with extreme fatigue, into a gloomy slumber. Some even assume, mistakenly, that awakening their dream bodies would be equivalent to undertaking another day's work and that they have absolutely no energy left for these "absurdities" of the night. In reality, unraveling the several selves of our dream reality requires very little "extra" time. Rather, it requires a cohesive stead-fastness and an integral awareness at all times. In fact, the effect may be entirely opposite from what you expect. The more you attune to your dream body, the more your time will seem to stretch positively in your daily life. To your own amazement, you will also experience a heightening of your overall physical energy. In fact, you may realize you don't have to spend any extra time at all, but that in the midst of your normal daily activities, the possibility of opening to the dream body is in your hands at any moment. Before I assert too many engag-ing promises, however, let me emphasize that reaching these optimal conditions of awareness demands a considerable amount of learning for every true dream seeker.

The dream body breathes behind you throughout your daily activities and is attached to you through the kidney center, entering your physical body at the navel. Both the tonal spirit animal and the nahual animal guide live in the dream body. This center of *intuition* abides inside you in your midsection, behind your navel. It is also called the gut. The dream body is attached to you with an invisible umbilical cord (some call it the silver thread). This subtle body voices its reality through your inner intuition, the source for your power of discernment. In other words, if intuition and will are not properly developed, you cannot achieve the incisiveness that discernment may confer on you to know reality directly and to see beyond the surface.

The dream body's presence can be felt as a swirling, yet steady and calm, power just behind and above you. At night, when your physical body is asleep and silent, it departs from you. It leaves your daily con-scious awareness to enter the dream world of immediate feeling. Whether or not you follow your double with your consciousness depends on your inner lucidity and the intuitive levels in your daily life. This will determine what you can remember of your dreams when you awaken.

Needless to say, this delicate body should be treated with all the reverence due its subtle and sacred nature. The dream body manifests exceptional qualities of alertness and awareness, beyond your conceptual mind. The impeccable memory of the dream body is far greater than what you may imagine. Most humans, however, truly give harsh treatment to their dream bodies, hampering any possibility of extending their spirit. The dream body of each person reintegrates fully with the physical body within two to three hours after the night's sleep. This moment of critical passage for both bodies should be observed with much lucidity.

A very ancient, native dreaming practice consists of fasting in the morning until the spirit-dream body and all the remembrance of the nightly journey are thoroughly with you. Contrary to what many Western doctors say, ingesting a copious breakfast immediately after waking is the worst treatment you can give to your dream body. The energy necessary for its lucid return will be employed in digestion instead of in the refined attention of every subtle movement of the dream body. In fact, the physical body does not need any food in the early morning. This is a myth, a bad habit of the mind and stomach. The morning restitution of your dream body feeds both your soul and your body, carrying back a vital inflow of fresh energy from the other reality for the morning, or even the entire day. It is not food that gives you energy in the morning, but your dream body. This is accompanied by an even greater awareness. The body, which has not yet undergone much vigorous physical activity, does not need food that early. By fasting, you allow your subtle body to slowly merge with your physical being, bringing back the awareness and memory of your night life. Much knowledge and spiritual training is given to you through dream time, by guides and other subtle spirits, especially if you have a clear mission on this plane. Whether you recall them consciously or not, these nightly teachings influence the steps you take in your daily awareness. To be conscious of the return of your dream body in the morning allows you to strongly attune to this reservoir of knowledge.

Think of this: How many rush out of bed, roused by a deafening alarm, jump into a cold shower to wake up, or do intense physical exercises to "boost" them up. They rush to work in their cars, trying to put on a tie, or eat breakfast, or read a newspaper while talking business on a cellular phone—all while driving! This may make you laugh, but it should not. In reality you need to ask yourself these questions: "What happens to the dream body in this hasty daily start? What happens to the other self, that most intimate essence?" What happens is simply that many of the subtleties of the night are lost to memory and consciousness forever, permanently slipping into other realities of the dream world. And this is the great loss.

After many treatments of this sort, your dream body will be scared away and will start removing itself from you, leaving you disconnected from your own intuition and inspiration of life. This is quite serious, as you can see! Your power animal may also remove its protection, leaving you vulnerable to all sorts of accidents and diseases. You will feel more and more empty as each day goes by, disconnected, ungrounded, and depressed. This is not to be taken lightly. It is absolutely necessary in the morning to develop a silent discipline and to allow time after awakening to meditate. Sit with a hot beverage and contemplate the coming day. Offer a morning prayer to greet the Sun, or take a gentle walk in nature to readjust both beings so that your day is harmonious and clear, and your sense of self, whole.

Once you have attuned properly to your night body, it will flow easily through you at any moment of the day. You may even notice how much more relaxed your physical body becomes, even if your work tasks have not decreased. The feeling of constantly running after yourself will have simply and magically disappeared from your existence. When your dream body is perfectly linked to you during the day, you may sense that it moves your very body, walking you, talking you, with a minimum of muscular effort on your part, all the while conferring on you a maximum efficiency to achieve your daily labors. In brief, it is your dream body that gives you all the energy you need to live intensively.

Your dream body allows you to move beyond any tension of the mind-ego. The ego is the being, the "entity" within us, that pushes, rushes, forces, overthinks, plans in a disconnected way, grasps with willfulness. It impedes your awareness of the dreaming witness. Once your intuition center is fully alert, your third eye, at the forehead, slowly awakes from a timeless nap, hurting slightly for a brief period because your inner consciousness is increasing. This is when you start receiving visions.

Many people read too much, constantly filling their minds with written information and visual images, in an incessant seeking for new ideas and theories. This hinders considerably the process to meet with your dream body. The written world of mind concepts can only trigger a certain level of inspirational, intellectual understanding. True knowledge is direct and cannot travel through the mind, because the thought process is much too slow. Your dream body vibrates much faster and at a higher frequency than your too ponderous and complex mind, heavy with all sorts of arguments, discussions, doubts, and preoccupations. The dramatic reality is that the great majority of people, living in their clouded brains, determine each of their daily gestures through this obstructive rational mind. It is your dream body, however, that should rule your inner guidance and life decisions.

How can people allow their rational minds to govern their spirits? This puzzles me—always having another entity (the mind) between your true self and the astonishing world, a mind that is naming, repeating like a parrot, explaining to you what reality is, as if your soul needed a translator for what you know and perceive already. Perceiving directly with your dream body forces you to put this farcical watcher in its true place. Your mind should be a powerful executive tool for your actions and strategies, but never the sovereign witness of the essence of the world.

Allow the dream body to discern within the true you the great vastness. Your twin is dreaming you now, in the most profound and earthy experience of spiritual nature, flowing from one situation to another with ease and appreciation. "Hunting your dream body" is to dream this world, a process of not struggling against the river of life. The key resides in training your mind and being still when meeting with the great dream of this reality. This is the hunt. For this, you must constantly catch and watch yourself when entangled in your personal concerns and your ego's neuroses. When you are caught in the supposed, normal identification of society, you think that the way you or others may react, your likes, dislikes, and your temperament, define who you are. For example, people who are convinced that they do not like being in nature, or do not like windy days, may be convinced that this defines who they are. This is not true, but only the stratagem of a malicious mind playing the game of the ego. It is not worth pursuing.

In reality, there is nothing to think about. Your dream body is below all of this. Underneath the emotional world of doubts and insecurities, it feels directly, on the spot, what is true and what is false, which is the correct step and which the erroneous one. It just knows. Your dream body, your spirit, sees that everything is equal in this universe, that everything is important or that nothing is important. This sort of wisdom is total attention, for it dwells in complete silence and allows the intent to flow, to touch and to be, beyond time conditioning. In its eyes, the world is not linear, but spiraling.

Life is a movement that holds the seeds of this inward transformation, of this complete internal revolution. The dream body never carries any negative residue. It is always clear and purified, although it mirrors you, your own preoccupations and illusions. For instance, most people dream only of their worries, waking up more tired than if they had not gone to sleep. The first step to attuning to your dream body is to perceive that what you do during the day directly determines any reflection in the mirror of your dream body. Whatever you have not wanted to see of your own shadows is reflected at night. In a true native perception, the human "subconscious" is absent and does not really exist, because pure and total consciousness dwells at this very moment within you in the landscape of eternity as a whole. Whether we perceive this eternity or not belongs to the capacity of every human to live in inner silence. There is nothing really hidden beneath your consciousness, except that you may have forgotten your true self somewhere. Your deepest memory is, nevertheless, there and moves each of your actions. In the dream realm, time is juxtaposed. It is time behind time, beyond the time, below and over the time, as well as the space. It is the same with consciousness. Total consciousness is always there, in various levels, and is the very essence of the universe. It is just that we do not have full access to it, but perceive it only in fragments. In this sense, there is no subconscious, only the great vastness of this conscience dreaming called the Great spirit.

THE PATH OF LUCID DREAMING

In order to have a lucid dreaming, it is essential to create a good place to sleep. Choose a clean area, free from any electric frequencies. I have seen people who keep a whole library by their bed, right where their heads lay while they sleep. If the dream body is pure silence, why would you want all these words to accompany you and hinder your dreams? The general precepts for lucid dreaming are:

- Carry a light stomach in the dream state;
- Have enough fresh air (aeration during the day is good to clean the energetic field of your room);
- Sleep on a hard mattress;
- Keep your mouth closed as you sleep;
- Don't watch television in your room;
- Don't drink any strong coffee or alcohol before going to sleep;
- Avoid all conversations and intense discussions in the room where you sleep;
- Don't read in your bed.

It is also helpful to smudge with smoke, to leave behind your worries of the day and call for clarity of dreams. If you sleep every night with a partner, sleep in two single beds or a fairly large bed so your two dream bodies do not touch and can breathe separately. In this way, you can experience your own dreaming more clearly. Or you may want to practice dreaming together.

There is an ancient Maya practice that I have found very useful in enhancing dreaming and the reminiscence of dreams. It consists of creating a dream altar. The altar should be by your bed, usually to the side, and must have on it a silver bowl of water. Both silver and water are remarkably conducive to dreams. On the altar, put some minerals, such as black obsidian and green jade, that induce dreaming and reaching the Other Self. These stones are grounding and powerful in helping you to come out of a dream when necessary. They bring you back so you don't get lost. The altar is used primarily as a strong focal point. Smudge it with smoke before sleeping to help your dream body find its way in the dream time. It is also a good place for meditating or praying in the morning to call back the dream body.

Lucid dreaming starts during the day, with the examination of the big consumers of your energy, energy that is absolutely necessary to access your dreams. Everything toward which you turn your attention is a direct receiver of your precious energy and constitutes a potential loss. Because of this, you must choose carefully where you focus your energy during the day. This includes what you do, what you say, and what you think, as well as what you see, for you dissipate a lot of energy through your eyes. You must avoid looking fixedly at someone, for this is a big dissipater. For natives, it is often very intruding to have someone look steadily at us for many minutes while conversing. People do this all the time. Their attention is caught easily in meaningless and superficial things, actions, events, situations, and especially the wrong-doings of others. Each time your attention is drawn toward something or someone of lower vibrational force, your energy is substantially depleted and you may feel drained afterward. However, by giving your attention to Earth's frequency, natural elements, or positive thoughts, you charge your soul with that energy. A practical exercise to prevent the harmful tendency to look too much involves gazing or slightly crossing your eyes at times during the day to undo the hypnotic effect of the tonal. You must also be discerning of how other people may directly draw your energy for themselves and learn how to protect yourself with your power animal.

In Western society, I have often observed that it is considered discourteous in a social meeting not to talk and share of yourself. In the native ways, however, this shows a total lack of sensibility and an invasion of privacy. Natives do not overwhelm others with questions or start sharing about themselves without first being invited. Curiosity, in this sense, is unhealthy, for it is based on insecurity. Natural curiosity, though, is a gift that should be cultivated and must be expressed in a detached way.

Every obsession holds damaging power, as do attitudes such as irritation, intolerance, and dispersion, all of which seem to be the disease of the century. Inner obsessions are caused by the need to grasp people, things, ideas, even teachings—the list is long. In order to cease the obsessive, vicious circle of your mind, you must drop any chaotic thinking and logically consider only what is needed to live your life, to cultivate renewing thoughts, and avoid distorted judgment and prejudice. This is the use of *true reason*. Any thoughts of fear, based on obsessions, are caused by internal aggressiveness, which is often translated as an inner struggle between you and you. This internal split causes pure suffering, often projected outside as blaming and resenting others. An awareness of your dream body will help you to detach and see beyond.

In the large range of dreams, we find *prophetic dreams* and *reversed dreams*. It is tricky to discern between the two, because reversed dreams are contrary reflections of what may happen to you in this reality. There are some people who dream reversed. This means that, if they dream that everything goes wrong in a situation, it will actually be fine in their lives. The contrary is also true. With a circumspect observation of how your dreams mature and how they consummate in the tonal, you may distinguish when a dream is premonitory and when it is reversed.

Analyzing dreams is a waste of time. Analysis is a process of the mind. Yet many dreams cannot be interpreted with the mind. It requires intuition to understand their full significance. Paying attention to the quality of your dreaming is of utmost importance. A dream that is recurrent must be looked at seriously, especially after dreaming three times of the same occurrence. I recommend, therefore, that you acquire a better remembrance of each dream, rather than analyzing them. Among natives, a group therapy is often the solution for obsessive dreams. This helps by acting out the dream, making it real in the presence of the affected, in order to purge it once and for all. I remember an Indian woman who, though not a horsewoman herself, often had dreams of falling off a horse and landing on her head, to the point that she developed a terrible obsession about horses. One day, we helped her act out her dreams. With the help of a medicine person, and in front of her family members and friends, she was asked to simulate her dreams safely, thus falling from her horse in the exact way of her dreams. She repeated the scene many times that day. After that, she was completely cured and never had this dream again. This seems more effective than any analysis.

There are feminine and masculine dreams. Most dreams contain colors, although some appear in black and white. In dreams, some of our human senses are more engaged than others. Your hearing may be quite sharp, and you may experience tactile feelings of hot and cold, but rarely of touching. If you dream of eating, you will not taste the food and it will never reach your stomach. Dreams can easily give you insight into your physical organs, as a kind of internal "barometric" evaluation. For example, dreams of fire and smoke, dead spirits, and awful creatures are symptoms of a heart problem, either physical and/or emotional. Dreams of wars and weapons, hard travels, endless streets where you are lost, or wavy oceans, reflect lung imbalances. Dreams in which you are exhausted and powerless, trying to run away without success, suggest kidney insufficiency. Intricate jungles, inaccessible mountains, or barren plains, often indicate liver problems. Discussions and fights with familiars, friends, or work partners, or gatherings of many people connote a congested gall bladder. Strangulation and suffocating dreams reflect an asthmatic condition.

As to the emotional significance of dreams, a general state of sadness and melancholy denotes a kidney insufficiency, and will be expressed in various signs such as mists, fears, impotency, prisons, or graves. Dreams sent by a deficient heart will carry symbols of smoking stoves, hot coals, fires, reddish skies, and sparks, all reflecting a seriously advanced state of inhibited anger and aggressive emotions. In contrast, dreams induced by beneficial spirits are watery, calm, and profound. Those of freedom contain ecstatic experiences, such as flying. Dreams of hope are symbolized by stars, lightning, and great heights. Sexual dreams, when not directly literal or suppressed, may be expressed by various symbols, such as roosters, serpents, and snakes. In understanding these signs, however, this is as far as a native analysis should go. What is required here is mostly a direct knowing of your own dream signs.

To clearly remember your dreams, it is imperative that you examine the nature of your memory. Memory is not like a file folder or a diskette. It is not a piece of furniture in which you can hide your "stuff" or classify your collection of souvenirs in an inner drawer. Rather, it is an inconceivable faculty with which humans have been endowed since the beginning of time. Memory should be regarded as your most valuable spiritual faculty, for, without it, the world would be incongruous. The magical perception of the dream body is not linear, but juxtaposes impressions of eternity within you, by the very act of memorizing and remembering. The memory of the dream body is perfect. When you are trying to recall an event, you just have to attune to it, instead of banging your head on the wall! Both past and future are the *now* for the dream body. For a native mind, the succession of events is not important when telling or recounting an incident. For the dream body, two events that hold the same significance—for instance, two similar and amazing signs of deer appearing thirty years apart—are part of the same time continuum, one sign explaining the other with no separation of time in between. These two events become juxtaposed, but are of the same nature, and they are both in the now. This is called *the magical mind*. The way memories are brought up in the

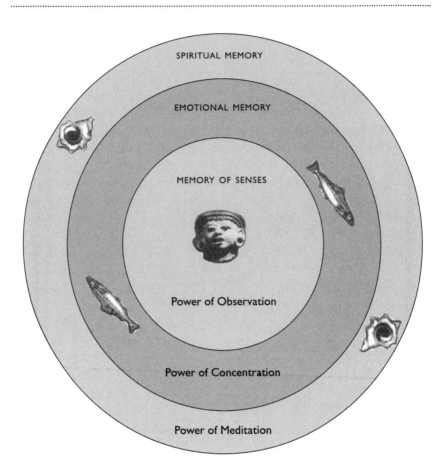

Figure 2. Awakening the Three Powers of Awareness.

dream witness differs from how they are handled by the rational mind. Association of symbols of past and present are one in this continuum. There exists no separation between past souvenirs, this very moment, and what will happen in ten years. When remembered, events exist again as vividly as in the now, by the mysterious reversal operation of the time continuum. We can even predict the future, because the awareness is in the same continuum.

In this wheel of eternity, where time is not leaving you as it does in normal consciousness (where you must run after time) but is reversed and constantly coming at you, time appears for the dream body to be expanding rather than contracting. Memory is your very consciousness and will follow your soul until the end of time throughout all your incarnations. Memory is a wondrous organ and you must exercise it, otherwise it may fall asleep along with your spirit. This incredible aptitude has many levels and types of memory (see figure 2). The first we develop as a child. It is the *memory of the senses,* also called the power of observation. Our *visual memory* is the observation of reality as a form of contemplation. This memory is two-dimensional and can easily be twisted (as can all other memories of our senses), according to the likes and dislikes of the ego, which qualifies what is looked at as better or worse in the analytical comparison of the rational mind. But the direct observation of reality through impersonal love confers an immediate knowing that increases the accuracy of this visual memory.

The auditive memory is also subject to ego interpretations. We hear what we want. This is the first sense to be born in the mother's womb and the last one to fade in a dying person. Being strongly connected to the dream body through the kidney center, it is the memory that contributes to the development of pure intuition. *The memories of smell, of taste, and of touch* are also very important in supporting our practical memory of this reality.

The second type of memory, the *emotional memory,* is the body memory. It is directly related to space memory, endowing us with the power of concentration. When emotional grounding is good, this memory is unconstrained. By remembering how your body felt at a particular moment, you can recall perfectly the specific situation, through letting the remembrance of these emotions come back gradually, in precise detail. Moreover, this memory provides you with the knowledge of direction in your life's walk. I think everyone has felt, at some point, a feeling of déjà vu—a feeling that you have already lived a moment or already seen a place, unknown until now. This is induced when the body memory awakens to other-life remembrance. This memory is intimately linked to the dream-body memory.

The third type of memory is the *dream-body memory,* or *spirit memory*. This memory gives the total memory-awareness of the moment (and all moments), as in telepathy. It is the power of meditation. Also called the psychic memory, it is drawn upon in divination, prophetic dreams, and augural insights. This memory will not be awakened until the other two memories are well developed. Telepathy has within it three levels: emotional or instinctual telepathy, as between animals or mother and child; mental telepathy of thought transmission; and spiritual telepathy or soul merging. The dream-body memory belongs to the realm of true feeling.

Awakening these memories is not easy, but can become a daily practice. Start with simple things, such as willing the intent in a relaxed manner, then remember a little more each day, recalling things like names, phone numbers, grocery lists, people's faces, events. Next, be more attentive to textures, thoughts, hearing, and feelings. This will considerably enlarge your power of perception to access the dream's awareness. When the three awarenesses—the powers of observation, concentration, and meditation—are concerted in harmony, you will achieve true balance within and your dream body will live indivisible from your essence and your daily awareness.

THE SMOKING OBSIDIAN MIRROR

Throughout the teachings I have shared on the power animal and the dream body, I have constantly referred to the shadow side we all have, following us at every moment. At this point, you are probably asking yourself: "What exactly is the shadow side of my being?"

To understand shadows, you must know that they are often expressed within, as an internal struggle, as a fight for life and death, between your ego and your dream spirit. In this struggle, you are revealed to your Self, you look into your own internal obsidian mirror, your inner Shadow Lodge. This is where your dream body emerges from the west passage in the medicine wheel. It is also the entrance tunnel into the Underworlds (or Lowerworlds).

The dreams come from the Earth and the West is symbolized as a deep Earth's tunnel and the ultimate death. It is where the Sun goes every night to die before being reborn in the East. The West is also called the Black Lodge, where are found the powers of introspection, humility, and true power from the Earth. The wall of the West is called the wall of dreams, but also the wall of inner terror and illusions. It is illusion that creates vanity and self-importance. This wall is represented as a big ball of millions of mirrors, similar to a discotheque ball hanging in the room. It is as if you were trapped inside this ball of mirrors. There, inside, you are reflected endlessly into thousands of mirrors.

At first, the images of yourself that you are reflected back please you and feed your vanity. You can go on for quite a while in this self-contemplation. But then the reflections become truly irritating, because you are looking in mirrors that are reflecting the same image of yourself an infinite number of times. So you see the same you, end-lessly. You become really bored and exasperated by this. You would like to escape, but where? You would like to change the image, but you can't. So, in your hopelessness, the mirrors then reflect your true shad-ows, not sparing you, making you see your ugliest sides, the parts of yourself that you are afraid to see. This is when you meet the smoking obsidian mirror within, interminably echoing what you refuse to see. You are now in a phase of pure denial, denial of everything within and without. You are absolutely terrified to enter into your shadows, eter-nally afraid of the night of your true self, and fearful of the profundi-ty of your feelings. "Oh! If I could return from where I come," you scream. "But how?" Now, trapped inside, there is no exit. "If only I could be as before, remain superficial as I was, as everyone else I know." Because no one else ever asked the true questions, never sought anything real. This is too perplexing, too bewildering. "It would be so much easier if I could remain as ignorant as always."

But you just can't go back. You now have to ask, "How?" You have to ask yourself, "Why?" You must start asking the real questions. By asking how, in searching for why, you have to go forward and jump into the mysterious abyss that the mirrors reveal to you. You have to jump into the mirrors of your shadows and meet your true power, your very spirit. For once, you have to be brave, because you are now facing the demons of Earth, the dark entities, shadows of the world about to kill you. And one particular shadow is a huge one—your fear of death. This is what the obscure entities on this planet wish for you, and for us all, that all humanity reside in this place of spiritual deprivation, bound to the mundane and materialistic fascination of these ego-mirrors, for-getting once and for all to quest for your soul's advancement.

Now, more than ever, you see the abyss and you are aware of these dark forces, hissing in your ears not to jump, not to find your libera-tion. They rejoice in enticing you with these appealing mirrors of mun-dane interests, keeping your mind busy for the rest of your life. With your mind busy on your vanity, they make sure there is no place left to look at your deepest self. The day that you awake, completely bored with this superficial world you have adopted, the day you awake, at last, with a true spiritual anxiety in front of the abyss, they will try to make your life impossible. They will impede you by all means possible, from breaking out of your chains, from breaking these mirrors.

This is when the inner struggle comes upon you, resulting in spiritual depression. This is when you start becoming quite aggressive. They are everywhere around you, constantly taking advantage of your weakest self, often appearing as merciless people, harassing you each time you wish to dedicate yourself to the true retreat into your spirit. They appear as dark influences within and without, as distractions, temptations, as endless problems, inciting you to destroy yourself by any means, inciting you to be angry at the whole world. They may go as far as providing an appealing life for you within this palace of mirrors, offering you total security and prosperity, so that you no longer desire to better your spiritual condition. If you undertake to fight these entities, you feel you are losing your mind. You become paranoid. All these voices shout in your mind at once, making you crazy. This is when you meet your second big shadow—the fear of insanity.

You are now in a state of complete vulnerability, so weak. You are a hungry and needy soul. It is now that you need to seek a spiritual guide. But you must proceed very carefully, for the dark forces may even hide in the disguise of a false spiritual teacher, who may do everything to possess your spirit, or even to create for you more temptations toward spiritual power. If you fall for all of these obscure entities and their telepathic enticement, they will have won you over. They will know you are now under their control, and will begin looking for other subjects, just barely awakening and of fresher taste than you are now.

But you have to be strong. This is when you are called to become a spiritual warrior. You have to be in the world of mirrors, out there, and yet you have to pursue your solitary quest with great veracity. For this, you learn spiritual strategies, because you cannot let this happen. You cannot die to your spirit. You learn to recognize these dark entities, and you also learn to preserve your pure essence. Your learn to hunt as a true warrior, because you know, out there, all of humanity is submersed in their influence.

You can now see them everywhere, at all levels, on television, in magazines, in the supermarkets, in the food your society tells you to eat, in the people who say they are your friends, at work, in a glass of whisky, in drugs, in the downtown streets, in the school systems and education, in governments. They are there, creating despair, insanity, death, and illness, in the common people, impeding them to awake to spirit. They can be incarnated in absolutely anyone—fascists and liberals, communists and capitalists, intellectuals and psychologists, doctors and artists, false shamans and common people. And you know now that you are alone, completely alone in this vast world. You learn to discern and this is your most powerful guide.

You learn to go in Earth, for your tunnel within is a safe place. There you can embrace your reflections of terror within, your mirage in the desert of your soul, and transmute all of this. If you are afraid of your emptiness, afraid of realizing you are alone and that you are absolutely no one, you will never see the passage. Once you have realized the presence of these terrible mirrors within, seeing them echo a thousand images of you, projecting intolerably your narcissism on a giant screen, you cry and scream in horror. You cannot live anymore with the perpetual illusions of yourself, disconnected from reality, where everything is centered around what you like, dislike, want, or need, as if only you exist. You cannot deny anymore this distressing semblance of yourself, never able to give of yourself, never able to lose yourself in the great void, always seeking more and more palliatives and justifications. You now have to jump. You cannot live in a secluded world anymore, a world in which you think everyone is watching you all the time, a world in which everyone is thinking everyone else is watching them. And, in the end, no one is watching any one. They are all too busy thinking they are being watched. This is a dishumanized world. But now, within, you learn that in the world, only death watches you.

You wish now to slip away, forever, from your ego's agony, to break the looking glass of a thousand reflections of yourself and escape from this house of mirrors and terrible loneliness. You long to find yourself lying at the foot of a calm lake under the night, reflected in the stars themselves. You want never again to stand in the blinding reflector of your inquisitive ego, asking you to believe exclusively in yourself, threatening you if you listen to anything that is not yourself. If you could only awaken from this nightmare. This, this moment of deep despair, is when you crack the mirror and slip through the fracture to see the other side of your obsidian mirror. And it is death that shows you the way, pointing out with a finger the real door, the path to your true liberation. As you jump through the crack, you learn to know your death and to fear no more.

On the other side you find yourself, but this time, with your real dreams within. You are alone with yourself, but in a great acceptance and serenity. This is when you reach the end of the West wall. Your firm determination to jump and cross this abysmal mirror is your impeccable canoe to the other shore, named true self. As you paddle, paddle, and paddle onto this wide looking glass, this river of life and death, the door to your old self closes behind you. The mirroring shore of terror you left is now so far behind, a vague memory, and you know now that you have reached your very spirit. You made it, with courage and perseverance, for now these dark forces will never touch you again. Never. You are free. You are free because you can dream, true dreams, where real hope exists. Beyond the internal terror and violence of the world, beyond this wall, is now the awe-inspiring vision of your spirit, the one that the great Earth is dreaming for you.

This open space of dreaming is our first and most primal reality as humans. It is the entrance into the fetal waters for all of us. It belongs to everyone, poor and rich, ugly and beautiful, ignorant and evolved. Dreaming is the very substance in which the universe spirals and manifests everything, even the inconceivable. Dreaming is our little corner of the cosmos, where we can cuddle in this dream shell, in the midst of the storms of life. It is the home of our spirit. Dreaming will follow you all your life as your shadow. In the labyrinth of dreaming, your dream path exists between symbols and realities. Here, inside and outside are banished. There is no left or right, up or down. By going through the walls of your inhibitions, one simple object may change into the subject of a whole cosmic dream. Here, the woods, deserts, and oceans turn into spaces of immensity and eternity, yet, at the same time, of enveloping intimacy. Here, in the ocean of absolute depths, there abides no weight or density. It is dissolved into the waters of your dreams. Here, dreaming is as round and circular as the universe, and dreaming of the Earth looms in realities of peaceful rest. Here, a succinct dream of fire surges as an infinite vision of inner illumination, a dream of the ocean dives you into the pure profundity of unknown and blessed feelings, and a wind dreaming you may materialize as a powerful soaring above your consciousness. For, right now, you are already dreaming and remembering all of this, for eons past . . .

THE RED LODGE BEYOND THE VEILS

EMERGENCE INTO THE CAVERN OF DREAMS

METAMORPHOSIS THROUGH NATIVE HEALING WAYS

THE SPIRIT ANIMAL BEHIND THE SOUL

THE SHAMAN BENEATH THE COSMIC TREE

RESURGENCE INTO THE REGIONS OF MYSTERY

JOURNEYING INTO THE MAZE OF SPIRIT

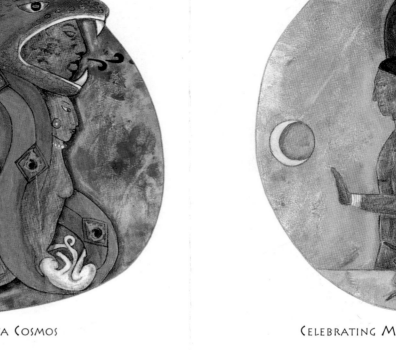

ECHOES OF THE MAYA COSMOS

CELEBRATING MEN'S AND WOMEN'S TWINNESS

CONNECTING THE WORLD MEDICINE WHEELS

CONVERGENCE OF GREAT CYCLES

THE RENAISSANCE OF THE TRUE HUMANS

4
LIFE

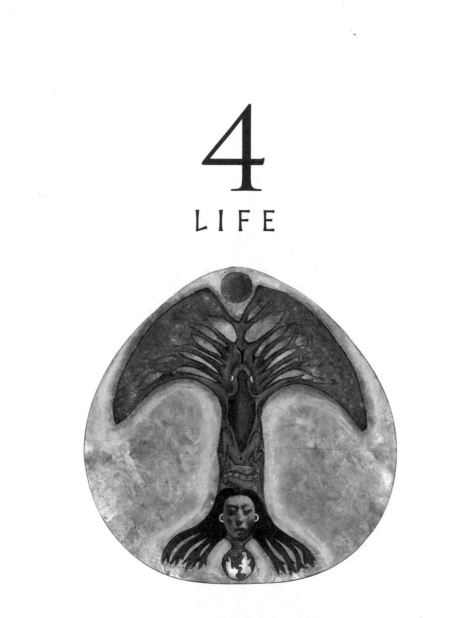

THE SHAMAN BENEATH THE
COSMIC TREE

There are many old Maya stories that chant of the pure consonance of ancient times. One of these songs related in the land of the pheasant and the deer recalls the myth of the tree of light of the East and the shadow tree of the West. The dark tree of the West is named Chechem, the Eastern tree, Mother Ceiba. These huge trees grow in the warm climate throughout the Maya land. They were planted there at the beginning of time.

In order to grasp the enchanting world of the ancient Mayas, imagine yourself in the rich rain forest of Central America, the heat and the extreme moisture inducing a dreamlike state, the crickets droning their sibilant and hypnotic sounds all day and all night long. Everything seems magical and alive in this jungle setting. The tale suggests that the hunter who knows these trees will know his way. Chechem, the tree of the West, has a melancholic essence. The venomous thorns on its bark confer on it the singular power of poisoning people. This venom pervades the shadow of its energy field. When the air becomes suffocatingly hot and the Sun is high at midday, those in search of shade may be seduced by Chechem's shadow. If they rest in its apparently refreshing shade, however, they may never wake up. If they do wake up and start running away, realizing they are in danger, they may remain crazy for the rest of their lives. This obscure tree is a powerful deceiver and a master of illusion. It is seen as the punishing tree of shadows. Those who trust this enticing shadow of poisoned leaves will never again follow the true path, but become captives of the tree's irresistible power of shadows. Even birds do not make their nests in this tree, nor do deer rest beneath it, even if they are dying of thirst. Only ignorant people are lured to it.

In opposition, Ceiba, the tree of the East, is called the enchanted tree of life, known for its joyful spirit. It is a tree of fertility. Its strong and smooth body rises high in the sky, as a tall antenna pointing to the zenith. Its branches are like a cosmic roof, extending to the infinite horizon. Its shadow is one of pure light, therefore many birds nest in its flowering branches. She is the *Madre Ceiba*, the mother of all children of humanity, the sacred tree of life that holds all the knowledge of the Maya, every branch representing the human destiny of the people. The sacred flourishing Ceiba presides over the center of the village to protect the people. They were planted in the middle of the community as the cosmic center of life. Some villages were built around centenary Ceibas. It is said that only the good winds and spirits blow at the Ceiba's peak, which is always filled with colorful butterflies, depicting the Butterfly Rainbow Tree, as in many other Indian cultures. The old people say that, if you rest or sleep under her shadows, the Mother tree dreams you and you will awaken restored and peaceful, having dreamt the most joyful dreams you may have ever had. Her shadow is the shadow of happiness. She is the tree of regeneration that keeps people youthful and healthy. Her soil is always very rich to her roots, contrary to the poisoned soil of the Chechem. It is customary for old people to choose to die under the Ceiba, to ensure a good passage to the land of the dead, into the Underworlds.

Clearly, this ancient and beautiful myth refers to the tree of life and the tree of death. The Maya Chechem, mirror of shadows, is the passageway to the nine Underworlds to meet the nine shadow obstacles. On the other hand, the sacred Ceiba is the portal to the thirteen Upperworlds, representing the thirteen accomplishments of the warrior toward higher consciousness. In the path toward liberation, the spiritual warrior must voyage into the terrible shadows or mirrors of the Underworlds. The descent into the nine regions is often seen as the meeting of the nine roots of the universal cosmic tree into the land of the dead. There, seekers undergo a small death passage. If they are successful in conquering the nine obstacles through these intensive initiations, they start the ascent into the thirteen flowering branches or upper spheres of consciousness. Only spiritual warriors may become true shamans, and only when they have died to themselves and been reborn from the cosmic tree of life.

THE NAVEL OF THE WORLD

The ancient Tree of Life teaching is found in traditional native cultures all over the world, being one of the most intrinsic elements within the ancient cosmogonies. In all cultures, the sacred tree of life symbolizes the axis of the universe, one of the most ancient teachings, rooted in shamanic knowledge. The cosmic tree is the center of the world, a perfect model of teaching to the true seeker, as well as the community, for a harmonious society. The ancient tree is also called the Sacred Tree of Ancestors and the Great Central Tree of Freedom and Enlightenment, in which the spiritual warrior traverses the river of human spirit. This tree of humans is formed from the lineage of our ancestors. Each leaf personifies a human being on Earth; the roots are the foundations connecting us to our inner truth. By drawing upon the sap of life beneath the tree, seekers find the nourishment toward true beauty, the substance of the real people, the true humans, or *Nichimal Vinik* in Maya, the flowering man and flowering woman.

For the Mongols, the teaching of the great tree as a way into life embodies the perfect model of alignment for humans. The cosmic tree is holding the spine of the universe. This great axis exemplifies the human spine of growth, existent in one being, also connected to the center of the cosmos. This is the vertebral column of the universe within us. The cosmic pole is a dreaming tree that reveals the vision of our lives' purpose.

At the base of the cosmic dreaming tree is often found the hole of emergence, the entrance to deeper regions, the Underworlds and to the land of the dead, as well as to higher spheres of consciousness. This carries an extremely rich symbolism. The importance of this opening at the foot of the tree is so central that it is represented in almost every native culture: as the entrance of kivas into the womb of the sweat lodges, as the *sipapu* entrance for the Hopis, as the roof opening of their ceremonial mud building, as the aperture of the tall teepee of many poles, and as the Maya portal through which the gods enter their ancient pyramids. The emergence of humanity onto this Earth is said, in many cultures, to have arisen through these sacred mouths at the center tree and through these ceremonial openings.

In most cultures, the sacred tree is believed to support the roof of the worlds, often envisioned as the bridge to the other worlds, a rainbow bridge that often takes the form of a sacred ladder or a sacred mountain. Most importantly, the tree of life is always represented at the center of the medicine wheel. There are three major planes that are accessed through this tree axis: the Underworlds (below the earth), the Earth Mother, and the Upperworlds (the sky realm), all coalescing in creation. There are many ways to enable the propulsion of shamans into the ancestor roots of generations or into the upper branches. Their travel through this great axis is expressed through powerful journeys, trance states and oracles (often accomplished with their animal spirits), in dances (with eagle feathers), and through prayers or spirit drums. It is common for the Mongols to seek the journey state by climbing a sacred pole erected in the center of the village. What is common to all shamans in traditional cultures, however, is the perfect mobility they have achieved between these worlds, thus attaining a complete spiritual freedom usually unknown to the common people. This is the great reward for the shamans, coming only after much hardship. Their journey to the tree of life is often called the magic ride over the winds.

The cosmic tree always presides over the center within yourself and is directly linked to the great zenith of our galaxy. The sacred zenith at the center of the universe, becomes the culminating point of guidance, always showing the way into the true path. And it is from the rainbow tree that the shaman may witness all the other worlds, through rituals of celestial ascension and tellurian descent. He or she develops the faculty to fly, sail, and travel great distances in seconds using the dream body. In this way, the shaman penetrates the magical time of the primal cosmic ocean and, through the hole of emergence, becomes immersed in other dimensions.

In the ancient engravings of the Mayas, the Ceiba tree is often depicted as the foliated tree of life, which gave birth to the sacred Corn God. The Ceiba tree embodies the holy cross, representing the four cardinal directions of the world, and was replaced during the conquest by the Christian cross. Nevertheless, behind it lives the sacred cosmic cross of fertility, persisting as one of the most powerful symbols of fecundity, even among the Maya people today. They believe that every corn-tree cross on the Mayan land has a soul and a voice that can be heard by the shaman seers.

If you travel in the Maya regions, you may often observe, by the sides of roads, three blue-green crosses standing together, adorned with flowers, votive candles, and copal incense. To many foreigners, the three crosses may appear to represent the Christian holy trinity or Christ's cross, but they do not. They celebrate an ancient representation of the three planes of the cosmic tree: the Underworlds, the Upperworlds, and the Earth's cradle of humanity. Moreover, there is likely to be a natural water hole wherever you see these Maya crosses, which also serve to bless the water spirits. The three fertility crosses honor the four ancestral rain gods, or *Chacs*, one for each of the four winds of the world. These important gods renew and regenerate the world, giving life to the water springs of the Earth. They are the sacred growers of the maize. On the three crosses, growing maize plants are often engraved, for the green crosses are the Corn God's trees.

Mother Ceiba as the Earth, the Chacs as the sky and the Corn God as the *Nichimal Vinik*, the flowered people, are incarnated in these three blue-green crosses as the three levels of the Maya growing tree. The most astounding of all this symbolism is that, through these three painted crosses, the Maya people have fed their sacred cosmic tree for over 10,000 years, and still have not ceased doing so. For this, they have survived, with their world and their ancient myths, through centuries of slavery, extermination, and oppression.

There are other clear parallels that indicate that all native cultures share the Tree of Life teachings. For the northern Indian cultures, the cosmic tree of life can be related in the same way as the Maya trees to the sacred forked tree, the tree with two arms. One branch represents the Moon Lodge of inner shadows, the other, the Sun Lodge of freedom and life. In another variant of this ancient teaching, the Moon Lodge also symbolizes the very roots of the tree, and the Sun Lodge, its flowering branches. Both lodges represent the two, inseparable, and opposed twins of our consciousness, in the same way as the two Maya trees.

Just as the Chechem tree may poison you, descending into the seducing Moon Lodge of your own shadows or fears may poison you and make you crazy for the rest of your life, if you are unable to withstand this powerful initiation. This is the meeting with the nahual and the dream realm in the west passage. The Chechem tree of the Maya, considered a punishing tree, reminds me of the teachings of thunder cloud beings of the West, once widespread among all North American Indian cultures. The thunder cloud birds have the power to strike (as do the rain gods, or Chacs), choosing whether to punish us or to protect us, depending on whether they consider us humbly aligned or too self-important in the face of life and death. Both teachings refer to the power of our shadows that may kill us. In both native myths, only the true warrior is granted a return from the west passage of death. Only the very pure can pass through all temptations and obstacles of the ego and become a shaman.

The other branch of the forked tree belongs to the Sun Lodge, the flowering tree of the tonal. It offers a model for humans to grow in a strong path. The Sun Lodge blooms, representing the greatness and enlightenment of the human race. The ancient teaching, however, mentions that we cannot reach the flowering of our life tree as real people without a true understanding of our roots. We all must meet the ancestors' roots of the Moon Lodge, and heal our race. Moreover, the teaching instructs that there is no reason to give too much attention to your Sun tree. It just grows by itself. You should center your care on your Moon roots, which confer the sap to your tree. Your mind, your being, and your spirit, must be in the Earth to grow long roots, in order for you to grow tall. After all, the vision tree of the Sun depends on the roots of the Moon dream tree for its sustenance, and every spiritual warrior must develop a deep capacity to reach far into all the Underworlds. The roots of the cosmic tree also represent all the generations of our forefathers, sustaining us through the roots of the great tree of life, and the branches, the coming faces of the generations to come.

The Cosmic Tree of Life teachings, be they Mongolian, Maya, or North American Indian, are a remarkably abundant source of wisdom, offering one of the most important of all teachings. They are a map providing guidance that every human should follow on the path. In all these cultures, the shaman necessarily exists at the center of the community, for he or she embodies the cosmic tree for the people. The shaman, who is a spiritual warrior who has undergone all the initiations, is the zenith for each being, the true spiritual guide, a light for all, connecting the upper branches with the roots of the tree. The shaman is the oracle, the ritual calendar, the guide, and the healer of the community or tribe. He or she stands at all times at the emergence hole of the tree, at the center opening of the medicine wheel itself, as the voice of the people. And the people, as a whole, live and breathe around his or her presence. In a perfect circle of cohesion and growth around the medicine wheel, all communities of the Earth were ordered this way a long time ago, in the most rooted and immovable societies the Earth has ever seen.

THE SHAMAN'S ZENITH

Each time I travel to the United States, I am very surprised to see how many people claim to be *shamans*. This word is now used in almost every "spiritual sauce." In light of this, I would like to share my understanding of what true shamans are, as seen through my teachers' eyes and through my own experience, for apparently there is much confusion around this.

Because true shamans are certainly one of the rarest species, not simply found on every corner, most people may not have a clear reference, and cannot easily discern who is genuine. Often, someone with channeling powers may be mistaken for a shaman, but a true shaman is much more than a channeler. Naturally, shamans must have clear divining powers and may often be healers themselves, but not all the good healers you meet are necessarily shamans. The distinction resides in the fact that a healer has learned a technique, a practice, and is dedicated to the healing of illnesses, while a shaman is not only a doctor of the body, but of the soul and spirit. Usually he or she focuses more on the prevention of illness among the community as well as on the training of the chosen warriors.

In order to grasp what shamans are, we must start by looking at the essence of shamanism. Actually, the word shaman is from Mongolian Siberia and for every ancient cultural language, there is a distinct word for shaman. Looking into my English dictionary under the word "shaman," I see that the word is also related to the word "sham," which means untrue, fraud, fake, bogus, and impostor. This reflects the distorted misinterpretation that the respected and conventional Western world has always held about shamans, our medicine, and our holy people. In light of this, it makes me laugh to think of the numerous Westerners who now fraudulently claim to be shamans.

It is important to differentiate between shamanism and shamanic ways. In reality, we cannot talk of shamanism as an "ism" like materialism, capitalism, imperialism, communism, or socialism, because a shaman cannot be put in any category. There is no fixed structure that determines the study of shamanic ways and its inherent natural laws. We shamans acquire knowledge from ancient teachings, and, inspired by these, develop our own particular ways. Nor is shamanism a religion or an ideology, for true shamans have reached the other side of the Self, undoing and breaking through any mind patterns, always in search of the highest kind of internal freedom as the chief goal of their lives. Shamans live to the fullest the manifestations of the spirits on Earth, with extreme, yet centered, intensity—

what I would call *spiritual passion*. And this cannot be contained in any "ism."

Living in the center of the cosmic tree and being at the center of the community as true guides, shamans can only become shamans themselves if they have conquered the center of the great medicine wheel of life, uncovering all the walls blocking consciousness and mastering all the distressing obstacles of the lower regions. Life teaches us that our passage here is essentially impermanent and transitive, so the passion of shamans is to plunge into life in all its forms, and to be one with the universe. Thus, shamanic ways cannot be classified in any philosophical or metaphysical system.

The center of *life* within the physical body is located at the first, or sexual, center. It is from this energy center that you tap into the sap of life from your inner roots. This center provides the vitality to your medicine field and infuses you with tremendous dynamism in order to awaken the other inner centers. When well activated, it also gives a tremendous power of grounding into the Earth.

Because shamans have this center highly developed, they can expand their understanding of energies through their own direct experience and their personal conception of life. They seek to be the exact axis, the perfect balance between the tonal and the nahual axes, performing the super-human exploit of standing at this delicate point on the Earth, while at the same time sustaining alignment with the zenith above. The tremendous amount of energy required to maintain this perfect equilibrium and not fall to one side or the other of the wheel demands a constant clarity, a supremacy over the ego and the human senses, as well as a strong spiritual capacity to withstand the blizzards of life and not lose the center of gravity. Needless to say, only shamans can perform this! They are the spiritual acrobats between the worlds. They always walk on the edge of the obsidian blade. Their flexibility, adaptability, and, at the same time, their solid moral principles, allow them to question the deepest strata of thoughts and feelings. They are usually the greatest thinkers of all, due to their freedom of mind, their incredible perspective, and their detachment. They are not intellectuals in the conventional sense, but, somewhere deep within, are extremely practical people, beings of action.

"Shamanic ways" is perhaps the best way to refer to what shamans do. In every tradition and lineage of shamans around the globe, although there are some recurrent patterns, we encounter an endless number of ancient shamanic practices, with so many variations that they cannot be fit within any system. However, many similar natural elements—Sun, Moon, Earth, tree, rainbow, fire, mist, and clouds—resonate strongly among shamans in their direct relationship to the universe. The spirit expression of their inspiration for the natural elements through ceremonies is a motivating factor to unite the people. Many times, shamans follow their own intuition in the performance of rituals. Nevertheless, the ancient practices and rites they are entitled to pass down to their own apprentices are transmitted and performed with strict observance and respect for the traditions.

Most shamans are true weather people, possessing the capacity to predict and call the rain, the Sun, or even a snow storm. The weather spirits are their allies. For this reason, they are the best meteorologists that have ever existed! Besides curing illnesses in the community, they maintain the ceremonial calendar, perform the oracle and divination rites, assist at marriages, baptisms, and rites of passage, prepare the warriors for good hunting, seek lost people, guide all funeral ceremonies, and talk to the dead souls and the ancestors.

Clearly, to become a shaman is not an easy task. In our ways, we know that there is no true shaman on Earth who ever wanted to become a shaman. You are born a shaman in the very soul. It is not a career you can choose and study, like any other occupation. No one who is called to become a shaman ever really wanted to follow this demanding path, although, at one point in the quest, a shaman must challenge death, knowing there is no other door, and only one path to embrace. I often have people ask me to teach them how to become shamans, yet, at the first sign of hardship, they just disappear in the bushes! Unlike common people, strong warriors and shamans are chosen by the great powers and are given the privilege to chose their death—the when, the where, and the how.

Shamans are also the great specialists of the soul and of human nature, knowing the destiny of peoples and of individuals. Although shamans are true travelers of life, we are all nomads in our own souls, as a Mongol shaman once told me. Nevertheless, shamans always care for the well-being and the survival of their communities. In order to provide for the people, they must enlarge their proficiency to foresee, to prevent, and to cure all possible disturbances affecting the community and restore life where it is disrupted. This is accomplished in special ceremonies, in which the shaman incarnates the disturbing spirits and casts them out of the village. For this, good shamans always prevent evil spirits from filtering into the circle of people. In this resides their greatest achievement.

Other shamans may prefer not to live close to the community, so that they may dedicate themselves to heightening their nexus with spirit in a purer way and enter sacred realms inaccessible to the common people. These shamans are often erroneously mistaken for *brujos*, or black witches. The difference between a brujo and an isolated shaman resides in the fact that even the isolated shaman is truly a spiritual leader or holy chief, holding a place of respect in the hearts of the people, while the *brujo* is feared. Isolated shamans often operate closely with the community's shaman, exchanging information from other realms, for example, or working together toward the proper guidance of the people.

Despite these distinctions, all in the shaman world is based on inner power. These are the spirits who always validate the path of the shaman. An apprentice can be chosen by the great powers in two ways: through a hereditary transmission of knowledge, or by being chosen by a shaman to become an apprentice. The destined warrior, however, is always called by clear signs to the shaman and, ultimately, in both situations, it is always the great powers who "propose" the future shaman as apprentice and guide him to the teacher. No one can become a shaman without the direct and living instruction of a master teacher. One of the major deeds effected by the shaman is to properly align the apprentice, even without his full awareness. The shaman, who is elected by the powers to carry on a tradition, is usually given great protection from the lineage itself. Thousands of years of unbroken and preserved lineage confers great power on the teachings.

Needless to say, no one can learn to become a true shaman through books. People may acquire personal practices for centering themselves and enlarging their spiritual understanding. But to pierce through the human essence and understand our temporal condition, as well as the passage through each obstacle of life and death, can surely not be accomplished solely through books.

It is universal that apprentices, especially male apprentices, called to master this path, whether from a lineage or in a more solitary way, may resist this path and take a long time to be trained by the shaman teacher. Women apprentices usually understand more promptly the wisdom of not resisting their true path. The powers must stalk the seekers, until they desist and surrender in this battle with spirits. This is the death passage that apprentices must endure. In the Underworlds, the destined shamans, whether men or women, are entrapped in a corner of life, and are forced to defy an ostensible dead end. This dead end is the death of the old self and the only tiny opening is for the apprentices to heal themselves and accept their destiny.

In the inescapable death passage beyond the self, the future shamans are dismembered in order to renovate their inner being and be reborn. When at the edge of the abyss or against the wall of ego, the apprentices must choose between physical and spiritual death, and their destiny as future shamans. In reality, it is all a mirage. There are no real choices, only the path to heal the self and be reborn in spirit. It is through suffering, death, and resurrection that the warriors and shamans are given new blood and awaken from the long sleep of their unconsciousness. This is something that cannot be chosen consciously. It happens only when one is ready.

During this dramatic spiritual crisis and intensive seeking of great beauty, the apprentices experience inward isolation from the rest of the community. It is in loneliness that power is gained. This period of solitude induces the vision to appear, through dreams and lucid awareness. These signs are a chief prerequisite for the universe to designate the students to their teachers and this is usually when the true spiritual guide must be sought. Shamans never seek the apprentices, but arrive at the rendezvous when the apprentices, previously prepared by the merciless hand of the universe, are ready to learn.

Usually, when the sincere seekers look for a master guide, it is never to learn the shamanic ways. It is usually to protect themselves from the powers that are constantly wrestling with and persecuting them. At that moment, the great powers trick the apprentices and win the battle. The future warriors, out of fear and despair, totally exhausted, abdicate in the hands of a shaman, who takes over the sacred duty of teaching the rebel apprentices, and through many ruses, leads them to their fate. Without the alignment and protection of the shaman, the apprentices may go insane and the powers may lash back on them.

THE GIFT OF THE GREAT POWERS

At the time I did my vision quest, I was already stalked by what felt like some dark forces. Many "bizarre" things and enigmatic signs were recurrently occurring on my path, showing me clearly how little I knew and how spiritually weak I was. This was one of the major reasons why I reluctantly decided to undertake my Vision Quest—to become stronger. Even though I knew that embarking on a Vision Quest meant taking refuge in spirit and connecting to the harmony of higher self, my experience was a different one, a true death passage.

I undertook my Vision Quest alone. I decided I didn't need the help of my medicine teacher to prepare or protect me. After all, I thought to myself, I am a Mohawk and I know of these things. That was my warrior presumption, I guess. The second night of my Vision Quest, while I was many miles away from the closest town, I was caught in a huge forest fire in the middle of nowhere. In total obscurity, I tried to take a small path leading out of the approaching fire, but, after trekking a mile, I could see the flames coming my way again. I returned and took another path, but the fire came again my way. Then, I was struck by the realization that the powers were hunting me. The fire was moving in a large circle. I was trapped, unless I faced my death once and for all, and said goodbye to this world. Because I had no other option, I sat on the rock where I had previously hidden my power objects, wrapped in my Indian blanket. Suddenly, out of nowhere, a man stepped out of the forest and invited me to follow him. I asked myself how he had gotten to me through the fire, for I hadn't called out. Needless to say, I didn't respect the "rule" of not talking or giving attention to strangers during the Vision Quest. I had no other choice but to follow him and, by then, I was ready to abandon this "ancient Indian" stuff about Vision Quests!

Then, in one flash of mind, I became certain that this man had been sent to me by the same forces that were chasing me. Once I was "safe" on the other side of a large river, I asked myself what these powers wanted of me. Late the next morning, after the helicopters had put out the fire, I returned to my "vision" rock. The landscape was devastating to observe, the smell of smoldering burnt wood everywhere. The fire had only come as close as five feet to the rock where I had left my things, circling the large boulder, leaving my power objects perfectly intact. This came as a deep revelation to me, and I cried about my own ignorance on this sacred rock. In the midst of the powers wishing to destroy me, were also my greatest protectors. I had no other choice, at this point, than to let them kill my old self and to find protection in my newly discovered spirit. I knew that the social career that I had set for myself as my life's path would be put aside forever by these revelations. I knew I had to seek the full guidance of the shaman who would become my main teacher, Thunder Man. This great fire was, in all ways, the same manifestation as the fire ball of my childhood. The loop had been made and now the circle closed and a new one began. The only thing left for me was to accept my fate, whether I wanted to or not.

This is when I realized that the only true thing left for me was to develop a profound sense of appreciation for all the wondrous gifts along the path. It is also when I realized that signs are extremely important along a warrior's path—and our only true means of guidance.

I often hear stories of people who mistake the signs of spirits for the gifts of power. They do not seem to know how to understand the significance of signs. Signs are not necessarily gifts of power. They can also be warnings. They can show the path to follow as you walk. A gift of power usually comes after the hunt, when a circle is closed. When you have pursued it with all your sincerity and courage, the universe grants you a gift of power. And you know it for what it is. In both cases, signs as gifts may come as animals, people, a sunset, or certain situations. They can occur anywhere—in the woods or in New York. They can take any form—a spoken or written word, or an object or a natural manifestation. It is as if the moment, however it manifests, just talks to you and only to you. It is as if time just stops, magically, to reveal its deepest secrets. You need intuition to understand this language.

No one wishes to undergo a small death, unless they are already insane. Because of the cultural taboos of Western societies, most avoid speaking of death and shadows at all cost. In fact, future shamans do not ask to shoulder this enormous responsibility. Although an intense, inner call, that turns into a veritable obsession, breathes deep inside them, true apprentices attempt to evade this responsibility at all cost. But the call reveals itself to be stronger than anything else in their lives and the universe makes sure of that. When they desist from this internal battle, an everlasting peace impregnates the seekers, as they reach authentic humility. A virtual renunciation of the old, limited, social and "educated" Self takes place. The new life of the future shaman begins, but with an intense separation: detachment from loved ones, from society, from old forms, habits, and activities, all of which now appear entirely irrelevant. From now on, these seekers will always refer to their real birth as the moment when they were reborn into their new destiny, after the Vision Quest.

Our new family becomes those who seed the new spirit in us, the family of shamans or medicine people. Even when apprentices leave their new family, after years of training, the shamans follow them all their lives, in spirit. They are bound together in a very special manner and sometimes the training even proceeds in dreams.

The death passage may happen in various ways. And not all people who have died physically and returned to their bodies are called to be shamans. The death passage of a future shaman can also happen during dream time. In this instance, apprentices may dream of being pulverized, their bones made into dust and sent by the winds to the universe. This pulverization is created by the internal fire (spiritual passion) of the future shamans, who have no way out other than liberating their awakening spirit in this way. This is a very striking experience. Other death passages that I have heard about, from shamans with whom I have worked, have occurred when apprentices fell on their heads from a great height, when lightning struck them directly, literally killing them, or when they suffered a deadly snake bite, or extreme convulsions, similar to an epileptic seizure. In all these cases, the shaman-to-be suffers a change of essence and of spirit animal.

Once the warrior-apprentices have gone through the worst, they become shamans. They now have great power to exercise their energy. Because of their new power of concentration, their great memory and capacity of discernment, it is hard to fool them. Their diligent discipline gives them the ability to undergo a lot of stress without being affected, drawing on a seemingly endless reservoir of vitality. Shamans constantly endure great pressure, one of a spiritual nature. This is a state of being already disillusioned, already deceived. I also call it *spiritual dissatisfaction*, referring to the endless quest into the mystery of life. Because of it, shamans are among the most balanced and grounded people walking this Earth.

In fact, all the shamans I know seek to be the most normal people, enjoying simple, ordinary life at the center of their shields. Their normal existence is not bound to restrictive conformity, but lives in poised simplicity and quietness even in the midst of their numerous activities. They are all poets of life and jokers, despite their great seriousness. In addition to their ordinary and neutral traits, however, all shamans are truly obsidian mirrors.

Among the Mohawks or Iroquois, shamans are known as the False Faces Society, because of the powerful and distorted masks they wear in their healing appearances and ceremonies. In Mongolia, people say that shamans have two faces, one that laughs and one that is very serious. Shamans may display their powers directly, as confronting mirrors, or as powerful soothing protectors who teach you by their contrast to the dark side. Most shamans scare people if they wish to, for in doing so, they destroy your self-image right in front of your eyes, clearly uncovering the essence of things.

In all cases, however, it is a myth to think shamans live in the complacency of performing all sorts of magical exploits. In fact, true shamans are very discreet about this. They are more concerned about helping and aligning people toward a strongly centered path than indulging in hallucinatory practices and extravagant magic.

The greatest peculiarity of shamans is that they are truly puzzled about how to refer to themselves. Most do not like to say they are shamans, medicine persons, priests, or whatever term is common to their denomination. In reality, they do not care at all for names, feeling beyond them. In the spirit, these labels do not exist.

Shamans' great love for the Earth is their ultimate freedom. They pursue the mastery of knowledge at all moments, the higher consciousness beyond consciousness itself. They are not interested in the meaning of life—there is no time for that. The only real thing is an utmost respect and appreciation for everything on this path—where knowledge can either kill or teach you—and the pursuit of the vision. They are constantly fighting to effect inner and outer revolution on Earth, in any way at hand.

Being more sensible to all aspects of life and more conscious of the intangible mystery of the universe, shamans are more vulnerable than common people. Therefore, to shield themselves is a crucial matter of life and death. As good hunters, they must know all points of protection and the direction of the winds in their life. Every step can be irremediably deadly. They always walk on the sword's edge, knowing the winds of death can take their power at any time. The winds of death can be anything, or any person. Contrary to the average person, therefore, shamans are always hunters and never the prey, never the hunted ones. As all hunters, shamans are connected to survival, especially spiritual survival, through the power of their intention. They know there are good and bad days to hunt, and they wait patiently, for their time of power, always with a knowledge of the enemy and a recognition of the trails and ambushes.

What we shamans hunt is our vision. All shamans are people of vision. To "kill the vision," for medicine people, means to have dreamed it first into the Earth, by totally surrendering to her force and to have "died" for their visions. After receiving the seed of her dream, and after acknowledging the vision, we start killing it, which is essential to making it come true. Otherwise, the vision will lurk around and try to kill us. Because a true vision holds much power, if it is not killed into this reality, it will have no place to go, and all its power will destroy the one who received it. A vision is a responsibility, and to kill the vision into reality is a complete act of power.

Although everyone can hunt and kill their vision of life in full realization of themselves, it is not given to just anyone to call themselves a shaman, though all are entitled to find their own warrior within and to develop all the skills of the hunter. In fact, everyone should dedicate themselves to this noble task. Knowing what you are hunting in the spirit world confers the spark of life and rewards you with the greatest awareness of the stalker. Nevertheless, most people fear killing. Of course, I am not talking of killing people or animals directly, for this is not our purpose here. The perfect aim of every warrior is the killing of the higher vision. In killing your most meaningful vision of the world, you must first give it a death in the dream realm, then give it birth into this reality. True seekers do not fear killing, for it is an honor that the prey grants them, agreeing to give themselves for the accomplishment of the spiritual hunters. The prey consents to shed blood for the warrior. Being a coward, refusing to make the kill, and letting the game escape after you have hunted it, is the worst offense you can make and the powers will make you pay for it. Unfortunately, many do not understand this, and still live in the naïve "Disney" world of their childhood.

When you integrate your spirit animal, it will show you the ways of your hunting skills and teach you not to be afraid. You may practice under its guidance, learn when to remove yourself and let nature move things in its own way for you, or learn when to act on the spot like a hunter, to embrace your prey and perceive its way.

Hunting and killing the vision involves the highest and most absolute responsibility awarded to the true humans. The prey, in many cases, becomes your own ego. This is what a spiritual warrior does. People are usually afraid of hurting and being hurt. They were taught that this is wrong. In reality, however, this has nothing to do with being hurtful. It is only the fears of an injured ego that make it so. If it is your turn to offer of your Self, because a greater hunter has captured you, than it is also an honor for yourself. Most people grow fearful of their truth, of real power, and refuse to assume it thoroughly. So when they give their power away to others, they do so in a completely unhealthy way, and not with the conscious grace of surrendering love.

To hunt is an art and, at the end, shamans who all their lives have hunted in the spirit world, will die there, never here. The old people say that dying shamans will be greeted with all the great distinctions at the Feast of the Council Fire of Spirits as true chiefs. This is where our true family is.

When shamans perform their last drumming, their last dancing and singing, their whole lives pass in front of them. Their last act on Earth is filled with great sentiment and power. It is the only way that they can transform what their lives on Earth were into a sacred time. It is the only way they can meet death with respect. For in the end, they know that death is just the beginning of another journey. The shamans leave this plane with the awareness of the greater signs that have marked their lives. They know that these gifts of power were the greatest manifestations of spirits that have blessed their lives, manifestations that they have painted on their life shields and empowered along their paths. They know that the rainbows appearing in their lives were the myths of Earth, that the fogs were their inner shadows, that the mists of their feelings were the sweat of Earth and that their most sacred visions were transitory legends echoing the dreams and hopes of Earth.

As they die, they undertake the last journey, following the rainbow path opening before them, leading them to freedom and enlightenment. They project their soul and spirit to the sacred zenith, underneath the cosmic tree, where they will dwell in immortality.

5

WISDOM

METAMORPHOSIS THROUGH
NATIVE HEALING WAYS

The shamans-to-be come to the realization, in the death passage, that their soul is deeply ill and out of balance. So there is no other choice for the future warriors but to learn how to self-heal before healing others. Learning to *metamorphose* the old self into the new self is absolutely indispensable. Hence, discovering to effectively shield against all the dark entities is of the utmost importance. Healing knowledge is essential to all warriors so that they may eventually be prepared for the appalling meeting with the terrible guardians of the nine shadows of the Underworlds.

For native shamans, the body and the ailment cannot be separated from spirit. Native medicine is, above all, *soul medicine*, and cannot be understood in any other form. All internal, soul disorders brought by the nine Underworld guardians, inevitably affect the body and create inner imbalances. This is the fundamental conception of the cause of illnesses and the main focus of all native medicines. Western medical practices, which primarily study symptoms, do not take into consideration our essential concepts and most often evade any deepening on the subject. Native shamans and medicine people concentrate on the soul dilemmas before anything else, with careful observation of the body and soul as a whole, and their relation to the universe. The relationship between body, soul, and spirit is seen as dynamic and interdependent. Whatever affects the spirit will alter the body, and vice versa. We do not necessarily see illnesses as evil and health as good. Rather, the two cooperate to mirror the balances and imbalances of the human nature. Diseases are transgressions against the natural order of the universe, creating serious disorders that are then manifested in physical ailments. Only through disorder can the shaman learn universal order. Illnesses are even viewed as an indispensable process that helps to adjust both soul and body and reach a perfect balance. We know that a world without disease is a world that is empty, lifeless, and without growth.

To heal imbalances of the body, we must first heal the soul, for it is intimately living with and attached to the dream body and sustaining the physical. The vitality of every human being is obtained through the regeneration of energy in this subtle body. We know that illnesses are always caused by an alteration of the harmonic relationship we maintain with the universe through negative emotions.

Shamans examine and recognize the physical and spiritual aspects of the universe, and restore harmony to themselves, first in their quest, then in learning to heal others. In other words, most healing, in a native sense, consists of retrieving and replacing a piece of the universe to the soul, a piece that has been lost somewhere. If the piece of the universe is not lost, it is out-of-balance and must be acknowledged and renovated. To do this, we shamans must ascertain in which level of the nine Underworlds the soul is captive or lost.

In the native world, elemental rules reflecting the movement of energies can easily be disturbed if not understood and maintained properly. All energies of the cosmos, despite their great vulnerability, circulate cyclically through the body at all times, in a powerful, perfect cadence. Therefore, the greater the imbalance, the worse the illness. All skilled and trained shamans learn to control and direct these energies, in or out of the ill body, depending on the cause and symptoms, throwing out the pathogenic traces of disease and directing the cosmic forces of regeneration inside the patient. Shamans must be perfect transmitters and receivers. As a result, they always confront themselves with the risk such healing operations may involve. They can become the target of these forces that are invited and called upon, if they are not channeled properly.

Maya shamans taught me that all illnesses are impelled from the Underworlds by the guardians of these regions. The illnesses surface to this world as winds, through mountains or caves, the natural vaginal entrances to the Lowerworlds in the belly and womb of Earth. What transpires on the face of Earth always causes immediate repercussions in the Underworlds' life. Some illnesses may be engendered by the legacy of the past, left by our direct ancestors, who are the conveyors of energy and the source of life for us. This rooted energy from our ancestors is accumulated in our bone marrow and kidneys, from generation to generation, giving a great percentage of our capacity for endurance and vitality. The weakening of the spirit of a family lineage, through constant violations of natural laws over many generations, creates the predisposition to emotional weakness and ailments in future generations.

These underground winds exhale in perpetual movement onto the human plane that also transports the bad winds through the reprehensible, negative emotions of humans. These heavy winds possess numerous "qualities," carrying cold or hot illnesses.

The polarity of hot and cold, humid and dry illnesses, refers to the battle between the gods from the nine Lowerworlds and the thirteen Upperworlds. In general, the Upperworlds are symbolized as the life forces opposed to the death passage of the Underworlds. All the cold and humid winds surface from the land of the dead in the lower regions. Most hot winds of sickness are created by the angry emotions of the spirit guardians from the Underworlds, and are afterward sent to the Upperworlds to be manifested as hot winds. The hot winds, lighter than the cold winds, naturally rise to the first levels of the Upperworlds, thus affecting human beings. Also, many winds of serious disorders are created by improper use of sexual energy, again reflected in the other worlds, upper or lower, and taking the form of illnesses.

For these reasons, we can observe how interrelated humans are in the omnipresent macrocosm and what responsibility every one of our emotions and thoughts holds. Perfect health is the balance between hot and cold airs. To reestablish health, in all the cases, these aggravating winds must be purged, as well as the underlying emotions.

For Maya shamans, *hot illnesses* appear in many forms: fevers, rashes and itching, all sorts of inflammations and infections, difficulty breathing, lip sores, swollen bodies, evil eye, hemorrhages, hair loss, vomiting, and diarrhea. *Cold illnesses,* by contrast, present themselves as heart attacks, rheumatism and arthritis, loss of strength, generalized weakness, colic, coughs and colds, cystitis, tumors and some skin spots, bone illnesses, and bad airs trapped in the back. Accordingly, there are *hot and cold emotions* generating these winds from within as well as from without, always created by soul imbalances and weaknesses. The hot emotions take the form of anger, aggressiveness, impatience, and hot tempers; the cold ones appear as contractions of fear, melancholy, depression, sadness and complaints, and fatigue and chronic diseases.

Before discussing some of these illnesses in depth, I wish to elucidate the various types of medicine healers dedicated to curing illnesses rather than preventing them. I found that Mongolian shamans possess an exquisitely refined understanding of energies, one more systematic than that of Native American people. However, North American shamans and healers have developed, over thousands of years, the greatest capacity for directly seeing spirits in the cause of illness. In the end, however, the diagnoses of all these shamans have proven to be very accurate, whatever their method, mainly because their inherent knowledge of the soul is the same.

When shamans learn their vocation, they dedicate themselves to specific practices and specialties. The *hierberos* heal with plants in many various and powerful ways, within and without, curing both the physical and vital body and expelling the intruding winds. The *hueseros* replace bones and remove the cold and hot air within the marrow. The *sobadores* massage specific spots to the same effect, and the *resadores* pray to the soul in need and in torment. We saw earlier how the retrievers and the blowers perform ceremonies to call forth the soul into the being, while the removers carry out an opposite kind of healing that consists of extracting the pains from the medicine field and body.

The prayer people, or *resadores,* are innate "pulsers." The Maya ways of pulsing differ completely from the Mongolian pulses, which is used as a way to diagnose the internal organs with a more methodical procedure. For a Maya prayer man, or *illol,* finding the cause of physical symptoms is done through a spiritual pulsing, consisting of holding the arm of the patient strongly in his or her hand, in order to hear the blood talking and thus reach the depth of the soul and illness. This pulsing may take a few minutes of long silence, during which the healers enter into your blood, where they remain until they locate the disorder, which speaks to them. Their soul diagnosis is always remarkably accurate, yet there is no technical procedure to learn how to perform this.

WINDS OF
THE UNDERWORLDS

These dark winds often manifest themselves as the Evil Eye and the *Mal Aire.* The Mal Aire is commonly a cold wind intruding on the physical body. It remains inside, hollowing its way through the circulatory and nervous systems, wandering around until it reaches the bones and bone marrow. Once there, this wind makes life quite impossible, causing sharp yet prolonged pain. These cold winds may be introduced into the body at many sensible spots, such as the kidneys, the ears, and even the hair. The healing process to remove a cold air involves much effort and patience. Both cold and hot air may also penetrate through the navel center, where life is given to us and from where death will take us. The hot and cold wind may also enter through the feet, neck, ankles, hands, breath, and eyes. Hot winds do not last long within, for they are frequently released in more dramatic ways, through fevers, rashes, or angry emotions. For the Maya *curanderos,* or healers, the principle applied in their healing practices is quite simple. If they have diagnosed a hot wind, it should be rebalanced with a cold element. For cold illnesses, something hot is required. Even though the principle is quite elementary, the healing can nonetheless be quite complex, requiring the most subtle completion. This includes the food ingested by the patient, herbal infusions, climate and surroundings, the colors of clothes, the kinds of activities, and the type of healing, all reflecting the hot and cold polarity balance. Here are some simple examples of food or drinks that are considered hot or cold. Chili, chicken or rooster meat, red meat, and sugar are all hot, as is chamomile tea. Mint teas are cold, even when taken as a hot drink. Salt and pork meat are cold. Some vegetables, such as spinach, are cold. Corn and beans are exactly between hot and cold.

There is only one exception to the rule of healing an ailment by its contrary. When an undefined hot air is lurking within the body and does not reach the point of the cathartic release after waiting, the healing consists of inducing more heat in the body to effect the liberating result.

A bad wind can appear as a dense gas that takes the form of an animal (often a scary one) created by the Underworld guardians. This gas becomes a whirlwind that often moves in the terrestrial space with much negativity. Many winds of the Underworlds may also penetrate through dreams and, unfortunately, many people are left defenseless, as they do not recall their dreams, their possible gates of filtration. *Brujos* and negative spirits may also give birth to these dense winds, taking the forms of awful animals, effecting this with the nefarious power of their dark feelings.

Some of these obscure underworld spirits are named *chanes* among the Mayas. They must be prayed to and revered with offerings, so that they will leave us in peace. Some chanes are small spirits, also called the rain dwarfs. All these chanes are senders of illnesses. They also often devastate crops through certain kinds of damaging rains. Other Underworld beings are night spirits, who may cause *espanto* (a disturbing fright) to those who walk at night in woods or dark places. It is said that night spirits may also wander as dark winds on the roads, waiting to push or to catch you, even in cities.

We strongly prescribe various ways to protect and shield against all these potential illnesses. We also recommend that much care be taken when in places where people may leave their diseases, such as hospitals, waiting rooms in doctor's offices, and healing rooms that are not cleaned afterward. Being where accidents occur or sitting where ill people have been may allow bad winds to jump from one person to another very easily. This is the most common way in which illnesses are transmitted.

Someone may be more prone to catch these winds due to spiritual factors. These are mostly engendered by weaknesses and transgressions of cosmic rules, whether individually or communally. The transgression caused by misbehavior is always an offense to spirit, whereas the illness can only be healed with repentence, prayer, sacrifice, fasting, and an apology to the spirits.

The Evil Eye is a hot wind that manifests itself in a different manner than *Mal Aire*. Evil Eye is transmitted by the eyes of a person who has extreme intensity of emotions. This hot wind of energy usually affects the stomach area. All natives know this and are therefore extremely protective, especially of their small ones. No one can really stay indifferent when looking at a baby, and anyone may project from their own eyes to the baby's eye. Even if what you project is an intense desire to cuddle the child, a hot wind may be transmitted into the small creature. Within an hour, the baby may start to vomit non-stop, suffering intense diarrhea and continual crying. It is common to see Maya mothers in Chiapas suddenly hiding their babies from someone because they sense that person is sending them the Evil Eye, even if there is no intention to harm the baby. The sender must then embrace and kiss the child, to prevent or cure the Evil Eye. Newborns, in their first days, are also prone to soul losses and must not be taken out of the home, for they may easily catch the Evil Eye. I have seen that for the Maya, babies can usually be shielded from this with a bead of amber tied to their wrists. It is interesting to observe that, often, the amber will crack to prevent the child from being a target.

Anyone, even adults, may catch the Evil Eye. Often, a man with intense sexual or emotional desires can throw the Evil Eye at a woman by catching her eyes. This can occur anywhere, even walking in the street. To develop prudence is imperative. You must learn to avoid looking in the eyes of unknown people, for many may capture or lose all sorts of energies through their eyes, without the clear notion of how or why. Without warning, the Evil Eye may, at the end of the day, make you feel sick, or you may awaken the next morning quite ill.

All pregnant women release a strong, dense hot wind from the force of life they hold in their wombs. This wind, although not bad, may readily affect small babies in their presence, who are more vulnerable to this energetic burst of power than adults. Fairly young babies (up to 1 month old) are thus best kept away from the sight of pregnant women emanating this energetic fluid from their navel, for it may penetrate the tender navel of newborn babies. This gas or bubble may remain trapped inside when the baby's navel seals, causing much crying and many stomachaches. Once the navel is sealed, babies are better protected.

A common healing practice for pregnant mothers consists of a shamanic cleansing of all these strong airs, for they may even endanger their own labor. This cleansing will smooth the way for the babies to birth easily. Otherwise, these hot winds are accumulated around the mother, generating more heaviness and tenseness for both beings.

In all circumstances, illnesses can be cured by *limpias*, a purification treatment of sweeping the body and medicine field with smoke, herbs, and flowers. Among North American natives, the ancient cleansing is accomplished with tobacco or sage smoke, with ashes or feather fans. For Maya natives, limpias are often elaborate ceremonies that require copal incense and free-range chicken eggs brushed all over the body. Raw eggs draw out any impurities from the medicine field and are extremely effective in removing the hot and cold winds from inside the body. Red and white carnations are then fanned all around the body, and other fresh herbs, such as basil, elder-tree leaves, rue, and laurel, are gently whipped on the patient. An altar made for the occasion is adorned with candles of all colors. These are brushed over the patient, so that once lit, they burn away all diseases and negativity of these bad winds. The patient stands in front of the altar while the limpia is performed. The shaman blows the blessed corn alcohol all around the medicine field of the patient. Once the healing is finished, the eggs, which now hold the disease, must be broken in a clear glass of water and read by the healer as a form of diagnosis. During the limpias, every detail indicates to the healer the internal and external disorder of the suffering person: the way the candles burn, which colors burn unevenly, which kinds of flowers fall on the ground as brushed, and the color the herbs turn after the ceremony. It is amazing to see the number of signs that are manifested, if only one can interpret them properly. At the very end, the patient must gather all the herbs, flowers, and eggs, and must throw them behind his or her back, while pondering on the full release of the illness.

It is important to understand, in terms of soul illnesses, that people predisposed to physical disorders, excess, and even apparently innocuous addictions, lack respect and don't care properly for themselves and the world around them, even though they may think they lead a good life. People commonly abide in a general state of weakness and emotional vulnerability that provides a direct passage for bad winds. Angry and dark emotions, envy and jealousy all irritate the subtle spirits that may send negative winds upon these persons. Many people constantly offend spirits out of cultural ignorance, and then are surprised when they get sick. Most display very little sensitivity toward spirit. As a simple example, many people, while walking in the woods, talk very loudly, yelling at each other from one spot to another, with no awareness that delicate and watchful spirit beings exist all around. Also, people who smoke constantly, without the least awareness of the tobacco plant, potentially call the dark winds upon themselves. In the sacred tobacco dwells one of the finest and most intelligent spirits of creation. Smoking out of nervousness or an addictive social attitude (never thanking this spirit), is thus a great offense. Instead of blessing them, the tobacco spirit may send unconscious smokers a series of bad events and physical ailments. Another proclivity to dark winds is seen in people who infringe upon the norms of their community. For this, they are at once spotted by all kinds of spirits (usually ancestor spirits), who send them illnesses directly from the lower regions. On the other hand, if the person's transgression is sensitive and in accordance with natural laws, the spirits will support those who have broken the rules, understanding that these social rules were not based on universal justice.

When disguised, illness may take the form of a weak emotion within. An overly emotional and false compassion for the world and pity for oneself considerably unbalances a person, allowing any of these winds to infiltrate the physical body and affect the judgment.

THE LOSS OF SOUL

The soul can become captive of different spirits through two forms of frights. The *susto* is manifested as a slight fright. It can be felt when something startles you—when someone sneaks up behind you, when a dog suddenly barks at you, or when you jump and something falls from your hands. Western people pay little attention to this. But for natives, many illnesses and bad winds can be contracted in this startling feeling of susto. Moreover, on the Maya land, each time this happens, as I have often been told by indigenous people, you must gather your Self on the spot, otherwise a bit of your soul may stay out of balance or will be left behind. Otherwise, you may sense this feeling of awkwardness after such moments of susto.

It is common and quite amusing in Chiapas to observe peasants, even in cities, taking off their jackets and beating the place they may have fallen or mis-stepped, in order to re-center their souls. The susto may not appear very serious, but may be the cause of more severe consequences later in the month, for it creates an opening for these bad winds. You may find yourself with a definite tendency toward nervousness and other small sustos, jumping constantly at nothing. All these little sustos may accumulate, creating a bigger feeling of fear and vulnerability. At night, your body may frequently jolt during sleep. A good healing to counter this lack of centeredness is to receive a few *limpias,* to vigorously whip and shake the medicine field with herbs to realign your soul. Another is to return to the susto site and stomp on the spot, beating the ground and replacing the soul in its center. Often a susto can only be healed with another susto of the soul.

The *espanto* consists of a stronger, frightening experience, in which the soul is really scared—serious accidents, big falls, dreadful fears, or dreams caused by bad spirits. Here, a total loss of soul may result, that may lead to death, if not retrieved. In dreams, the separation of the body and soul is momentary, but when the separation of the soul from the physical body is definitive, death occurs. If the espanto is not scary enough to produce a total loss, then a partial or small loss of soul may occur. This is called *the fall of the soul*. In the moment of the espanto, a spirit kidnaps your soul, imprisoning it and creating the loss, whether total or partial. The spirit that captures the soul is not necessarily a bad spirit. Any weakness or lack of consciousness can provide direct entrance. The healing ceremony for the espanto is a very complex one for which a true retriever must be solicited. When your soul is absent, you suffer a general depletion, day after day. Your body is not functional. You experience a definite lack of appetite, a complete loss of will to live, deep depression, emotional disturbances, and total disinterest. The spark of life is missing from your soul. In the worst of cases your spirit animal, now removed, is no longer protecting your physical body. This permits all sorts of illnesses to intrude. Usually, this depletion is immediate, following the espanto. In a big loss, if the soul is not retrieved soon, the person may even die within the next three weeks. Disquieting emotions are often responsible for this prominent state of deterioration, often causing the soul to escape in this frightening experience.

There is the espanto of water, the espanto of Earth, the espanto of fire, the espanto of the dark and of dead spirits, the espanto of animals, of lightning, of sacred caves, of weeds, and of mountains.

An *espanto of water* happens when someone almost drowns, being pulled under by water spirits. An *espanto of Earth* occurs when someone has a bad fall, the Earth grabbing the soul, pulling it into her. The *espanto of woods* is created by spirits of large centenary trees. Anti-social people can also induce espanto, especially those possessed by a dark spirit. All of these frights are primarily what the seeker will face in the initiations of the nine Underworlds.

There are also espantos provoked by ancient sites, in pyramids and sacred places, either caused by the visitor's lack of respect, or by their ignorance of how to handle power in such sites. Other spirits are extremely subtle, such as the spirits of springs, who are not likely to keep you captive, but may rather enchant and seduce you, leading you to lose your sense of self and proper reason. As a result, you may become abnormally obsessed and seemingly far away. In the case of an *espanto by fire*, besides fear of fire, improper sexual behavior (sexual energy surging from the fire domain) can be the cause of the small loss of soul.

Often, the soul is held captive by spirits of the lower regions who wander around where the accident occurred. It is important to bear in mind that, in the native world, no accident presents itself without reason. In our world, coincidences and accidents just do not exist. If the soul is firmly attached to the body, the "accident," however terrible, will not produce any soul loss.

The difficult task of the shaman is to discover the origin of the illness, even if the patient may point out the exact place it occurred. To know precisely which spirits are tormenting the soul belongs to the realm of the true retriever. A frequent practice of soul retrieval consists of calling the illness of the patient into the shaman's body in order to find out where the soul may be dwelling. The shaman retriever must work with the protection of powerful allies to guard against the imminent dangers. In order to perform the retrieval, the shaman must inevitably intercede, directly fighting with the spirits that are holding the soul hostage. If the espanto is caused by harmful spirits, shamans must be aware that these spirits hate them as well, because they defend and heal the souls of people. Consequently, shamans often come under attack.

The *chulal*, the soul, can also become the captive of dream spirits, who may push the soul into caves or other hidden regions in dreams. In the morning, you may awaken with an uneasy, depressed feeling. For healing the dreams, the retriever must then pray to the lords of a real cave and perform a ceremony in such a place.

In a completely different field, there is another type of espanto that appears as the intrusion of an external spirit into the soul and body. This is a possession of the soul, as opposed to a soul loss. Here, the soul lives under the domination of another spirit. The result may not necessarily be a state of serious physical weakness, but rather one of spiritual and moral weakness. Intense inner struggle, past traumas, and numerous personalities create the essential condition for such a spirit to begin controlling you. Physical symptoms, such as loss of appetite, sleepiness during the day, depression, a feeling of strangeness, and wandering physical pains, can be observed. Often, a spirit may capture a soul after an espanto, then a possessing spirit may take advantage of the soul loss, entering the empty body and living in it. Such people may function on a daily basis, although they may appear ghost-like and unrecognizable to all their familiars. These possessed people may, in turn, create espantos for others and can therefore be quite dangerous.

In all these possibilities of soul loss and soul possessing, it is absolutely necessary to urgently call on a strong shaman or a medicine person, depending on the kind of spirits with which you are dealing. The shaman must perform the retrieval ceremony, if possible, at the place where the espanto occurred. Only those who have the gift, knowledge, and permission to recuperate souls can perform the following Maya healing.

The medicine person first creates a sacred altar at the very spot of the espanto, if possible. If the patient is too weak to walk up to the site, he or she must be transported. Otherwise, the retrieval ceremony may be executed at the healing space of the shaman. On the altar, the healer lights four or five dozen small candles, of all colors, lit at the same time of day that the fright presented itself. These will burn for a few hours afterward. Three young pine shoots should adorn the altar, along with other votive candles, flowers, corn alcohol, and pine needles, to purify the patient. The pine spirit is said to be a beneficial and rejuvenating one, who always bestows help in such retrieving.

As the copal incense spreads its fragrant and purifying smoke through the entire room or site, the ceremony commences, with all the candles illuminating the whole area, lighting the path of the soul. Copal is said to be the sacred resin of a jungle tree given by the heart of the heavens. A small *tecomate*, or tiny dry squash, containing some water is used to produce a specific tone of music that awakens the spirit possessing the soul and calls it forth. A red or white rooster, depending on the sex of the patient, is then offered and purified with copal. Because the rooster's sacrifice serves to invoke and to please the imprisoning spirit, it releases the soul in the form of a trade. It is believed that the soul returns when it is exchanged for the rooster spirit. All the candles, flowers, incense, and the living rooster are meticulously passed over the patient's body. Once the shaman has interceded and "negotiated" with the spirit, the rooster is then sacrificed and the blood given to the Earth at the very site.

Returning home along the same path, the *curandero* sprays alcohol to bless the passage for the returning soul, and blows the tecomate to ensure that the soul is following. Once in the house, the patient is laid at the foot of another, similar altar, and the shaman prays while smudging and blowing the soul back into the body. In the meantime, a woman cooks the *caldo de gallo* (rooster broth) with many regional vegetables. This crucial bouillon is then blessed and given, first to the patient to help him or her regain strength. Then the caldo de gallo is offered to the shamans, in gratitude.

This fundamental ceremony has some variants, depending on the nature of the illness. Among Mongols, I was taught by the shamans to bring back the soul in my own fist, as if I had caught it, and to blow it into the patient's ear. Native American retrievers often blow in the chest or third eye. Among the Maya curanderos, it is blown with the help of the tecomate.

Retrievers commonly consume themselves more quickly than any other healers, for they give a piece of their light each time they retrieve souls. It is thus very important that these healers be compensated in one way or another. I have met many people who think that spiritual rituals and teachings should be free, requiring no compensation. This is a very wrong notion. Some native healers may ask openly for whatever voluntary donation you wish to give—a blanket, a meal, corn, tobacco, money, even a watch. Other shamans may tell you directly the "fee" for their service. Both methods are valid, within reasonable bounds, of course. Natives know that, without this acquittal to the shaman who performed the healing or the ritual, the spirit allies of the shaman will be offended and the healing may have diminished effect, if any.

THE ILL POWER OF ENVY

One of the fiercest and most hypocritical human emotions is envy. Envy can create another form of harmful winds. A wicked wish from someone who cultivates jealousy and bad thoughts toward you is a great danger. Persistent bad thoughts and abusive intents held toward someone else may ultimately take the form of a real entity (a dark wind, spirit animal or others). Good warriors thus learn to shield themselves from other people by practicing solitude.

Each time the sender of envy thinks and emits this black emotional thought-entity, he or she targets it toward the unprotected medicine field of a person-receiver, thus creating serious diseases and emotional problems. These bad feelings ally easily with obscure Underworld entities, attacking the person who is the target of the envy. This often occurs within dreams. When the envy is conscious and sent deliberately, the harm is even more terrible, appearing as a sudden illness in the person's life, with no apparent cause.

In most traditions, natives exercise careful demeanor in order to avoid being the target of people's envy. Utmost discretion and true humility regarding one's material and spiritual wealth, even with close friends, is the best guardian. People who constantly show off are not prudent, exposing themselves unnecessarily to all sorts of life's tragedies without knowing it. Obviously, many people are not aware of this, for they continue their pretenses in an unconscious fashion. This seems to be a cultural peculiarity of Western countries.

The majority of people on this planet constantly emit and discharge their bad thoughts and bad words onto anyone at hand. Unfortunately, this is a behavior that is never truly reproached and that is, to a certain degree, accepted in many strata of the society. In fact, this is nothing other than a complete lack of education in these supposedly "cultivated" societies. In the end, everyone sends potential physical and moral harm to everyone else, even through their most intimate feelings and thoughts. Most people are not even aware that their envious thoughts may make someone sick. They constantly unload their heavy temper and negative emotions onto others, instead of assuming and transforming these in their own core. This is one of the ways that the dark forces have filtered into us. By disposing our emotional garbage on others, by getting angry at others, or blaming them, we assume we have freed ourselves of it. However, energies do not operate this way. Not only do we harm others, but, instead of freeing ourselves, we create a vicious circle. And one day our negativity returns to us, at the end of the circle. It returns with more force because it has accumulated all the negativity of others in this process. To metamorphose such endless absurd attitudes, a warrior's self-control is required, as well as an immediate aptitude for feeling another's moccasins. We must acquire, in our spiritual learning, a discipline that redirects our negativity toward the natural elements. For example, there are countless practices to release negative emotions: by hugging a tree, breathing into the earth, swimming in water, or burning the object of our suffering in the fire. Natural elements hold the power to truly transmute the shaman's human emotional garbage, unlike other humans, who are easily entangled in their own negativity. The earth will transform our negativity into inner power, the fire will transmute it into light, the tree will absorb it into its own roots, and water will help us forgive.

Sometimes envy or bad thoughts may try to insidiously enter into your energy field, without piercing through if you are strong. If this is the case, it immediately bounces back to the sender's field, who may in turn become ill. At other times, the envy that took the form of an obscure entity may well discharge itself onto a close familiar of the targeted person. Unfortunately, children are often perfect victims because of their greater openness. It is, therefore, important to bless and smudge your entire family, asking for protection.

The native ceremony for healing and protecting against envy involves three consecutive days of alternate fasting and continence observed by all the members. This healing process also invariably requires a physical sacrifice of some sort. The process ends with a sweat lodge and prayer ceremony. Prayers are a continuous part of our life, for, through them, we disclose a profound deference for such rituals of purity. Often performed in a standing or squatting position, a native prayer, as a rule, says what is essential. It may be repetitious, thus forming a chant and inducing a slight trance state. Whatever form the prayer takes, it must always come from *the heart center*, the seat of love and wisdom. When the heart and faith in spirit are strong, our protection is inevitably powerful. We have prayers and chants for everything that requires our true appreciation of life, even during the hard storms, or even during the eclipse times of our lives.

Ceremonial altars can be erected for various purposes. They provide a telepathic vinculum and a place of focus for the shamans. Altars are the center of the universe for us. They are our cosmic tree, the emergence hole through all the levels of consciousness that are accessible to us. For these altars, any object can be transformed into a sacred element and a power object. One stunning example is the use of Coca-Cola in the Maya altars. The curanderos, or healers, believe that the gas expels bad spirits of the stomach. Therefore Coke is very sacred to them! Knowing what Coca-Cola represents, which has nothing to do with spirit, I can only say that this example expresses the purest magical mind. I have also observed 100-year-old women healers worshipping plastic containers on their altars, because the durability and non-fading colors of the plastic stands in contrast to their aged and cracked clay vessels! In a native mind, anything is good and can become sacred and precious.

Despite their great humor, old shamans are usually very serious when talking of their conception of illness and the human transgressions that produce it. What they have taught me is primarily that we cannot destroy energy, we can only transform it. In light of this explicit principle, we are all recipients of the stupendous inner potential to self-heal. A good warrior must unveil and reveal this inward capacity. To mature into a powerful healer, however, there are rudimentary precepts of protection that it is imperative to possess. The daily practice of a regenerative discipline to maintain the amount of energy made available to us by the universe is the distinguishing characteristic of a strong warrior. We are the perfect mirror of the energies into which we tap. We become undifferentiated from the energies with which we merge, whether we use them properly or misuse them through harmful activities. This should be our daily reflection and prayer. Because we function in this way, as a mirror, we must be a perfect receptacle so that we may teach others not to unload their negativity, but to positively transform it through our heart. Our hearts must be, at all moments, the heart of the universe.

The greatest recipe for happiness for native shamans is as simple as breathing in the very early morning. It is a way of living. It is a way to integrate these four daily precepts of wisdom to ensure the perfection of our spiritual warrior within:

Purify the body and spirit through fasting and the perpetual cleansing of the unbalanced passions, wanting, and needing of your ego;

Pray to invoke beneficial morning spirits to bless your home within and without;

Sacrifice to give of yourselves, reciprocally, to the powers, for the magnanimity and abundance of the universe in our lives; and

Appreciate the magnificence and beauty of the encompassing world, in the same way that children glimpse it at every moment.

6
SILENCE

RESURGENCE INTO THE REGIONS OF MYSTERY

 Within the passage of the celestial bodies in the sky realm, the star gods of our solar system (Sun, Moon, Venus, and others) in their intrinsic cycles, descend through the nine Lowerworlds of the west death passage. There, they rebirth and resurrect in the East, to the thirteen Upperworlds, that they ascend during the day in their course through the sky.

In their descent into the regions of mystery, these gods must conquer the trials of each of the nine lower regions, roots of Xibalba, so they may be received, with all the honors of gods, in the celestial realms. The following ancient Maya teaching presents a chart of guidance to the spiritual warriors in their subterranean descent. Any warrior or future shaman is given the potential to find their god within eventually if they are capable of passing the nine trials, thus defeating the nine guardians of this night passage in the womb-belly of the Earth mother. There, life is generated as the subterranean richness of seeds, precious stones, and crystalline water. Also abiding in her core are the eternal fire of destruction and the land of the dead.

For the warrior, undergoing a small death during the course of life means experiencing what all souls necessarily face during the final death. The nine regions of mystery symbolize the nine roots of our human cosmic tree and correspond to the nine medicine centers (chakras) of the human body. When a dying person passes away to the other world, the energy of life and the soul gradually leave the body through these nine centers. While life departs the body through each of the nine energetic centers, the soul must review each one of the nine challenges to our shadows. If this quest has not been undertaken in life, it must be dealt with at the moment of dying. And there always exists the potential risk of spiritual defeat while the energy of the body is slowly leaving. All true humans must, therefore, confront themselves with the small death experience in their lifetimes, so that they may have continuity of consciousness during the death process—so their souls may leave with clarity and freedom.

Many dying people who have never met their spiritual challenges in life may never find the ninth region of the land of the dead, due to their lack of spiritual and moral strength. They risk being detained and vanquished in any of the prior regions. Some souls never find their way out of the lower regions and, if they are pulled to reincarnate, they may carry all the heaviness of these regions in their next life. On the contrary, the dying warrior who successfully attains the Happy Hunting Ground of the ancestors at the ninth level, may leave the lower regions to ascend into the higher realms of the Upperworlds, where important spiritual training is given before rebirth.

According to ancient, native knowledge from North to South, all dying persons must traverse the sacred river of blood and life in a small boat or canoe, accompanied by a black dog that guides the passenger through various portals to the other shore, the first lower region. In ancient Maya knowledge, the dying person, or the seeker of the lower realms, may arrive at a crossroad. They must solve a riddle, which grants them passage to meet the nine initiations of Xibalba. Special privileges are given to the previously initiated—powerful warriors, shamans, priests, and those killed by lightning. They can pass directly to the ninth region without living the torment of these terrible obstacles because they have mastered the art of dying during their lives. This is also true for women dying during labor, because of their courage, as well as for babies dying at birth. Because they come from the pure realm between life and death, they will also attain the ninth Underworld and immediately begin their ascent into the thirteen Upperworlds.

The passage into the nine Underworlds is the way between life and death. It marks the soul's journey from ignorance to the knowledge of the initiated. This subtle passage of the soul is as thin as a silk thread or a woman's hair. In the subterranean regions, everything is contrary. When it is night there, it is day here. When it is hot here, it is cold there. When it is happy here, it is sad there. This explains something I have observed among the Mayas. They often place their images of gods and saints, or other fetishes upside down. Sacred objects have also been found upside down in ancient gravesites, reflecting this same belief.

To properly undergo the death passage, you must have dealt with your fears during this lifetime. Fears are the inherent reality of this physical plane of adversity. You must face and overcome them. If you have not met your fears during life and not extended to a good level of consciousness, you will abandon your body through one of the lower centers, such as the navel center, or, at worst, through the anus. The soul may also leave through the mouth, nose, or ears. For most people, the soul departs through the navel. This is where life is given through the umbilical cord in the mother's womb. However, when the soul is already enlightened, it will depart, at death, through the crown center to avoid falling into a low state of numbness in the other medicine centers of the body. This occurrence requires great discipline and mastery over the mind and awareness. This departure always occurs from the bottom centers, up to the crown. The soul often struggles with all the body's knots of tension, stress, sickness, and fear, at each of the nine energy centers before exiting. This is exhausting for the dying person, who could employ that precious soul energy in reaching the upper realms directly through the crown, without going through the hardship of the lower regions. If this is not achieved in life, the soul must then travel through each of the nine lower levels. For this journey, the dying soul must gather sufficient energy to meet the challenges of the nine regions. Therefore, it is important before dying, to clear all blockages not released during one's lifetime and to adopt a serene attitude.

Simple practices can help—envisioning a personal star force and drawing the soul-chulel through the crown center, visualizing it flying and departing with the power animal. An individual who has attained a fairly high level of consciousness during life by meeting and reflecting on his or her death is given the aptitude to choose the time, as well as the manner and the place, of death. This is only granted to true warriors who have defeated the obstacles and allied with the nine lower guardians.

Another ancient and powerful discipline that I have found throughout the Mongol, Inuit, American Indian, and Maya traditions involves enlarging the consciousness of one's death in daily awareness. Called the Circle of Skulls Journey, this meditative practice invites you to visualize yourself approaching the first lower region to meet the presence of your own death, in a circle of human skulls, in a desolate, desert landscape where death awaits you. After entering the circle and sitting at the center of the skulls, you invite death to meet you, while your power animal witnesses and protects you from above. A prayer to your ancestors is then offered. You start peeling off layers of skin, muscles, and nerves, until only your skeleton is seen, sitting on the ground in the middle of the circle of skulls. By visualizing every one of your bones being pulverized and spread in all directions, you are left with only the consciousness of your soul. You must now perform a last gesture in this world, before freely departing to travel to the nine regions. This final gesture can be your last drumming, a dance or chant. It must convey the force of your ultimate moment upon this plane, recollecting your life's journey of learning throughout your life's accomplishments. This is a good preparation for your eventual journey to the nine regions.

XIBALBA,
THE PLACE OF AWE

The *Xibalba* of the Mayas is the mysterious realm, the region of those who have vanished into the infraterrestrial world. The nine god-guardians reveal their nine obscure faces and exhibit the nine mirrors of your inner shadows. The Mayas call these regions, *casas*, or houses, literally lodges. Each house of initiation holds a test, a small death passage represented by a god and a goddess counterpart. The teaching I am sharing here loses itself in the depth of remote times. Some of the ancient sources that I studied are often contradictory in relation to the order of the regions. Here I will give a version that recollects this archetypal knowledge in terms of the real passage of the dying person through these nine energy centers and trials. In reality, the human body has thirteen medicine centers, one for each of the thirteen Upperworlds. In the death passage, however, the soul deals with only nine of these centers.

In the ancient legends depicting the passage into the Underworlds, warrior-heroes were capable of conquering the inner torments of the human shadows and becoming *Nichimal Vinik*, the real humans, only by demonstrating temerity, astuteness, and fearlessness. Any souls who did not pass the test of a certain region, died in that failed region and were reborn on Earth to undergo the missed initiation in life. Here, we will undertake the journey that a spiritual warrior, a true seeker, must inevitably encounter in his or her life passage, just as the soul of a dying person would do (see figure 3 on page 116).

THE FIRST REGION: In the first region of the *Inframundo* (Underworlds), the seeker finds the *House of Illness,* also named the *House of Vices.* As we saw, illnesses and immorality surface to our world

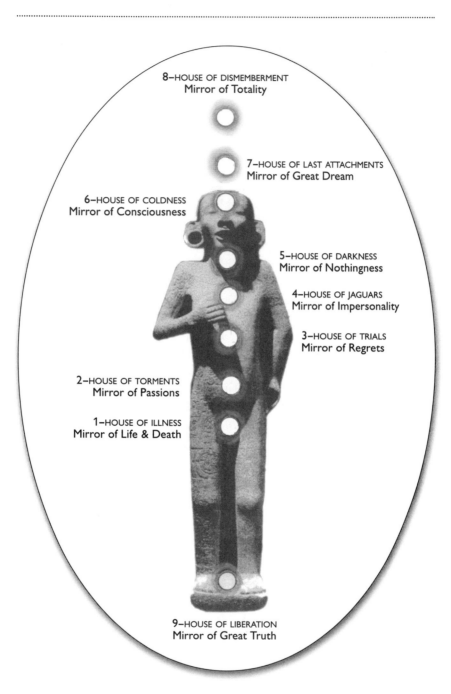

8–HOUSE OF DISMEMBERMENT
Mirror of Totality

7–HOUSE OF LAST ATTACHMENTS
Mirror of Great Dream

6–HOUSE OF COLDNESS
Mirror of Consciousness

5–HOUSE OF DARKNESS
Mirror of Nothingness

4–HOUSE OF JAGUARS
Mirror of Impersonality

3–HOUSE OF TRIALS
Mirror of Regrets

2–HOUSE OF TORMENTS
Mirror of Passions

1–HOUSE OF ILLNESS
Mirror of Life & Death

9–HOUSE OF LIBERATION
Mirror of Great Truth

Figure 3. Dying through the Nine Lower Regions of the Underworlds.

through caves and mountains, carried by winds originating in the first region. This region is guarded by the Fire God, Tohil, and his wife-goddess. Both hold the mirror of our imbalances. The House of Illness corresponds to the first energy center of your body, the sexual center (also called life), which, when harmonized, provides the vitality in your dream body. If these gods are appeased properly, they help us transmute negativity and the sick energies of their realm. When you show clear disrespect for all sources of life, however, the fire gods use their power to send illness, usually of a hot nature. They teach that sexual energy must be venerated in the same way as that of a fire spirit, for both are very subtle energies. For this reason, the Mayas consider that making love in front of a fire is a great offense. These gods hold the Mirror of Life and Death, also called the mirror of immortality. For the dying soul, this passage grants the opportunity to understand the illness that is causing it to leave this plane, the one that has brought death. This level also gives you the mastery of mental and physical sanity during your life. If your soul is truly debased, it will not gather enough vital energy to pursue your other body centers and regions, and may simply leave through your anus. Reincarnation of the soul is a belief common to all native cultures, and our wise people know that those souls who are defeated in the first region will have no possibility of a superior incarnation in the next life.

THE SECOND REGION: In the second region, you find the *House of Deceitfulness*, also called the *Lodge of Torments*. This is where warriors meet and conquer all fears of the flesh. This house is guarded by Kisin, the God of Earthquakes, and his wife, Xtabai, also named Crazy Mother. These embrace the traveler of this region, seducing and rendering him or her forever crazy in this cave of desires. These gods are adorned with necklaces of human eyes, and earrings of dead bones. They hold for you the obsidian Mirror of Passions, the shadow mirror of internal terror, that reveals your true beauty on the other side. This place is also called the *House of Noises* (probably for the disquiet of our clamorous ego) and is related to the navel center (called intuition). The trial here is to embrace your shadows and overcome insanity by allying with these gods. As the soul reaches the navel, the fears not faced by the dying person during life are now met. They can appear so frightening, that the soul may leave the body right at the navel, wandering for a long period in this region of inner torment.

THE THIRD REGION: In the third region, the seeker finds the *House of Punishment,* also named the *House of Trials.* The thunder gods (chacs, gods of lightning) preside over this region. This is where the lightning reaches when it strikes Earth. Traveling into this level, you are either destroyed or protected. It could also be called the house of karma, where you must review all the causes and effects of all your life actions. This region is connected to the solar plexus center (our center of discernment). In a positive sense, it is a place of important evaluation, and, in a negative sense, this judgment house is where we all face our inner weaknesses, remorse, guilt, and the nightmare of the soul. Once you review all actions and succeed in overcoming this house, you are positively aligned with the great powers. This level is also called the House of a Thousand Bats (or Zutz), each bat holding the Mirror of Regrets of our shame and guilt.

THE FOURTH REGION: Here, in the *House of Jaguars,* lives the sacred knowledge and secret teachings that are revealed to those who unearth them by conquering the power of the jaguars, who stalk within this region. The heart center (called wisdom) corresponds to this region, watched over by the Sun God, Balanke, and his female companion, the Moon Goddess, Ixchel, who guard this passage into the lower worlds. For the dying person, the passage of the soul into the heart is crucial, for, once the heart is reached, the journey to the upper energy centers may occur much more smoothly. To challenge and acquire the power of the night jaguar in this lodge is to enter into the realm of the mirror of personal concern, also called the Mirror of Impersonality, where your relation to hate and love is reviewed and where the prospect of choosing your future incarnation is awarded.

THE FIFTH REGION: This region leads to the *House of Darkness.* It is the *House of Nothingness,* of total emptiness. Those who die believing there is no life after death often lose themselves in this region, unable to find the way out. In this region, the traveler meets with the evanescing thought process, as part of the great void. In this region four guardians are found, named Ikim, the Owls of Great Silence, messengers of death. They hold in front of you the black Mirror of the Nothingness or the mirror of the spiraling void within. This level is directly connected to the throat center (power of truth). Here, the initiation of the warriors is to keep their inner light shining amidst the obscurity.

THE SIXTH REGION: The *House of Ice,* or *House of Coldness,* lies in the sixth region. This is where the warrior must face unbearable winds, incessantly blowing. It requires a lot of strength to withstand the winds of death of this realm. In the dying process, when the energy is truly leaving, the body becomes colder and colder. It is the beginning of the end—the moment filled with ancient memories. You have a feeling of joining the great meeting of the lineage of ancestors. In this region, the return to life becomes harder, because the will to live has predominantly left the body. This region is guarded by Kukulcan, the Maya plumed serpent, also called the evening star. He dwells here in his passage to the Underworlds, before he is reborn in the East as the morning star. He holds the Mirror of Consciousness that opens the third eye (higher consciousness), the body energy center of this region.

THE SEVENTH REGION: In this region, the seeker finds the *House of Knives* and Obsidian Blades, the *House of Last Attachments.* This is where you sever the invisible umbilical thread that connects your soul to your physical body. It is said that the passage into this house is filled with extremely sharp knives and the thorny torments of grasping desperately onto life and people. After cutting all attachments at the crown center (or divine order), you return into the Mirror of the Great Dream, of the universe. This mirror is held by the vulture guardian, Zopilote, who assists at the final separation of each traveler in this region.

THE EIGHTH REGION: Here is found the *House of Dismemberment,* where the Earth Goddess, Coatlicue, was herself dismembered. This is the place of the small death for shamans and warriors, where their skeletons are pulverized. This lodge is also called the second death. It is the return to the fetus designating the star center (called totality), just above the crown center, where the animal guide dwells. It is the last post before dying completely. This test of endurance is as far as shamans may go in the death passage, or anyone, for that matter, who will return to life with the knowledge of having died. The House of Dismemberment is supervised by the most ancient creators of the Maya universe, the old god and goddess, Itzamna (also symbolized as an iguana or a crocodile at the center of Earth). This two-fold deity also presides over the Upperworlds as celestial lizards, holding the heart of the sky with the four Mother Ceibas at each corner. In Xibalba, they hold the Mirror of Totality to the warrior seekers.

THE NINTH REGION: Here resides the *House of Death, House of Final Liberation*. This is where we find the light at the end of the tunnel, after the cessation of all physical life. The Death God and Goddess, Ah Puch and his wife, are always represented as happy gods, holding the Mirror of Great Truth. These gods are always depicted as skeletons, dancing and rejoicing at the great banquet of all dead souls. The land of the dead, the Happy Hunting Ground, is the place attained by the immortal souls of the worthy warriors. From here, all souls, after passing through all nine trials, may begin their ascent into the thirteen higher spheres. This final region corresponds to the energy center of the feet (of unity), symbolizing the departure from this world and the new walk to be undertaken into the land of the dead.

There are many gods and spirit animals who have the capacity to meet all nine regions of Xibalba successfully. Even if they are represented here in only one region, they can travel in all regions of both the Lower and Upperworlds. The great jaguar god, the plumed rattlesnake of transmutation, the warrior vulture, the dreaming lizard, and the sacred eagle are all animal spirits who can travel easily from one region to another.

THE GREAT NIGHT JAGUAR

Some old Maya legends describe the passage of the Sun God into Xibalba, the west passage. Every night, our solar star shape-shifts into the night jaguar, and then is reborn every morning as the great rattlesnake. In the early Maya matriarchal civilization, the Jaguar clan was a high cast of priests and priestesses. The jaguar at the house of the *heart* center was one of their most important totems, and sat at the center of their medicine wheel, at the foot of the Earth Goddess' throne. This is the place of totality and complete remembrance, where the tonal and nahual axes meet. The priests and priestesses themselves dressed in jaguar skins, with jade necklaces symbolizing the rattlesnake totem, a clear sign of their spiritual distinction. The priests, in these early times, were people of great spiritual elevation who had previously undergone much suffering in each one of the initiations within the regions of mystery.

The night jaguar, called *Balam,* is a contrary jaguar. His skin is black as the night sky and he carries the stars on his back as yellow spots, as little suns. At night, if you are outside in an open space and look at the stars, you can reflect that you are inside Balam's own belly, his womb, that you are looking at his skin from the inside and that he is digesting you. Even if the ancient Mayas referred to the great Balam as male, this animal spirit was considered to be the greatest feminine shield of all animals. This is true primarily because Balam portrays the Earth realms. It is the night jaguar who regulates the movements of the stars and planets of our solar system, the cosmic winds and the rains that provide sustenance to all Earth beings. He also causes the eclipses, for these are an Underworld manifestation. It is also the sacred jaguar that makes the sky move and rotates the stars around the Pleiades in the night sky.

In ancient times, to become a jaguar priest involved mastering *the art of shape-shifting*. The jaguar inspires us to use this great feat of control as a medicine of great influence in the world. Being connected to both the mysterious, sexual center and the heart center, the jaguar occupies the place of immortality and impersonality in relation to the teachings of these specific centers, because the jaguar spirit being lives in the alter ego realm, the realm of the dream body.

Jaguar medicine is still very important in the Maya world, even today, because it is a medicine of initiations and mastering all dimensions of the Underworlds. Maya priests say the jaguar spirit is returning in these times to help the true seeker to meet the human roots of our cosmic tree. Consequently, this is a very important medicine for warriors to call upon in their passage into the Lowerworlds. The jaguar is the greatest hunter of the lower realms, the magnetic teacher of fearlessness and of embracing our shadows. The jaguar also confers on seekers a great protection, keeping them from falling into the grip of insanity. It is a powerful totem of death and rebirth that incites us to die for our passions and be resurrected, unfraid of becoming lost in the void and burning in the fire of our vision. The jaguar understands how the universe grants power, always seeking the hardest situation possible to prove his spirit's strength. He will go so far as to sacrifice himself for the sake of others.

Holding the place of power, yet always seeking peace, the dignity of the jaguar priests forces them to go to great lengths to keep consensus and harmony among the people. This captivating medicine always works to implant reforms and help those in need. Without this purpose, the jaguar spirit has no reason to exist. In his cycle of power and his mastery of intent, the great jaguar of the night shows us, through appropriate fierceness, the courage and the true gracefulness in the circles of our life.

Stalking every one of us silently, in the corner of our shadows, in our passage into Xibalba, this totem demands that we all strengthen our spirits, and deepen our inner visions. He demands that we find the light and hope of the red Sun in our darkest night. This is the teaching of the plumed jaguar. When he has reached the highest level, the jaguar grows feathers and, ultimately, flies in all the upper realms.

Balam, jaguar of noble spirit and unbeatable mind, carries the staff of authority of the Earth, for he opens the path to the people, as proclaimed by the ancient Maya teachings and prophecies.

With his infrared vision, the jaguar spirit sees perfectly in the dark, overlooking great distances, moving in the vast territory of the mind, from one region to another, reading our minds, revealing our truth. The night is his realm, for it allows the expansion of consciousness. He walks with clouds on his paws, in the great silence of the regions of awe.

EARTH BURIAL CEREMONY

The Earth consciousness is receptive, but not passive. She possesses immaculate intuition, pure knowledge of your shadows, and she dreams, with you, the conception of the universe. In her womb, you plant the seed of your true spirit. For you are only feelings and you can only truly perceive your immeasurable nature with the knowledge of your death.

The Earth Burial ceremony is a powerful practice of *deep healing*. Earth energy has the great power to absorb all disease, though in a slower manner then the transmutation ceremony with fire. A complete burial ceremony entails fasting for nine days, the number of the nine regions. In it, one surrenders into the entrails of the Earth goddess. I have found that this ceremony is one of inner disintegration and of the dismemberment of the old Self, moving toward true, spiritual awakening. The retreat into the Earth thus not only permits the healing of disease, but also confers *a true regeneration of the soul.* In the womb of the Earth, you reach the point of losing the sense of your own body and the boundaries of physicality. This is why it is a ceremony of small death and rebirth.

It is important here to understand the difference between the Vision Quest and the Earth Burial. Many have asked me if they could make their Vision Quest in the Earth hole. No, for no one can find their life purpose in a hole! A Vision Quest consists of fasting and praying, usually on top of a mountain, to manifest to all the spirits of the universe your need for guidance and ask them to help you meet your destiny. The quest calls forth the power to find the vision and your purpose in the world. It serves to show you, through this lonely time of four days and four nights, that you are not alone and that spirits are guiding you. A Vision Quest creates a masculine shield in your life. It is the entrance into the womb of the cosmos and is a necessary rite of passage for you to grow into courage and warriorship. The Earth Burial, in opposition, is used more for internal spiritual and physical healing. It connects you with your feminine shield within. It is a return into the womb of the Earth.

Although, in both rituals, you surely face fears of all sorts, the Earth ceremony may strongly encourage you to ground yourself and to meet your inner complexes more directly. In the Earth darkness, you meet, face to face, your mental and emotional imbalances, neurosis, insanity, and shadows by releasing your ego into the sacred hole. This return to the fetus and your primal awareness must occur in total nakedness and darkness. In the Vision Quest, you find yourself naked in front of the Council chiefs, your spiritual guides. In the Earth womb, you are unveiled in front of your very Self, with all your wounds open. This is where you will breathe and release forever all past hurts into the sacred Earth. In the sacred soil, disintegrated, you may conceive that you are nothing and everything at the same time. You may die to find your life. In the Earth, you can only encounter real inner silence, the same silence that created the universe in the great dream of the void.

The medicine center of *silence* is located in the back of the neck, at the base of the brain, in the medulla. It is also called the Moon center because it is marked by a little natural concavity that you can find when you touch it. It is said by the ancients that in this little hole is found the essence of your spirit, that here your universe is expressed. This center is related to silence, for, to discover spirit, we must be silent.

The Earth Burial ceremony is very appealing and many ask me to share its secret. Some important warnings are necessary, however, before you undertake this ritual. I strongly recommend that you seek the help of a knowledgeable assistant. The assistant may help you with breathing at specific times, give you some water if needed, and help you by providing a sense of normality during and after the burial ceremony. It is strongly recommended that you prepare ahead of time for a complete fasting. In any case, you must be left entirely alone, because disintegration is always dangerous. The assistant must not disturb you, but should stay outside, at hand for any problems. A couple of days of burial preparation is judicious to start with. There are two ways of performing the ceremony. The seeker may lie in a hole-grave, completely covered with earth, with only a small orifice through which to breathe. Or the seeker can sit in a deep, narrow hole, six to nine feet in the earth. In both cases, the ceremony should be performed in complete darkness.

During the period of gestation within the earth, you must allow yourself to die to your old thoughts and past hurts. You can also practice various journeys to sink into each region of the nine energy centers of the body, to locate and challenge your inner knots and obstacles as described in the teachings of the nine underworlds. This is the principal occupation you will have in your hole of regeneration—looking at your fears.

After the period of burial, you must reintegrate yourself, slowly emerging out of the grave with a clear understanding of this rebirth. Newly healed, a light sweat lodge to clean your body and a light meal are advised. Before returning to your normal life, a few days of quiet are needed after such an impacting passage. Rushing back into your life is surely not prescribed.

After the sweating and bathing of your body, the grave should be smudged and blessed with herbs and personal offerings, then well covered with earth, for you must leave no trace. A prayer of thankfulness for the courage that Earth has given you in this impacting dismemberment ritual is necessary to end it mindfully.

This ceremony of small death passage is similar to the real death passage. Indians, for eons, have insisted, through their traditions and ways of living, on the importance of burying the dead properly and the sacredness of burial grounds. All these teachings come from the Underworlds, either from those who died and returned to teach humanity, or directly, from the spirits and ancestors. For years, in my work, I have observed people seeking and needing guidance to assist their loved ones in dying properly. This is important, and I have found that the White culture teaches very little on the mourning ceremonies of this essential rite of passage. If these rites are not properly done, the departing soul may wander forever and may even strive to come back and haunt humans.

Traditionally, among the ancient Mayas, priests were cremated, for they were masters of the eternal fire and their ashes were deposited in small clay receptacles, over which pyramids were built. The common people were not cremated. They were buried, at sunset, in an earthen hole, always in a sitting position, in large clay vessels, facing the west entrance of the Underworlds. Nevertheless, in all Indian traditions, the dead are buried with their sacred power objects, regardless of the level of the soul, to ease the path into the nine realms.

The dead are usually feared, for we believe that they may take their closest relatives with them, causing deep grieving, pain, and depression to those who remain behind. It is, therefore, essential to perform the proper ceremonies for the soul, so that it may leave freely and choose a clear future incarnation. Any rituals performed for the dead do carry dangerous aspects and are traditionally performed by shamans or priests who know what is involved. For instance, a dying body dispels a strong, invisible gas that may seriously harm anyone too near. The shamans help the soul to leave and not come back, to depart from this plane in a most proper way.

I remember years ago, a native man and woman knocked on my door, asking if I could heal their son. A 16-year-old man was then brought into my practice room. They sat him on a chair. He looked almost like a vegetable, never pronouncing more than deep, painful laments once in while, as if he were already in another world. I approached him and looked into his eyes. The light was quite gone, but his body remained alive, barely. He would not talk. His parents said that, for the last year, they had had to attend to all his necessities, as for a newborn, for he was completely unable to see for himself. They said no more. I then started the journey to meet the soul of this young person and, after an arduous meeting, found him to be the captive of another soul. I was told that it was his brother, who had died a year before and hadn't received the proper ceremonies at his burial. This had kept the living brother captive. I asked the parents about this and they looked shameful, as they both said that this was true. Their older son had died a year ago. I asked what happened and they replied that there had been an accident. Asking them if he had received any ceremony at his burial, they said only a simple one.

Now, this sensitive younger son sitting in front of me had so much unhealed pain about the death of his brother that he had chosen to depart as well. But he had forgotten to take his body. This is what we mean when we say that the souls of the dead can take you with them. This is extremely dangerous. So I prescribed that the parents create the proper altar for their deceased son, and I undertook a number of healing practices to call back the soul of the younger son. It was not easy. He was truly gone in spirit. Finally, after several attempts, I journeyed myself to meet the soul of this young man in the other realms, scolding his soul to help him understand the reality of where he was dwelling. I urged him to make a decision, whether to return to his body now, or to depart this plane entirely, to cease the pain he was causing. After various attempts, which at times appeared hopeless to me, his mother brought him for his usual ceremony. That morning, she knocked on my door, I opened the gate and saw the young man held by his mother. He was barely walking, as usual, but there was a light in his eyes and I heard a young man's voice saying; "Buenos dias, Ohky." He was back.

To meet death properly, it is important to come to the realization that *you are born alone and that you will also die alone.* In most spiritual traditions of the world, dying people leave the community and retreat to die in solitude. *Birthing into the death passage* is the only sensible way to consider death and the dying process. Therefore, a dying person needs time alone and silence, but surely not the morbid atmosphere usually created by family members. Dying people sense everything more than usual, and they simply abhor seeing people crying around them. And a dying person hears everything, hearing being the last sense to die.

In an Indian sense, it is important to overcome any pain while in the presence of the dying person and, instead, to encourage them powerfully into their passage. Creating a small altar in the room where the person is dying helps to remedy much sorrow. Lighting some candles on the altar assists the deceased in finding the way through the nine Underworlds and finding the light at the end of the tunnel. Among northern Indians, a sacred fire was customarily lit for four days and four nights. This is the normal time a spiritualized soul will take to pass through all the lower regions and reach the ninth, the Happy Death God. However, in these days, with all the grasping complexities of the psyche, the mind, emotional blockages, not to mention stress, people may take a number of weeks to traverse all the regions through illnesses. They may unfortunately, stay entrapped somewhere in between. In the worst cases, I have seen the wandering souls of dead take years to reach the ninth stage of liberation, due to improper living and lack of preparation toward dying.

The altar for a dying person should be adorned with flowers, a bowl of food, and a bowl of water, for the soul may get thirsty and hungry through all these arduous passages. An altar serves as a point of convergence on which the soul may rest, as well as a place for the assistants to place their emotions. There are many native traditions of chanting for the departing ones for four days and four nights. This considerably helps the soul to lift up, as well as to release the grief of those who remain. Chanting for the soul creates a vibration, a music that will inspire the soul not to lurk around, lost and caught in everybody's pains of the physical realm.

It is common that many unprepared souls, as they leave, do not fully understand what is happening to them in this passage. Resisting and seeking to come back, they hope to touch their loved ones, trying desperately to talk to them. It may take time for the soul to get used to its new state. Even after death, for a number of days, words of encouragement and of joy for the wandering soul are thus absolutely imperative.

Death should be as joyful as birth. The passage into the womb of life is as beautiful as that into the womb of death. Only projections of people's fears about death have made funerals a boring and painful matter. Any heavy, painful emotions are directly received by the soul even days after death. The encouragement serves to support the soul to leave promptly and swiftly. It also keeps the dead from taking anyone with them emotionally, spiritually, or even physically, which is a current phenomenon. How many have lost the will to live after the death of someone close to them?

It is absolutely essential to reassure people who are dying, and not disturb them with words and memories of their own lives.

Although it is true that many dying people review their lives, they do this in a timely way. Interfering with their process can be quite aggravating. And, of course, grasping onto them and urging them to remain as long as possible is the worst of all. Alternatively, giving clear guidance to help stimulate the crown center with a small, clear, single-pointed crystal may incite the soul to choose this doorway to find higher awareness.

Even though many elect to depart this plane in the fastest way possible (in accidents), the majority choose the long process (in agony). Usually, dying people will not leave until some matters are solved in their family situation, such as a reconciliation among family members who have not seen each other for years, but are now reunited at this death. I have seen this very often when assisting dying people. It seems that the agony lasts forever and everyone wishes it could be over. The people who are dying are suffering and so is everyone around them. But the departing souls know the time is not ripe yet and that this is the last meeting for this life. This time is as precious as a birth. This is why true reconciliation between family members at the bed of an agonizing loved one becomes powerful healing for all.

One of the most ancient customs among native cultures consists of burning the teepee, breaking and burying all the belongings of the deceased, even killing the horse of the dead. This allows the soul to cut any material attachments and leave free, at peace. Only the sacred power objects of the deceased accompany them into the hunting of the lower regions. This ancient custom can thus be an inspiration to clear away as much as possible of the dying person's belongings, before and after death. The liberation of the soul should have priority over the grasping of whatever the dead leave behind.

Veneration of the dead body is also indispensable. The body must be cared for with utmost respect. An Indian belief affirms that autopsy after death desecrates the body and certainly impels the soul into lower incarnations. The giving of organs after death, something that has become the subject of a spiritual controversy, represents, for the ancient natives, the utmost profanation. Every physical organ carries our very essence while alive and this essence remains in our internal organs long after death. Giving organs to others is, to a certain extent, forging karmic chains with unknown people.

After the native funerals and rituals (lasting four days and four nights), the family and close friends conclude with some ritual baths or a sweat ceremony to mark the end of the grieving period, clearing any gas and ensuring that the soul does not cling to them. Afterward, the name of the deceased is never mentioned, nor are they overly thought about. This allows them to live at peace wherever they may be and encourages them to leave us at peace. This is Indian under-standing. I have seen some people leaving a personal object in the grave of a deceased, and, even after years, they cannot get over their lingering sadness. The dead, departing with a part of these people, will be forever pulling on them, unless a shamanic ritual is performed. If we receive or take home any object of the deceased, we must also be conscious of possible effects.

The Day of the Dead is an important feast in Mexico that has ancient Indian roots all over the three Americas. This day is celebrat-ed on November 1st for the small, or infant, souls (*almas chicas*), and on November 2nd for all the big, or adult souls (*almas grandes*). I have come upon northern native customs that also honor this date from remote times. Among the Iroquois people, the Day of the Dead is usu-ally feasted on November 4th. This day is a time of veneration of the ancestors and all the dead, to solicit protection and guidance in our lives. It is believed that the dead return among us during this time. The customary altar for the Day of the Dead among the Mayas can be quite elaborate. An entire wall is covered with a large, dark-blue drap-ery, symbolizing the sky with stars, and adorned with a profusion of flowers, candles of all colors, photos of the deceased, sugar cane, sweet calabashes, blessed corn alcohol, and many fruits. This altar is a true feast for the eyes.

On this day, everyone meets at the grave of their respective fam-ily members, for the entire day. They eat with their dead. The whole cemetery is transformed into a giant, colorful altar, filled with flow-ers, candles, and people dressed in traditional clothes. It is a day to reflect on death itself, as a way to unite our consciousness with the true meaning of our personal death, keeping alive the essential vin-culum to our ancestors and the link of life.

Because death, as the absolute end, is a concept created by the mind, our belief in permanent separation is only a fatalistic view of reality. Death, in its transitional essence, teaches us that we cannot consider ourselves immortal in this life. You should ponder that every moment of your humble existence may be your very last one, that you can never really know when death may embrace you. Every instant should reflect your heartfelt appreciation of the bounty of life. To give importance to material things and emotional attachments creates, to a certain degree, violent emotions that bind you to depressing ways of living. In the abysmal eyes of death, everything exists with perfect and absolute detachment. All else is futile.

7

IMAGINATION

JOURNEYING INTO
THE MAZE OF SPIRIT

In their passage into the sky, all the star beings undergo a small death passage into the Underworlds before resurrecting in the Upperworlds. In his daily voyage, the Sun is born in the East every morning and climbs the Upperworlds of the sky during the day. When night falls, the Sun dies in the West, the Earth's womb, to enter the *Inframundo*, or the Underworlds. All through the night, the Sun visits the nine lower regions to be reborn in the morning again in the East. The same travel happens with the Moon. Although born in the East at dusk, she traverses the Upperworlds during the night and the Underworlds during the day. Venus, as the morning and evening star, also crosses the Underworlds, dying in the West and the Upperworlds, and re-birthing in the East. This occurrence doesn't take place every twenty-four hours, as with the Sun and Moon, but has a larger cycle of 584 days. This is the great journey of the star beings in their paths in the cosmos.

This natural passage also takes place in the whole of our little universe on Earth. Every creature is bound to these natural cycles and experiences the small death and resurgence from the Underworlds as a resurrection. So do we, as children of Earth. There are various cycles circling on our paths and in our way of being. As the Sun, Moon, and Earth, we are ruled by a twenty-four-hour cycle. At night, while dreaming the nahual, we enter the Underworld realm, and in the day of the tonal, the Upperworlds. There are also larger cycles in our lives, upperworld phases of expansion and realization, where the lessons are about giving, sharing, and opening, and then phases of internalization, of small death, where all the lessons are seemingly around detachment.

In the traditional way, these natural passages, from light to shadow and shadow to light, from life to death and vice versa, are governing our physical, emotional, and spiritual selves. These passages represent the important journeys of our path whether it is our journey in death or in life. It is the responsibility of each one of us to observe and attune to all these minor and major cycles within our being as well as our journey in life. It is a journey that is inseparable from our true life vision. This great task should be our primary aim in life. For the most part, all our internal and external problems, as well as any lack of balance, result from being disconnected from these natural cycles, from this original vision; they come from our resistance to opening and attuning to it. This resistance always comes from the mind. The mind opposes the small death and resurrection cycles with all its rationality. When it is time to "die" on our path, and the mind had previously scheduled the contrary, then the result is internal chaos. When life asks us to expand and bring forth full realization, the mind often resists, especially when we had thought of having a break, only wanting to crawl under the blankets! And of course, with this sort of resisting mind, the worst always happens when unexpected events come along our way.

It is not easy to learn how to journey powerfully in your daily lives or on your life path. To learn to unravel the secret of how to journey properly is to learn how to hunt as a warrior and eventually discover how to become a real master of your path. The shamanic ways offer various teachings on developing your journeying. Some practices are simple and may help open the medicine center in the body that develops the awareness and capacity of journeying. This center is called *imagination* and is located within the brain at the pituitary gland.

Imagination is a powerful faculty that has been misunderstood by the Western mind. When you experience an extraordinary perception—let's say you heard a bird talking to you—if you tell this to a scientist, he would probably tell you, "This is all in your imagination," as if it were nothing. But if you say this to a native medicine person, our answer would be, "Oh! good, so what did it tell you?" because we know you really had the experience. So if you truly heard the bird, whether you heard words, or sounds, or only meanings, you will start telling us your journey. This is the same with life or with death. Examples and manifestations like this happen all the time, at every moment. To open to the vastness of this great mystery surrounding you, you must learn how to journey. You must learn how to open your imagination center, as well as your intuition, to perceive the essence of all things. And in order to learn how to journey on your life path, you must inevitably discover how to journey in your daily life. This helps to recognize magic in the little ordinary things around you. Journeying in your daily life does not mean you are daydreaming or that you "space out." On the contrary, you connect so intensively to the world around you that with your new perception, the world, space, and all beings become more alive and full of life. You realize you are not in a world of dead objects anymore, and that living beings, plants, animals, and natural manifestations are on their own journey as well. And, ultimately, the larger awareness you develop with the imagination center is that all living creatures and things, as well as yourself, are in fact journeying and dreaming *together* at this very moment and at this very place.

The tall cornstalks by my window are moving with the breeze as I am writing this. They look as if they are human beings dancing, the sounds of the gentle ruffle of their leaves seems as if they are talking to each other. Are they holding an important council? Probably. The crows on the phone line seem to be listening to their talk. These tall corn chiefs seem to be telling their old legends, songs of their origins, how the first corn spirit came to be on Earth for the survival of the Red people. As I am listening to their great council meeting, my 5-year-old daughter comes out of the small wood near our home. She enters the cornfield looking for worms that are crawling under these corn beings. She gathers a few of them, sits on the ground, and tries to place them in a circle. As I am watching the scene, she starts talking to the worms, scolding them not to disturb the corn. It is as if she knew what I was perceiving and journeying about from my window a moment ago, when the corn stalks were whispering their sacred songs. She simply knew because children journey all the time. They just connect. Journeying links you to the subtleties and poetry of life, to the rhythm of the creation, to the mysterious, often amusing, wonders of the world. You do not need a space ship to travel to feel the universe; it is right here in your hands in the small details of life.

This leads me to mention what a shamanic journey can be for you. Again, there are all sorts of shamanic practices and journeying techniques "out there." Not that they are necessarily wrong, but the instructors who offer seminars on journeying don't explain what a journey is in essence. They only introduce the journeying practice, which consists of lying down, with eyes closed, to visualize entering a tunnel, going to the light, and finding a landscape, all of this while following the sound of a drum. They usually have people journeying and sharing their journeys with no further mention on how to integrate this practice in their lives. For a beginner, this may only help them open some internal gates to themselves. Although the practice seems to be relatively easy, to become a good "journeyer" is a complex one.

To journey in this way is to go in the first region of the Underworlds. When you dream, you meet the second and third lower regions. And when you die, you go even deeper in the lower realms, as we saw. With the sound of the drum, imagining and entering an earth tunnel is to enter the Underworlds. The journey state is said to be an altered state of consciousness. Now, what does this mean? Simply, that you enter the gateway of dreaming, but your normal daily awareness is not fully "shut" as it would be when you are sound asleep. In the journey, you are dreaming, yet you have the awareness of your tonal consciousness. This means that you are aware of the dreaming, of the journey. Like dreaming, your perception can go to all places in an instant, things will appear in front of your eyes, and so forth. Journeying is timeless and beyond space. Journeying should not limit itself to flying or doing all sorts of extraordinary things. This could be a simple waste of time. Your journeying, as well as your dreaming, needs a purpose. And more so in the journey, because your mind consciousness is not asleep. Therefore journeying becomes a safe way to develop your dream body as opposed to directly enhancing it in the dream time, where you could seriously lose yourself.

To journey properly, you need a focus, an intent, and a clear purpose. You must always start your journeying with the idea of discovering something about yourself, about the world that is around, about someone who asks you for a healing or the like. It takes much mental clarity and power to direct your intent within the journey. Usually, people lose themselves in all the visions they receive, and often these countless images are not real visions. I remember once, in a circle I was holding, I asked people to journey to Snake medicine for a teaching on transmutation. A woman had a long, apparently vivid journey that she shared with us. Her interminable journey had numerous experiences of flying in the stars, bathing in a turquoise ocean, becoming tall as a purple giant snake goddess type, and so forth. Everyone in the circle seemed to admire her journey. I asked her when she ended, "So what were the messages you received?" She could not give me an answer. Then, it was the next lady's turn to share. She timidly started to say that she did not receive anything, she had no visions. She said she saw nothing, she never saw a snake. I invited her to share what happened to her. "Did you come out of the tunnel?" "Yes," she replied, "I was in a barren desert. I tried to call my power animal to help me, but she didn't show up; I tried to call the snake, but none came. Nothing happened for a long time in this immense desert. I decided to sit on the sand. I looked at the small stones by my knees, everything was so real. As I sat there, I realized how awkward I felt, being in this vast nothingness. I realized how in my life I always try to make things happen, to fill this emptiness with things, words, and people. I suddenly felt so naked, I felt how all my internal chains keep me from being free. I felt so vulnerable, but nothing ever happened." After she finished I told her, "You got yourself a very good journey here, considering it is your first one. You truly learned something, you were true to yourself, you didn't try to make up things. You touched and let yourself be touched by the West desert of small death where you were. You had a good attitude."

This is how journeying begins, by being simply yourself, with the intent to feel, to touch, to learn, and to discover as if you were really traveling. Otherwise, you are a leaf in the wind, going from one vision to another, and however vivid and extraordinary, this is not true journeying. You have no real warrior's intent, no clear purpose. And if there is no particular purpose at this time, or if nothing seems to happen on your journey, then to experience the void is the only really sensible thing to do. If you stay in this void, you will begin hearing the essence of life, sensing the great truth of all things, including yours, feeling the vital clarity that the knowing of your death confers. You will notice that this great void also takes you to the depths of a universe, a universe that is also just right here in your being. And, as in my journey that I am inviting you to read, this is because a good journey is the most powerful mirror of your true human within.

MANIFESTATIONS OF THE SPIRIT

Listen, see with your ears the silence in the breathing . . . the wind of breath . . .
Listen, behind the wall of sound exists the silence . . .
The resonance of your breathing is the sound of Earth, the cadence of her Heart . . .
Your heart, drumming into your ears like the pulse of the Universe . . .
Intonations of the spirit-drum, the voice of the cosmos . . .
Replenish yourself with the inflection of the universal resonance.
Empty yourself with the vastness of the beat and pulse of the Cosmic Heart,

For somewhere at the end of the Galaxy, at the end of the silence,
you can hear the sonority of the void.
You can listen to the secret voice of Spirit, revelation of wholeness.
Along with this melodious articulation, eternal and infinite in
your very core,
You can hear your intuitive voice as one with the symphony of
the infinite space . . .
This spacious interval called Spirit . . .

In this never-ending space, you listen to the dignity of silence.
There is a wind whispering . . .
Only your Spirit can hear it.
Listen, listen . . . In the holes between the silence exhale the wind
of your higher Self and the voice of the void . . .
Waves of Visions, winds of harmony are pouring as a gentle
rainfall on your Soul
And you oscillate in the euphony of Creation,
The thundering utterance of the Rain Gods in the faraway
reaches of your mind.
Your ears are the ears of the Universe . . .

Everything has a vibration, and an energy made of sounds.
Undulating tones which create matter . . .
Listen to the resonance of substance . . . Sounds create matter . . .
The world is a concerto of notes in the emanations of the
Macrocosm
And Light is a sound made substance, escaping in this gap . . .
Objects are not objects, they are light in a space that creates notes
and tones,
They are sounds in a space that gives light. Enigma beyond your
sensual perception . . .
There is no such world as a world of objects . . .

Wind whispering on the waves of the sea, fire crippling,
River flowing over the staying stones, all creating in diapason, a
resonance by their frequency of light,
By the way they receive their pulsation from the core of the
Universe,

By the way their heart vibrates to the quintessence of the cosmos.

Listen to the sounds you cannot hear . . . Detect the Holes of Emergence between the beats of the Great Heart . . .

Reverberations of sounds originate uninterruptedly from the source of the Creation,

Noises are distortions created by the human Ego, but sounds are the voice of the void . . .

Is your voice the reflection of your Ego or your Spirit?

Discern between the sounds . . .

In silence, listen to the voice of your social personality, the one that you speak with to the world . . .

Hear the language of your intuition within your abyss, the one that talks and whispers into your womb . . .

Have you veiled your voice within, in order to conceal your Soul from others?

What would your voice reveal if you let the inflection of the void articulate in your being,

The voice of the Universe expressing with the same pounding as the rhythm of the Heart of the Great Stillness?

Unclothe the dark cloud that shades upon the very spring of your essence . . .

Remember carefully this instinctive place, for in this sacred Shelter resides the riddle of your being . . .

Have you left there a fragment of you?

Can you distinguish your very Spirit after such an eternity?

Witness carefully this place, this region of mystery,

Can you capture it back within you or is it already existing in you, part of you,

As an ancient drifting memory . . . always and forever . . .

Huge, obscure and pessimistic shadows are now rising upon us in the closure of this era . . .

Though the family of humans is surviving the great cycle, a contingency conferred to us

Through the spiritual trial of global understanding, and human assignments

To ultimately transcend all our walls of consciousness.
These dark penumbras from Xibalba are but a simulacrum of
*   our own ignorance, our eclipsed knowledge . . .*
In reality, these black brumes perpetually existed as reflections of
*   thought-forms we have all created.*
Nevertheless, they are shaped more evidently, as the discernible
*   and intelligible light forces of the planet grow sharper and*
*   enlivening every day.*
We are at the eminence of a Great Momentum . . .

It is not possible to witness this cleavage on Earth
Without each one of us asking "where is the place of our
*   spiritual responsibility?" . . .*
Have you alienated and fractured your very Self, even in your
*   deep conscience?*
Do you help the world to achieve its destiny, to remove the
*   always-existing danger of being collectively destroyed?*
Remember, you cannot transmute toward light unless you have
*   clearly endorsed your own darkness.*
Do you still trust the course traced by the Great Powers?
Are you still capable to impart love, or are you drowning in the
*   skepticism of your own shadows?*
See the obscurity and the radiance in all Life . . .
Behold, the shadows and the lights are sharper on the horizon of
*   the landscape in this end of millennium.*
More defined, more brilliant, even more beautiful.
See, with the Eyes of Earth that touch the Essence of Life . . .

And the nightfall of the Regions of Mystery is coming out of
*   sleep, dawning upon us to awaken us . . .*
As a day and a night Jaguar over all Creation, he moves you,
*   he touches you . . . Open . . .*
Oh! Chacs, Gods of Rain and sacred Thunder, fertility of creation,
Gods of water falling from the sky.
In the Earth Womb where Jaguar dwells, is contained the clay
*   vessel filled with sacred drops,*
Sperm falling from the sky, that penetrates Earth, that conceives
*   Earth,*

Soil of fertility, where the seeds will sprout and grow back to their
origins, reaching the Heart of Heavens . . .
This is the Great Vision of the True Humans . . .
The mist that rose from Earth when it was still dark,
When the first rays of the Red Sun created the protective shelter
of Earth
In the aurora of our emerging and awakening.
Mist, shadows concealing our beauty, feminine magical coating,
which imbues the air, and then rises to ether . . .
Another act of love, the male fecundates female principle . . .
Kukulcan, Plumed Serpent of renovation descending from
the Sky,
Plumed Jaguar conceiving into a sacred vessel to receive and to
hold the divine water from the vault of Heaven,
Immortal void where everything returns in an eternal cycle.
Then the Sacrifice to honor the mysterious Regions of Creation is
requested of you,
The offering is the ritual of transformation, sacrifice of the Self,
Skin of the visible, in pain, in birthing, shedding to release,
denuded,
Finally achieved in the dust of nothingness, inevitable nakedness,
To be holder of the Universe, arms raised to the Upperworlds . . .
To be your Spirit, at last . . .
To be renewed, to be dressed with the mist of times,
To be covered with the iridescence of nature, green as jade,
precious as the Nahual eyes,
To be adorned with the majesty of sacred Plumed Serpent, songs
of ancient codes,
Whispering voices of Xibalba embracing the mysterious mantle
of its nine regions,
Holding the precious liquid falling from the Sky, to refresh all
guardians of the Regions from their thirst,
Finally being a source of truth, where the occult wind flows from
origin, to be at peace at last . . .
Coatlicue, Earth goddess, Ancestral Mother, guardian of the
Truth of the Great Matriarch,
Goddess of pregnancy, unceasing creative Fire of her womb,
Female guardian of the rhythms, of the cycle of our being,

Of the secret oracles of our birthing,
She who shepherds into the labyrinth of the Underworld, she
walks trails of beauty . . .
Coatlicue is waiting for you . . . there . . . beyond . . . she is
receiving you in the meeting place of your unseeable Self.
Watch her carefully, she reposes on the largest turtle's back . . .
She nudges you to the doorway of your deepest feelings . . . follow
her . . .
Where the twins of your essence meet at the roots of the Cosmic
Portal,
Male and female, one substance . . .
Where the sentiments surpass all duality, all emotions . . .
Incisive feelings in the underground chamber of your intuitive
discernment . . .
Your clandestine and internal voices to be introduced to the
Light . . . to the river of beauty . . .
Open to her subterranean passage within,
To the intensity and to the immeasurable tangibility of her world
of feelings . . .
These might surprise you, they might scare you, they might
seduce or capture you.
In one way or another, you have often censured them, your very
feelings,
Forgotten them for a millennium,
They were too compromising, too grounding to assume,
They appeared so obscure in the desolate crater of your
intuitiveness, too absorbing to conceive . . .
Inhibited feelings often twisted into your being, shadows that
search for light . . .
Now the time of eclipse is over in this end of millennium . . .

Spirit powers of the Red Sun are drawing near to revoke your
coercive form of being.
Its heat is piercing through the tempestuous and resisting
carapace of your Self.
Receive the Sacred warmth within your being . . .
To recognize all the shadows and the darkness accumulated in
the luminous Shell of your Soul.

*They are of the same essence as the black spots at the surface of
the Star Sun.*
*Realize how these tenebrous clouds have stained the Sun, our
brother, the light of our Life . . .*
Intruded by human's negative thoughts . . .
Understand how sensitively Nature responds to Life and Death.
*We humans have forgotten to acknowledge and celebrate the
Beauty of the Life-Giver,*
The joy of its company.
*We have shaded our light like the dark marks on the Sun, tears
of disconsolation . . .*
Host the purification of its brightness and the power of discerning.
*You are a Star Fire who exhales in all directions as beams of
wisdom.*
Central Fire of your essence, ancient knowledge in your middle.
*Cleanse yourself of Life, absorb light in the most obscure alcove
of your existence.*
Dances of embers sprout from your hands as bouquets of Light.

Trails of flames illuminate through your feet as fibers of joy.
Rays of lightning emerge from your hair like arrows of Fire.
Offer to the sacred altar, all the Beauty contained within you,
*To renovate the somber haze of the Sun in a pure gesture of
celebration.*

*As you emerge from the Regions of Mystery, the flame of
Consciousness radiates within your Mind . . .*
Yet imperceptible for others. Creative and clear in your core,
Acknowledge it, contemplate with the Flame of Mind.
See the shadows and light onto the Creation slithering
As a divine serpent, soaring over all things.
*Behold, the shadows and the lights are sharper in the landscape,
in the horizon.*
More defined, even more beautiful.
*Everything is ever moving, ever growing, ever living and dying
under the Red Sun of Xibalba,*
*Bear in mind to contemplate with the Eyes of a child, full of
newness and curiosity,*

To contemplate the world in all its power, yet in all its fragility.
Ever detached . . . Ever blessed . . .
Then you will hear the dignified Heart of all your brothers and
sisters as one with yours.

A WARRIOR'S SOLITUDE

When we journey all our senses are involved—completely alert. Our hearing and visual and intuitive senses become enhanced to discern other levels of feeling, to explore the depths of our solitude. This is why it is so important to have a purpose, in order not to lose our sense of self. And there comes a time, after years of developing this awareness, when there is no more need to formally journey in order to do so. Shamans and medicine people, true artists, sacred warriors, fine poets are constantly journeying, living at the edge between the two worlds, at the edge where true signs and meanings are revealed. They are always aware of this tiny door between the abyss of life and death. To illustrate the sacred quest of the true humans, here is a moving poem written by the native medicine healer and companion who led me to the mysterious world of the ancient Maya.

This time, time does not exist in distant solitude
as a flame of the changing fire and of the changeable mask
Only breathing stays in the midst of the profound silence
in emptiness reigns the mystery without end and with courage

Expanding in the faraway the quietness of this moment
between silences and sounds as enigmas of wind
strong wind, soothing wind, take the feelings away
to profound solitude that approaches as reflections and sentiments

The death of the day is reaching, masked with the sunset,
strong colors of buoyant clouds always changing, always dying.

Powerful twilight, obscurity eats it all, origin of Xibalba
the cold wind of death penetrates deep in the bones
impressions of longing that liberate the spirit
as a strange music heard in the far away

The cold embraces as a fire, the smoke as a pathway,
the wind guides the dance of the warrior
the palpitation of the earth, in tune with the drums
reveals the road for the warriors of the soul

As if the night reveals her old secrets, the wind blew in the foliage,
taking the dust of time and the sentiments in uncertain places
The illusion of time at last stopped, everything stays here,
as a feather suspended by the breath of spirit
emanating from the silence

In this constant immensity of contraction and expansion,
death walks close by and my existence lost in a breathing

The night waits, elegant with stars, scents of eucalyptus that trespass
beyond the confluence of dream, the time whirls dragging memories
the sunset opens, the wind is coming east and the breeze of illusion
    is gone,
fragile deception that catches feelings creating worlds of reason, reasoning

At the end, again with solitude now returning,
solitude that hunted itself in the region of delusion, now is back,
    into my heart
this detachment of Life for Death, this suffocation into the earth,
this memory of origin as the unique fascination of mystery

Always at the edge of the obsidian blade, interminable resistance
    for Spirit,
waking in a strange world, where people have no allegiance for they
    live in spiritual idleness,
the warrior is dancing to the sound of the four winds, to the flight
    of crows
that tear their incantation at dusk as if between Life and Death[1]

---

[1] Eliberto Jimenez, Maya artist and medicine healer, Chiapas, Mexico, 1993.

PART TWO

THE
GREAT VISION
OF THE
TRUE HUMANS

"With tears running, O great Spirit. . . . And may be the last time on this earth, I recall the great vision you sent me. It may be that some little root of the sacred tree still lives. . . . Hear me, not for myself, but for my people. . . . Hear me that they may once more go back into the sacred hoop and find the good red road, the shielding tree!"

–Hehaka Sapa, Black Elk,
Sioux holy man, Black Hills, 1931

8

UNITY

CONNECTING THE WORLD
MEDICINE WHEELS

When shamans enter in and out the Under- and Upperworlds through the center of the great cosmic tree, we emerge to other circles, other worlds within the infinite, spiraling womb of the universe. Comprised within this greatest wheel revolve billions of smaller wheels—as large as the galactic wheels to the star systems, and as small as the circle of self within. To perceive the place of humanity in this circling vastness, however, we must first understand the interrelation to the first wheel of our world, the Earth circle. I have given you a description of the three Maya crosses that define the three planes that humans can access from the tree of life. The first cross represents the Underworld plane into which we have already journeyed. The second, which interests us here, is the circle of Earth of humanity, the flowering humans, or the *Ongwhe Onwhe*. The last cross represents the Upperworlds of the sky realm.

In this intermediary plane at the surface of the Earth, everything in nature proceeds in cycles. Trees grow in rings, nests are round, and the year moves in a cycle through the seasons. This is the natural and primary law of our world. On the Earth, all beings living in the plane between Earth and sky move in circles, even without knowing it. Accordingly, we all physically face one direction or another on the horizontal plane. Even within the thickest walls of our prisons, we are still facing a cardinal direction, wherever we may go. For this reason, the medicine wheel provides a way to attune to this horizontal plane by recognizing our first basic hoop. For example, the first relationship of a child to the world is within the horizontal circle and is never vertical. This is easy to observe when a baby is old enough to sit by himself on the floor. Babies discover the world of objects around them in a horizontal manner, touching what is at hand, on the ground, within their own circle. But as children grow older, they are inculcated with often unhealthy patterns of behavior and thinking, patterns that are opposite to the natural circle of being.

The Medicine Wheel ways are represented as a circle of eight stones lying on the ground and a ninth one in the center. This appears to be one of the simplest representations of the universe, yet the wheel ways comprise an ancient and complex body of spiritual teachings. These ways of great transcendence describe levels upon levels of awareness. The medicine wheel teachings are almost endless and by creating a medicine wheel of stones, we form a natural circle of energy that unites the Earth and the sky realms in the horizontal plane of the cardinal directions in which we live. The power of the natural wheel is circular by nature and always holds a true center, contrary to a more linear perception. Each time we enter a wheel, we bring our minds back into a circular manner of thinking contrary to Western educational systems that have conditioned the mind to perceive in a linear and square way. In such a linear conception of the world, the mind's need to establish beginnings and endings inevitably turns into an unhealthy mental addiction, a prevailing tendency in Western society.

Throughout history, entire civilizations bound to destructive mind concepts have forgotten the horizontal plane of understanding. Many Western religions have and still do profess verticality as the only way to God, often rejecting anything secular and of the earthly world. This obsession for verticality has only expressed the false concepts of spiritual evolution caught in a pyramidal edifice. But in the great wheel of the universe, when we think we have climbed the ladder to God and are therefore more evolved, this is a mere illusion, for we all are equal in the circle. We will all return to the same place around the wheel, at one point or another in the circular cycles of life and death. In fact, we just go around the circle and this is the only thing we really do, so there is nothing to be so serious about in our lives!

THE CIRCLES OF THE EARTH

The foundations of our Earth circle are time and space, and neither is linear. They are both circular. In the true circle of being, achievements are not what count, but rather the way we journey in our sacred circle and the dance of life. It is not *what* we achieve spiritually that counts, but *how* we achieve it. When shamans ascend the Upperworlds or descend the Underworlds along the vertical axis, we always do so with a constant awareness of the primary circle of Earth. Without a firm foothold in the plane parallel to the horizons of the four directions, we may lose ourselves or become totally insane.

This teaching on the medicine wheel is thus connected to the body center of *unity*. This center is located at your feet, and represents your dance of life, your capacity to walk and to fight to bring forth your true vision. When you do so, you can only expand in *unity* within and without.

You can only perceive the circle of Earth from where your feet are, from wherever you travel. It follows you. The true understanding of yourself and all other beings of the universe is given with the discernment of your inherent place within the circle of Earth. Without the knowledge of where and for what you stand, your consciousness cannot enlarge toward the great wheel of life. You cannot self-heal and learn how to heal others and become *a true human*.

The Center of the World should be where your feet are. To gain the awareness of the center of your natural circle is the only healthy process in life. Not perceiving from the center of your own wheel creates a pyramidal mind that sees superior and inferior. This is contrary to a full alignment to your tree of being. At the foot of your tree where you can rest, there exists *no less and more*, but only a place to be, *here and now*. The Underworlds and the Upperworlds are not, respectively, inferior and superior, because these two necessary circles are both part of the same great tree.

In pyramidal verticality, there is only defensiveness, not true protection. Only within the circle are you really shielded. In Western cultures based on the subordination and domination of humans, there exist only false shields. At any moment, anyone may fall off the monolithic structure. And if one falls, all the others follow down the skyscraper. But in a circle of society, someone who leaves may create an empty space for a while, but the circle remains alive. It has nowhere to fall. In a pyramidal human structure, people live constantly scared and dependent on one another, unable to breath and move freely. As a result, there is a constant denial of the true responsibility of the self. Usually, the one at the top is the most fearful, depending on everyone below. To ensure their place within this structure and eventually to make their way to the top, everyone must step over their neighbor and everyone must be ready to kill. Intrigue, corruption, conspiracy, and treason are the leitmotifs of these weak and ill concepts of being. This eventually leads to coercive and authoritarian states, where intolerance is the chief motivation, everyone putting on a mask of rigidity and falseness in order to survive. In the world of today, many people are still caught in this outmoded behavior. They spend most of their time acting out the model imposed on them.

In the natural perception of the Earth circle, however, you live at the center of your inner wheel. This is beyond egocentricity. It involves a natural awareness of what is around you. This may easily expand to the peripheries of the circle, the eight directions, and farther. Limits are not imposed according to an oppressing above, a weak below, and constricting sides. Here the only limits that the wheel knows are the natural boundaries of Earth, like a stone thrown in a river creating rings to the infinite. In contrast, egocentricity is only found in the shallow pyramidal structure and is expressed as disconnected individuals obsessed with saving their skins, never able to view the whole edifice in which they are trapped. In the circle of presence, however, it is given to anyone to see everyone around them, for no one obstructs or inhibits your perspective.

It is important to understand that all the problems of humanity arise from a disconnection from the natural wheel of being. We can either enlarge or close our understanding of the circle of Earth. In this truth resides the principal difference for the future of humanity.

The minds of the majority of people in Western societies are still inwardly trapped in this disconnected form of thinking. They have abandoned the natural wheel. This is, of course, the cause of most depression, empty feelings, and frustration within people. In your hoop of self, you should be with your feet. Your mind should be in the Earth. Everything outside your own circle is only fantasy and does not really exist. For example, the minds of people are constantly thinking over matters that are beyond the scope of their natural circle and the range of the moment, the here and now. One instant, your mind may be in China, while the next, you may be thinking over things that are not your business. One minute, you think about what your mother-in-law might be doing, and the next, you are thinking over the problems in Europe. After that, you come back to dwell on your neighbor's problems, and then you are in the Pleiades, and then back to China, and so on! Such a hectic mind, thinking in this haphazard manner, is not living at the center of its wheel. It is a mind that has no center, wandering precariously beyond the real boundaries, allowing thoughts to dwell on things that are not centered with the path. Many people are affected by and concerned with everyone else's troubles. It is no wonder there is no peace in the world, for almost all humanity carries the sort of mind that is constantly deliberating, judging, analyzing, separating, and identifying.

A mind in balance knows what to think about and what not to, when to think and when to stop thinking beyond the circle of Self and responsibility. It knows how to be in the moment. If you get obsessed over events of the past and projecting into the future, this means you have left the awareness of your protection circle. To allow the requirement of the moment to guide you with the perfect sense of presence and serenity is to achieve an incredible equilibrium. It is mastering walking with your sacred turtle at the center of the wheel. Many people are so caught up in thinking on and on about everyone else that, when it is time to truly give a hand to others, they cannot, they are so tired. In addition, many people with that sort of mind may help someone when they should not, when they are not invited to. In this great truth resides one of the greatest diseases of humanity—the imperialistic mind.

To stop thinking about people all the time, to be in your circle and look at your own circle, requires great mastery. Only then will you know when it is proper to assist others with a full heart, without being an encumbrance. Because of these truths, spiritual warriors and shamans never leave their true centers. Never.

By practicing the Medicine Wheel ways, you may begin to feel energies shifting in another manner in your life. One of the major teachings of the medicine wheel talks of the importance and the responsibility of justly completing the circles in your life. Most people create situations and leave them unfinished, with the pretext of being disinterested. Or they may excuse life's complications, or even become convinced they are through with certain aspects of their path's circle. These individuals never really complete the circles of energy, of situations. This necessarily gives birth to negativity. The circle is not properly closed and it leaves openings. Therefore, the first purpose of the wheel way of being is to educate yourself on the proper completion, closure, and activation of your circles of protection. It is to take responsibility for your own truth and for understanding and developing mindfulness toward others.

In the inner circle of your being, there is only *the way back home*, the way back to the center spiraling inwardly, to this mystery never really reachable, but barely discernible. Those who spiral outward have lost the trail to spirit, constantly pursuing superficial and external stimuli to satisfy and entertain their emptiness, even spiritually. This great mirror of truth is the wheel of reflection of every existence in the universe. It is a natural way to teach ourselves and to become true humans. It is called the Great Shield of Understanding and it teaches the great laws to all the people.

I am profoundly convinced that the imminent new era and new order of peace cannot happen in the air, but can only come with the return to the Medicine Wheel ways of life, the wheel of the self within. It is only in the center of the wheel that *real transformation* exists, nowhere else. Remember, energy cannot be destroyed, only transformed. This miracle of transmuting humanity's poisons can only happen at the center of the wheel, where all axes meet, the eight directions, the upper realms and the under regions, converging at the heart of humanity.

Whether made with earth, river, mountain stones or crystals, a medicine wheel always represents the powers of the eight cardinal directions on this Earth plane, the ninth one being at the center within. In the path of life, all humans, whether they know it or not, face spiritually one of the eight directions and the obstacles and walls, powers and perspective of that corresponding direction. This is true whether we follow another spiritual belief or not. This awareness is beyond belief, but is simply given by the natural forces of Earth.

The place of inner challenge with which each one of us is confronted differs greatly from the direction of the wheel in which we were born and the temperament we carry. For instance, someone may be born with a South temperament, which is emotional (as the water energies of the South), while someone else may be born with a way of being from the West, which is more introverted. Independent of the place we are born, however, all the great lessons of our lives necessarily belong to one of the four major directions. Therefore, the teachings really emphasize that we must learn from each position. This is our most sacred human responsibility. We must meet the walls of the four major directions, as well as gain these four powers. We must, therefore, travel in our life around the great circle. Someone who blocks and resists the passage through these four hills (lessons) of life is likened to a horse with four blinders, unable to see the larger vision and the collective circle. If you refuse to learn and to expand your awareness, you hinder the stream on the wheel for all other sisters and brothers near you. In other words, you block them from moving to other directions as well. We are all interdependent. This is how entire nations have been stocked in a particular direction, people refusing to learn, thus blocking the consciousness of many generations ahead. This is how prejudices, fear of the new, and racism become the inherited traits of a whole people, transmitted through the cultural conditionings.

To truly meet the four veils requires great courage and discernment. And once challenged and defeated, it will remain so forever. Many people have commented to me that they often have the impression of encountering a wall in their lives, fighting with it, considering they are through it, but, inevitably, they find themselves back again at the edge of a similar obstacle at a future time. This reflects two things: first, these people have not fully gotten through their wall, which will appear bigger at each phase of their lives, and second, the circle of energy inherent in the wall is not properly buried and completed, so it perpetually ties them to an eventual return.

The walls of each direction appear as heavy veils or curtains limiting our perception. In the face of these, only what is seen directly ahead is considered by people, nothing below or above, or to either side. This reminds us of the poor peripheral and pyramidal perspective of the mind. Only when you unveil the four major walls, and not before, is your vision clear, neutral, open, and vast. Only if you have defeated these veils and conquered the eight powers, may you stand and sit at the invulnerable center of the wheel, the perfect shield of honesty within. To properly defeat a veil may take many years, or a whole lifetime. Moreover, there are no strict rules. All relies on your inner strength. Once your full circle around the wheel is accomplished, leaving no entrance for negativity, you can experience true invulnerability. However, you will only achieve this when you learn real vulnerability by exposing yourself completely to these walls and to the consciousness of this tender and fragile part within. In the Maya cosmogony, the center tree is always the weakest, the most vulnerable, yet the most powerful, protected by the four large and strong Ceiba trees of the four winds, holders of the sky universe. The universal Medicine Wheel ways provide broad guidance to the sincere seeker to fully meet each one of the directions and their respective obstacles.

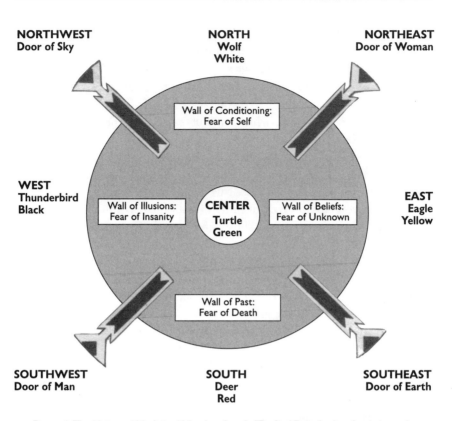

NORTHWEST
Door of Sky

NORTH
Wolf
White

NORTHEAST
Door of Woman

Wall of Conditioning:
Fear of Self

WEST
Thunderbird
Black

Wall of Illusions:
Fear of Insanity

CENTER
Turtle
Green

Wall of Beliefs:
Fear of Unknown

EAST
Eagle
Yellow

Wall of Past:
Fear of Death

SOUTHWEST
Door of Man

SOUTH
Deer
Red

SOUTHEAST
Door of Earth

Figure 4. The Universal Medicine Wheel. • **South**: The Red Deer Lodge. *Symbols* are the magical jungle, the Moon, water, and blood. *Powers of the Heart* are trust and regeneration; *The Wall of Past* reveals the fear of death. • **West**: The Black Thunderbird Lodge. *Symbols* are the desert, Earth's womb; *Powers of the Body* are intuition and humility; *The Wall of Illusions* reveals the fear of insanity. • **North**: The White Wolf Lodge. *Symbols* are the sacred mountain, the stars, and winds; *Powers of the Mind* are knowledge and wisdom; The Wall of Conditioning reveals the fear of Self. • **East**: The Yellow Eagle Lodge. *Symbols* are the blossoming tree, the Sun and fire; *Powers of the Spirit* are freedom and clarity; The Wall of Beliefs reveals the fear of the unknown. • **Center**: The Green Lodge. *Symbols* are the turtle, the seashell, the circle of sacred stones; *Powers of the True Self* are balance, perseverance, and patience. There are no walls anymore, it is a perfect opening. • **Southeast**: The Door of Earth is the Gate of Profoundity where the Guardians of Ancestors dwell. • **Southwest**: The Door of Man is the Gate of Truth where the Guardians of Dreams dwell. • **Northwest**: The Door of Sky is the Gate of Intelligence where the Guardians of Great Laws dwell. • **Northeast**: The Door of Woman is the Gate of Silence where the Guardians of Cosmic Awareness dwell.

In the walls, you constantly live in self-defense. If you are threatened, you will then feel hurt and you may withdraw, attack, or fight back. This is all reactive. But when you have no more walls, you are able to transform, on the spot, any attack into an act of love, of real openness and full acceptance of your aggressor. If you open and *let go*, you have met your wall, which, in this case, took the shape of an attack. To let go fully of a way of conceiving how life should (or should not) be is often very hard. It requires a tremendous sacrifice and capacity to see beyond. It starts with asking yourself, "What if what I am thinking is not totally true or adequate?"

Once you have let go four times in your life (as in the four walls), you find the inner state at the center shield. Once a soul passes through the long and arduous passage into the four walls and perspectives and reaches the center of the wheel, sometimes over many life times, then, and only then, it may be reborn as a true teacher, a born chief, forever free of the chains of cause and effect. This is why the center of turtle in the great wheel is called the Shaman's Place. It is the real place of alignment to the cosmic laws. There can be no real authority and mastery until this circle is completed.

In my path along the Medicine Wheel ways, I have encountered and worked with many types of wheels—American Indian, Mongolian, and Maya. It always struck me how similar they are, the significance of each power very analogous and the larger understanding of the circles of energy identical. This makes these ancient ways the most universal and ancient teachings humanity has ever seen. Of course, some differences are found from one cultural wheel to another, differences in certain colors and the regionalism of animals representing the four mountains and directions of the wheel, but these differences are quite minor and easily adjusted. For instance, in all these cultures, the center of the wheel is commonly green, the place of ultimate power, and the seat of the Great Turtle. Among the Mongol and Native American shamans, and for the Maya, I have found the cosmic center symbolized as a giant sea turtle, or, oftentimes, a great crocodile.

Throughout my learning and practice, I have been confronted with the dilemma of knowing which wheel of these cultures I should be "practicing," knowing the importance of maintaining the integrity of each one. After years of application of these ancient wheels in my daily practices, one day I found myself naturally with a fourth wheel, given to me by extremely ancient and spiritual guides, a wheel with all the universal elements of the aforementioned wheels into which I had been initiated, a wheel that resolved many of these cultural differences.

The **South** is the Red Lodge (see figure 4, page 155). It is called the Celebration Shield. The South is part of the tonal axis with the North. The sacred deer is the principal animal. It is the place of the heart and sacred blood of Earth, but also of the reflections of our emotional world. South is the place of water and the Moon goddess. South is where life enters this planet. It is, therefore, is the place of children. The landscape is the luscious and magical jungle. It is eternally summer. Trust, regeneration, and vitality are the main powers. It is where the drum for the Earth beats, where the red corn and beans grow to feed the children, and where the moccasins for the dance of life are symbolized. South is a feminine shield and the place of sexuality and procreation. Here are found other animals, such as the macaw, frogs, and beavers.

The wall of past burdens, called the veil of personal concerns, keeps us from being present. In this wall abides all the unresolved resentment, anger, and hate of the Self and other Selves. It is where we must meet our fear of death. Beyond this internal obstacle is impersonal love. What is required to pass through this wall and reach beyond is a firm commitment to ourselves, our spiritual path, and our healing process. Once we have released any residue of the past, we have overcome the fear of self and we are no longer afraid of our heart or of opening to others.

The **West** is the Black Lodge, also called the Dream Shield. This is also a feminine shield, belonging to the nahual axis with the East shield. The thunder beings (or Chacs) are the chief spirit and the power of lightning is the Earthly manifestation of these higher spirits—the lightning that strikes to destroy or to align forever. It is the shield of form and matter, the entrance into the Earth's womb. The landscape is the entrance of a cavern in a desolate desert. It is eternally autumn and adulthood. It holds the powers of introspection, intuition, and humility through which we receive the seed-dream of Mother Earth. It is where we meet our inner dream. It is the cavern of dreams, the first glimpse of the mystery beyond ourselves. We meet our egos in this labyrinth of solitude. Other animals of the West are owls, lizards, and rattlesnakes, as well as the horse and raven. Gourds, squashes, and blue corn are Earth symbols.

The wall of the seven mirrors, also named the wall of illusions, is where we meet with our internal terror, our fear of insanity. Beyond the wall, we find the place of absolute reality. What is required to crawl under this veil is complete nakedness and embracing shame as a true purifier. This is the death passage in the meeting of inner darkness, within the Earth goddess's consciousness.

The **North** is the White Lodge, also called the Purpose Shield, a masculine shield of the tonal axis. The main animal is the white wolf, but crows, elk, and buffalo are also important. The landscape is a sacred mountain covered with snow. It is eternally winter and the place of old age, symbolized as the highest peak. It is where the spiritual warriors hunt in their quest for the powers of strength, knowledge, and wisdom. Once we have found fecundity in the South and let the seed-dream in the West impregnate us, in the North we see the great vision of life. It is also the place of the Star Goddess, the place of mind and thoughts, air and winds. To climb the mountain and to kill the vision is the purpose of the North. It is the sacrifice shield wherein our life does not belong to us anymore. It allows us to accomplish our true work in the world. It is where we learn of strategy, beyond competition and ambition. Here dwell our Council chiefs (spiritual guides) teaching the Council ways of the people. It is a shield of understanding. Here the sacred pipe and tobacco connect us to the upper chiefs and the staff and talking stick call forth inner authority and peace among nations. The white corn also feeds the people.

The wall of limitations, also called the veil of conditionings, resides in the North and represents all the "shoulds" and "should nots" that constantly crowd in our heads. This wall refers to the external authority and power we have given away to other people, primarily to those who taught us. To meet the circle of chiefs who walk within us is to understand our human conditionings and find our inner guidance. Here we meet the fear of the self. What is required to climb over this obstacle is great courage and, so that we may learn beyond the hindrance of our minds, true wisdom.

The **East** is the Yellow Lodge, also named the Spirit Shield. The cardinal animals are the eagle, the hawk, and the vulture, soaring in the springtime of our lives. It is the place of rebirth in spirit in the nahual axis, opposed to the West death passage. The East is the place of the eagle, of seeing, and of the third eye's awakening. Beyond the limitations of the self that we meet in the North, in the East, we merge with spirit. It is called the never-ending shield. This refers to the total expansion met in the East. The landscape is filled with blossoming trees. This is the lodge of the sacred clown, who shows that everything in spirit is reversed and contrary, who prompts us to remove our masks and move beyond personal history and suffering. Here we encounter the light of total transformation, the eternally burning flame of the fire goddess. It is the rainbow shield of artistic inspiration for the Maya, with the hummingbird as its symbol. In the lodge of divine order, we undergo the journey to eternity and infinity, to the place of the great Sun, of total freedom and discernment. Feather fans and bird feathers, the smudging of incense of sage and copal, and the yellow corn to feed our spirit self are all found here.

The wall of religions, or the veil of beliefs, teaches that no philosophical systems and dogmas exist. The passage of this wall opens us as perfect vessels. Beyond falsehood is humor, which resolves all duality and the absurdity of life and death. It is to integrate the truth with two faces, teaching that sadness and joy coexist, that everything is equally important. What is required to fly beyond the veil of falsehood is absolute simplicity. For here we meet the fear of the unknown.

The **Center** is the Green Lodge, also called the Shield of all Perspectives. It is the shaman's zenith. Here the leading animal and landscape is the great Earth Turtle in the middle of a calm ocean, extending to the infinite. The powers found are balance, perseverance, and patience. Also called the ordinary shield, the tonal and nahual axis meet here at the entrance to the thirteen Upper- and nine Underworlds. This is the shield of invulnerability and cosmic guidance. It is the shield of all shadows and all lights, beyond limitations of reincarnations. It is total openness, a shield of great protection. The four directional powers now live within. In the center place, there exist no walls, for all the walls of the four other directions are transmuted here into pure wisdom. Its symbols are the turtle shell, seashell, and the circle of sacred stones.

THE DOORS OF
SOLSTICES AND EQUINOXES

Each time in your life that you move toward the wall of a direction to face it, you will naturally travel through a door that coincides with one of the intermediary directions—the Northeast, Southeast, Southwest, or Northwest. So in order to meet the South, you must journey through the southeast door to meet the South wall, then through the southwest door to meet the west wall, and so forth. Since every human is unique, the path is different for everyone. We are all unique and the way you choose to travel around the wheel of life reflects your inherent distinctiveness. For instance, you may uncover your own trail from the south shield to the north mountain and then, from the West passage to end in the East. This may take a whole lifetime. Your personal path around the wheel will vary according to the traits of your soul essence and that which you are ready to confront.

Passing through a particular door before reaching the corresponding wall illustrates the extreme transitions that many people experience at times in their lives. This is expressed as an uneasy feeling of great shifts and an unstable situation in your life, as if you almost don't know where tomorrow may land you. Generally speaking, the time span essential to pass a door may vary from a few months to a full year, the revolving cycle of the Earth around the Sun. And for slower movers, this may even require a few years. Of course, this depends on your inner ability to withstand such a transitory passage, for some may get lost in the door.

In many ancient wheels, the doors were even more important than the four cardinal directions. It is said that, if a door is not properly taken and traveled through, it is often impossible to conquer the corresponding wall of that direction. Passing a door in the correct way consequently minimizes the inner and outer crisis that proceeding through a wall may engender.

At every gate, a powerful wind of inner change embraces and seizes you, and it is impossible to entirely resist it. Journeying through a door always marks a time of great meaning in your life. When you do so, you enter in the sacred time of a new portal in the great wheel. In these important thresholds, you necessarily meet the sacred guardians, who may let you through so that you may reach the corresponding direction and its wall. Only then can your life settle more easily.

In a larger sense, the gates of the Southeast, Southwest, Northwest, and Northeast in the medicine wheel represent the solstices and equinoxes. Solstices and equinoxes are always points of great change during the year, when there is a special concentration of energy. In ancient times, all the medicine wheels were created according to this knowledge of the Sun's cycle. Solstices and equinoxes have always been meaningful times of the year that remind people to be conscious of economic and social responsibilities connected to planting, harvesting, and food distribution. They are marked by rituals to bring the people together, giving a periodical progression and orderliness to the community, linking it to the cosmic and the Earth forces.

The revolution of the Earth around the Sun creates a phenomenon that looks as though the Sun would be spiraling like a rattlesnake around the Earth in the passage of a year, manifesting the solstices and equinoxes around the globe, and forming a cross at the Northwest, Southeast, Northeast, and Southwest. Equinoxes and solstices express the divine duality of feminine and masculine energies through the Sun's itinerary, forming three major circles spiraling around our planet visible from the northern hemisphere (see figure 5, page 162): one at the northern position (the Summer Solstice of the northern hemisphere), another one at the southern station (the Winter Solstice), and two internal circles in between (the Spring and Autumn Equinoxes).

For the ancient Maya priests observing the night sky, these four major natural markers were announced by the position of the Pleiades, marking the zenith as the center cross of the shaman's place—the exact center within. This is why these four natural portals were associated with cycles of birth, growth, maturity, and rebirth.

The moments of solstice and equinox are of great influence when properly attuned to. If you attune correctly to these natural changes in the course of your life giver, you will receive an increased inflow of vitality and rejuvenation. Traditionally, performing ceremonies of energy renewal such as sweat rituals, prayers, or small spiritual retreats, fosters the release of the negativity of the season we are leaving, preparing for the new one to come. A doorway is a sacred pause when the cosmic energies stand in suspension and in silence. Not harmonizing yourself to these moments, therefore, allows undesired energies

SUMMER SOLSTICE
Northern position of the Sun

SPRING & FALL EQUINOXES
Center position of the Sun

WINTER SOLSTICE
Southern position of the Sun

Figure 5. The Spiraling Serpent of Solstices and Equinoxes.

to enter in the new season that may lurk around and filter through when least expected. If you hurry through your activities for the three-day period of each equinox and solstice, you cannot be sensitive to the cosmic rhythm and you will be off pace, off beat, and unbalanced during the corresponding season. In this state of stress, of course, circumstances cannot fall into place. It is not just a matter of things being unresolved inwardly. There are also troubles created by external influences. When you try to force the natural movement of energy, even if later in the successive season you may try to center and calm down, you will always be slightly off the natural current. So you are opening to negative energies of all sorts—missed situations, wrong movements, and energies, all of which are the natural consequences of not having taken the door properly.

The **Southeast** is the Vernal Solstice, when the Sun is at its northern position in the northern hemisphere. It is the Door of Earth, the gate of profundity, giving entrance into the summer of the South, and the wall of the past and personal concerns. The dwellers of this door are called the guardians of ancestors and ancient memories, teaching you Earth laws. These guardians confront you with a part of your ancient self you have forgotten and abandoned. In this door are also found the sacred midwives, who tutor the birth of your true self.

The **Southwest** is the Fall Equinox, when the Sun is at its central rising position. It is the door of man, or the gate of truth, where the guardians of dreams incite you to follow them to the West and meet the wall of illusions. They force the traveler to examine the vain illusions and the false dreams. They teach us the laws of the circle. We also encounter the dream of the Earth in alignment with our true aspirations. In this door, you find the medicine people and healers, mending your wounded soul.

The **Northwest** is the door of the Winter Solstice, when the Sun is at the southern position, as opposed to the summer solstice of the Southeast. It is the door of sky, gate of intelligence, where the guardians of universal laws teach you from the sky laws before leading you to the sacred mountain of the North. In this door dwell the mourners (as opposed to the midwives), who assist you in the final death of your ego after the west passage.

The **Northeast** is the Spring Equinox, as opposed to the Autumn Equinox of the Southwest. It is the Door of Woman, or the gate of silence, where the guardians of cosmic awareness dwell and force the seekers to examine the lack of mindfulness in their lives before entering the clarity of the East. In this door, we find the priests (and priestesses), guiding us in the path to the veneration of all life as sacred, teaching us the laws of the sacred.

By recognizing each door and by aligning with its specific guardians, you will receive the teachings to prepare you for the corresponding wall, in order that you may overcome it. If, in your natural passage during the year, it is important to attune to the equinoxes and solstices, these same conditions also exist in correctly attuning to the doors at the equinoxes and solstices of your own life. Often, the guardians may even appear as real people, accompanying you for a short while in your life, teaching or guiding you in this transitional phase, then disappearing when they are no longer needed. At other times, the guardians may appear as challenging situations that you have to confront. To pass a door, you are always asked to surrender to the powerful wind, to be the perfect witness, and to follow its motion. These passages are not times of strong, personal realization in any way.

You cannot resist or fight in a door, or you will spin and whirl and may miss the way out, possibly becoming caught there for years. On the contrary, you are required to let go of everything that cannot accompany you in the next phase of your life and surrender to the wind.

RESONATING CRYSTAL WHEELS

You may be asking yourself which wall, door, guardian, or direction you are facing. In order to find the correct path through all of this without becoming confused, I strongly recommend that you build a wheel yourself. A medicine wheel should usually be built on Earth, but you can make one as a home altar as well.

What is most important is that, to create a wheel, you must first dream it. This requires your dedication to it as daily practice. Dreaming your wheel is to allow yourself to be called to it, discovering what kind it will be, where exactly it wants to be, where to find the stones, and what will be its purpose. There is a proper and sacred way to build a wheel. The process of dreaming your wheel can come through actual dreams, through clear signs given by nature, or through a strong intuition to create one. I suggest that you meditate and journey to receive clear answers about all the specifics of these questions. Wheels can be placed in any type of landscape: on mountain peaks, in deserts, in the woods, by the ocean, or on natural vortices. They can even be placed in cities, but the stones should touch the Earth and not a concrete surface.

The building of an actual wheel is quite simple, but it is a sacred process. Once you know where you will place your wheel, you must smudge the spot with smoke to dedicate it. Then, go in search of the stones. It is best to find the stones on the same land where the wheel will be located. The stones should *call* you to them, instead of you seeking the stones. Every stone you come upon should have the qualities of each of the directions. For each stone you take from nature, you must leave an offering of tobacco or cornmeal in thankfulness. Once you have gathered nine large stones, bring them to your spot. Place the center stone, which should be the biggest, first. Then place the stones for the tonal axis, North-South, the nahual axis, West-East, and for the four doors, Southeast, Southwest, Northwest, and Northeast, in a clockwise manner. Afterward, smudge again and pray in the center to call the spirits of each direction to bless and inaugurate it. You can also walk reverently and drum or rattle in a clockwise manner. This wheel will then slowly start its own activation and will be a strong receptacle for your daily meditation or prayers.

Medicine wheels may have various purposes, but independent of its specific aim, each wheel is always a sacred altars and a spiritual temple. For us, it is our church. Among all the aspects to consider in the creation of a wheel, its true purpose is usually the most difficult to determine. Sometimes, it is only after years of working with the wheel that it may be made clear to you. Wheels can be individual, familiar, or collective, each with a distinct purpose. Dreaming wheels enhance dreams, prayer wheels are for individual or planetary prayers, healing wheels can be for yourself or others, teaching wheels help you learn about yourself or teach to a group, dancing wheels, star wheels, oracle wheels, justice wheels, as in a court room, council wheels for a peace meeting among people, journeying wheels to travel the Lower and Upperworlds—these are but a few.

Once your wheel is dedicated to one or several of these purposes, it should be respected, lest energies in the wheel become entangled and what is accomplished in the wheel confused. If you do not know the purpose of your particular wheel to begin with, but feel drawn to create one, you should simply keep the wheel as personal as possible, with a simple and clear direction—for instance, to find your center within and journey to the different walls and doors to receive guidance.

Every wheel represents the eight directions in the outer circle, the center stone represents the zenith of the cosmic tree. Wheels naturally have a female and a male axis. The female Mother axis of the wheel expands outwardly on the horizontal plane, and is a receiving axis. These energies may reach far beyond the circle of stones, even for miles around, especially when there are crystals on the wheel. The male Father axis of the wheel expands on the vertical plane from the center stone, spiraling energies up and down as a transmitting axis. If there is a crystal at the center, energies and prayers can sometimes reach into the cosmos. The vertical Father axis connects to the female Mother axis through the center stone, thus reaching every stone around the wheel.

In the medicine wheel practices, we emphasize the necessity of grounding all prayers and journeys, especially when working with the vertical axis. A well-activated wheel substantially elevates mental awareness, so I cannot emphasize enough the importance of fully grounding yourself in the Earth through prayers, breathing downward, and placing your mind within the Earth. It is extremely important to understand this in your personal work in a wheel, or when working with groups, in order to create the proper channel for all the powerful energies that may be opening to you. To properly align the wheel to its real purpose, all the ceremonies or practices effectuated must be rooted in the Earth Lodge below. Therefore, you need to be extremely conscious of how energies move within the wheel, for a medicine wheel can become much more than a simple circle of stones lying on the ground. It is a powerful circle representing the entire universe and can hold much force.

A medicine wheel must be primarily a way to return to the Earth Lodge. There is a natural pace in the Earth expressed as a heartbeat, a special pulse that humans should hear and adjust to, to be free of stress, disease, and troubles. Medicine wheels, especially ancient wheels, are sacred Earth keepers of this universal heartbeat. Most wheels can also have a connection to a specific star or planet. This is often discovered through the process of dreaming your wheel. This is usually done through journeying, whether individually or collectively, and afterward sharing your findings. Once the star connection is done, prayers can be sent through the vertical axis more easily to reach its intent.

The proper protocol to enter and emerge in a wheel must be simple and must be your own. Smudging each time, for example, is a good preliminary. Among the Mongols, I have found a simple and wonderful practice that serves to signal the entrance into the sacred space and time of the wheel. Strike together four times, two round and smooth stones that fit in the palms of your hands—one for the male, preferably black, and the other for the female, preferably reddish. The purpose of this is to announce to the spirits that you are ready. The entrance to the wheel should always be made from the South, the direction where life's energies penetrate onto this planet. From there, walk around the wheel one to four times before starting any specific activity. Moving counterclockwise around the wheel enables you to ground your negativity into the Earth, especially if you feel distracted that day. Moving clockwise, if your overall stamina is down, will uplift you. Once this is accomplished, you should take a few minutes to sense your wheel. Whenever the wheel is too activated or too strong from previous practices, empty it counterclockwise to prepare and ground the energies for the next activation. If your wheel is not activated enough, move in a clockwise direction to animate its power. Performing a simple salute to the eight directions every day will center you in your inner circle. This allows you to "carry" your wheel with you all day, wherever you go. Many beautiful, simple ceremonies can be performed through medicine wheels—Moon or Sun journeys, morning prayers, dream connections, and calling the spirit animal for personal guidance.

Crystals can easily be placed in your wheel and programmed with any intent or prayer that you may wish, but you must be sure you can handle their frequencies. Crystals are living beings that vibrate extremely fast. These special beings hold great power and can even disappear into other dimensions in front of your eyes. I have experienced this myself. Crystals reflect and amplify any emotions and thoughts more than a hundredfold—even more so when unified within a crystal wheel. Needless to say, you must be careful, especially when you feel emotionally agitated! When crystals are activated too quickly, or with too high a frequency, they may create discordant vibrations instead of pure and natural ones. You may even realize that your neighbors start to look restless!

If you are with others in such wheels, it is important to ensure that everyone involved can handle these energies. People live very unaware. They are not trained or raised to see levels of spirits. Many psychically vulnerable people can suffer severe emotional injury, especially if the wheel holds big crystals, as in the case of collective wheels and big planetary prayer wheels. Unfortunately, I have observed people leaving powerful ceremonies quite sick, because those who led the rites were not aligned and not sufficiently knowledgeable to supervise these energetic movements judiciously for a large group. A wheel that holds much power can create nausea or dizziness. Sometimes, a person will become sick a few days afterward. This is nothing to play with. Someone cannot just improvise as a ceremonial leader. It requires true training and a knowledge of ancient teachings and real traditions.

When all these things are taken in consideration, your medicine wheel can truly become a wondrous and incredible tool to enhance your dream body, ground you, and find your spirit. It may inspire you in the remembrance of the divine plan—why we are here, our true mission as humans. Humanity came here eons ago. We have now forgotten the great conscious plan of the Earth. By bridging time through the various doors and directions, the wheel allows us to re-link to our origins. A wheel, as an Earth keeper, can even hold the noble purpose of renovating the magnetic field of the Earth.

The medicine wheel is the teacher of these ways and much more. It helps us to reach the vision of the *Ongwhe Onwhe*, the true humans. Collectively, wheels share with us one of the most valuable understandings of all—the true meeting of our brothers and sisters in the great hoop of this world. As we all stand around the wheel, we can hear the stories of everyone and enlarge our own perspectives by putting ourselves in other moccasins. This is a very rich lesson for everyone. When we refuse to do this, when we selfishly insist that we, and only we, hold the truth, then conflict starts. This is how nations go to war against each other, by refusing to understand the perspective of people on the other side of the wheel of the world. If all people and nations would live the great wheel, such inflexible insensibility would not be possible, for everyone standing in the circle would force those at war to see their lack of consciousness.

Touching one another on a deeper level is the only way given to us to rediscover the true sense of sisterhood and brotherhood, now lost among so many nations. As given in the prophecies I will share later, these are the times to create numerous wheels and return to the Council ways as our form of community. Medicine wheels, wherever they are, however they are created, will always gather people in unity and community of mind, regardless of their background or religious beliefs. Circles of Earth offer a great way of moving beyond differences, and provide an effective path for truly meeting together at the very heart of the Earth. Only Earth provides the perfect vessel to hold the energies for all humans, because she is our Mother, the source of sustenance for everyone of us here. The wheel is a place to meet and to marry all the disagreements and misunderstandings within the context of the Council wheels.

Since very ancient times, wheels have been used for community healing, and especially for communication between tribes and people. Wheels were the *world wide wheels* (the www) of early times, when there were no other means of communicating at distance. Although I must say, in a more evolved way, that telepathic communication had to be indispensably enhanced in order to really work in its most refined application. Connecting the medicine wheels in this way was a form of long-distance communication between wheels, applied to unite consciousness and transfer messages. The return of this most ancient ritual of connecting wheels has revealed its pressing signs to me through much more than a dream sent by my guides.

Connecting the wheels involves at least two councils or groups, each with their respective wheel. In order to perform this, a definite knowledge of the wheels is an absolute requirement—knowing the star of each wheel, its specific purpose, the surrounding landscape, and so forth. To perform such ceremonies, all the participants should also be well acquainted with working in wheels, as well as have an awareness of the direction they may be facing personally in life. Then a day and a time must be agreed upon between the two groups to perform such a ceremony. Usually equinoxes and solstices are the most favorable times. Some early preparations during the day before the connection itself help adjust the two wheels to the same intonation. Each council must have worked previously with their respective wheel through meditations and journeying. Then at a specific time, the two councils directly connect the two wheels from a distance through a unified drumming, even if they are thousands of miles away. This allows the two wheels to reach the same resonating frequency at their respective center stones. Once the channel or conduit of energy is established, further reciprocal communication can be achieved through subsequent practices.

An expanded version of this ceremony consists of connecting four distant wheels to a fifth, larger one that serves as the central point of convergence for the others. Some preparation is again required to align each wheel to this purpose earlier in the day. At a determined hour, all four council groups, in their respective wheels, journey to the central wheel, each of the four wheels having been previously assigned to a specific cardinal direction in accordance with its inherent qualities. Each of the four wheels links to the stone of their assigned direction at the central wheel—one council in the North, one in the South, one in the East, and one in the West. The central wheel connects the converging energies at its own center stone. The council at the central wheel then journeys to each of its four stones. Thus the five councils are creating a large ring of energy to which all the wheels eventually connect and through which they communicate, through their respective cardinal space, as well as under the Earth. Afterward, all wheels may journey to each other (pray or even dream together), always joined at the central wheel. This practice can also be used to answer many important questions and solve various problems among the councils (see figure 6).

The purpose of this powerful work is to help the expansion and activation of each wheel, in order to create effective bridges and lines of energy of light between the different points around the Earth where these wheels exist.

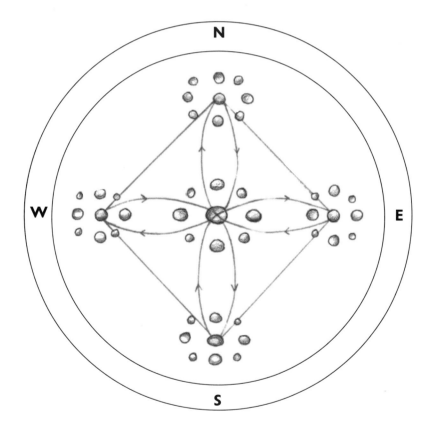

Figure 6. Connection of Five Medicine Wheels.

Over the past few years, with the help of my medicine council in Chiapas, I have been organizing various connections of wheels with several other councils that have formed around these teachings in other parts of Mexico and North America. To reach a sense of connectedness at the same day and time with sometimes up to fifty people, joining our spirits for a whole day, fasting, sweating, and performing the same rituals, even beyond the great distance, is always amazing to me. But the most astounding realization to us all was that, after the connection of wheels, when we e-mailed our "reports" (through the other www!), we all noticed the frequent recurrence of meanings and symbols received in the journeys of each participant, miles apart. This brought the spiritual fulfillment that we were all really connected in bridging wheels through rainbows of energies.

It also became obvious to all of us that medicine wheels actively change the linear mind-set. Therefore, the more people create wheels in a conscious, sacred way, the more energetic openings we create, the more we will help people to liberate their fixed mind structures. This, somehow, contributes to the cleansing of humanity of its internal toxins and impurities, as well as helping to cure the Earth's contamination, in the small way we can. At the very least, this is better than the "I-feel-so-useless" attitude that I often hear from people confronted with the world's problems.

In any of these extremely old practices of a medicine wheel, it is essential to align yourself with true and ancient teachings. Many amateurs, though well-intentioned, lack the understanding and depth of the ancient disciplines based on universal laws. The wise medicine people of primeval times saw and experienced for us all the perils, faithfully improving their ways and their understanding, providing a truly balanced way for the people. Their teachings are certainly not obsolete. In fact, they are slowly emerging again, from the very Earth herself.

The sweet medicine ways are a way of living and we cannot attempt to convert the teachings to fit our modern and busy existence. There is no such thing as the spiritual life separate from personal life that many people strive to create. When people talk, they divide all aspects of their lives, constantly referring to all their fragmented ways: "my personal life," "my social life," "my work life," "my sentimental life," "my sexual life," and then, at last, if I have the time or maybe next year, "my spiritual life." Here and now, all your supposedly separate lives breathe simultaneously, your spirit subsists in your body at every step of your life's exploration. The turtle's back of your true inward center coalesces both with your body and your spirit, keeping you from being dispersed in all directions without roots. Cultivating utmost simplicity is the essential requirement to meet your spirit at the pivot of your being. For this, drastic, yet positive, changes in your way of living may be necessary. This challenge awaits you in your efforts to meet these ancient ways.

What encumbers your spirit is often the sentimental and useless habit of collecting things, grasping events, and purposeless relationships. True humans must let go of these. A great sense of natural order and unity is what the medicine wheel provides for you. To understand, to sense, and to discern energies, your way of living must be lucid, simple, and filled with true humility, entirely unencumbered of artificiality and pretense. Then the great magic of living will reveal itself to you and you will meet the circles of Earth within you.

9

CONSCIOUSNESS

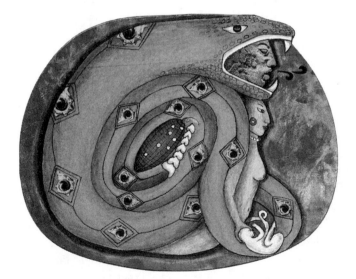

ECHOES OF
THE MAYA COSMOS

Here is the story of the maiden, Ixquic, daughter of a Maya lord, Cuchuma-quic. A strange story came to her ears, told by her father, and she became fascinated by the story of Hun-Hunahpu and the Xibalba Tree. This legend tells about the death of Hun-Hunahpu, great prince of the Maya land, wiseman and seer, musician, great hunter, painter, and sculptor. He and his brother were invited by the lord-guardians of Xibalba to play the ball game in the Underworlds with them. These lords had heard the bouncing of the rubber ball on Earth, making all the Underworlds tremble as in an earthquake, for this rubber ball represented the Sun on Earth. The lords of Xibalba were aggravated, thinking they were not respected and not feared anymore, for they heard humans on Earth were even now fighting above their heads. So the Xibalba guardians wanted to defeat these two princely brothers. All the Underworld lords had dreadful powers. Some required the blood of humans to shed in sacrifice, others caused humans to become swollen in an instant, others painted the faces of people yellow, making them forever lose their flesh, leaving only bones, while others created terrible misfortunes and hardships for humans. In order to challenge the virtuous princes, the lords of Xibalba asked the four owl messengers, *Ikim*, guardians of the four roads leading to the Underworlds, to invite Hun-Hunahpu and his brother into the lower regions. The men accepted the invitation, saying goodbye to their mother, Ixmucane, and left.

They started their descent on the road to Xibalba and then crossed a river of blood, where gourds with sharp spines grew on the banks. They arrived unharmed at the place where the four roads of Xibalba met. One path was red, another yellow, another white, and the last, black. They were quite puzzled about which one to take, for, in reality, only one would lead to the Lower regions. A voice rose from the black path of the West telling them that it was the path to follow. This was their first defeat, for they could not intuit the proper road. The west path lead them to the council lodge of the lords of Xibalba, who were laughing at them. They were conducted into the various Underworlds. In the dark house, they had to keep their cigars lit all night long and yet not let them burn at all. They were taken into the house of ice, where an unbearable frozen wind was blowing, into the house of jaguar, where many hungry tigers were waiting, into the house of bats, filled with their loud screeching and screaming, and into the house of sharp blades, shattering like broken glass. They came back unharmed from all these places of torment in the lower regions. But, in the morning, when the lords asked them to give back their burning cigars intact, they had failed. The tobacco was burned away. This is how the lords of Xibalba defeated and then sacrificed the two brothers. They buried them both, but kept the head of Hun-Hunahpu, which they hung in the branches of a large tree along the black road to Xibalba. As soon as the head was placed on one of the branches, the tree, for the first time ever, became covered with magnificent fruits. These were the first gourds that ever existed and this tree was named the gourd tree. The head of the prince was indistinguishable from the fruit, having itself been transformed into a large round gourd. The nature of this calabash tree was therefore considered magical. Witnessing this marvelous event, the lords of Xibalba ordered that they should never rest under this healing and enchanting tree, for fear of being seduced and defeated by its power of shadows.

However, Ixquic had heard this extraordinary story and become very intrigued by it. She decided to venture on the road that leads to Xibalba and visit the gourd tree. Once she arrived, she wondered what might happen if she were to taste of its fruits. Suddenly, the skull of Hun-Hunahpu spoke from between the branches:

"What do you want, young maiden? You must know that these round fruits are no more than dead skulls. Tell me, do you still hunger for one?"

"Yes" she replied.

"Well then, beautiful one, extend your hand to me."

In this instant, the skull spit his saliva into her hand. Surprised, she looked immediately into her hand, but the saliva was already gone, absorbed by her palm.

"In *my saliva*, I have given you *my lineage*," said the voice in the tree. "Now, my head has nothing else in it. It is no more than a skull of bone. This is how the heads of all the great princes perish, for only the flesh gives them a beautiful appearance. When they die, only bones are left and everyone is scared of them. But you are not. The nature of our lineage is similar to the saliva. The mastery and the word of the great princes when they leave is not lost, but transmitted. The image of the true human does not disappear, but remains in the faces and the words of the daughters and sons they procreate. This is what is in you now. Return to the surface of the Earth that you may not die. Trust my word."

Ixquic returned to her home, knowing now that she was pregnant with twins, knowing that only the word and the truth of noble souls are immortal and that only death itself can conceive the return to eternal life. For indeed, this tree was not one of shadows but a tree of life and of light.

But Cuchumaquic, the father of Ixquic, heard about the secret pregnancy of his daughter. He immediately called a meeting with his counselors.

"My daughter has been dishonored. Who is the father of this child gestating in your womb," he asked Ixquic.

"The truth is that I have not met any man yet, father."

At this reply, the father became so angry that he called the four owl messengers of Xibalba to sacrifice Ixquic, requesting that her heart be brought back to him in a gourd. The four messengers left at once with a large calabash, a sacrificial blade of obsidian, and the young woman. Once they reached Xibalba, Ixquic conversed with the owls:

"It is not right that you should kill me. I am being dishonored. This is an injustice. I went only to admire the dead head of Hun-Hunahpu in the gourd tree "

"What will we bring then in the place of your heart," asked the messengers.

Ixquic answered, "My heart doesn't belong to my father and his lords. Your home should not be here nor in Xibalba, nor should you tolerate that anyone force you to kill humans. Collect the resin of the tree of skulls in place of my heart."

Then a red sap poured out of the magical tree in a luminous red ball, taking the shape of a heart. The sap, resembling blood, coagulated inside the gourd. This is why this mysterious tree was later named the blood tree of Xibalba.

"Now leave the Underworlds, go to the Earth, and there you will be loved," said the young woman to the owls. "I must go my way now."

Not long after, she gave birth to twins, her son, who was named Hunahpu, and her daughter, Ixbalamque. The legends made these twins the famous heroes of the Popol Vuh, where this legend is inspired from this ancient Maya book. The twins were made famous, for they eventually conquered all the lords of Xibalba, defeating death in order to avenge their father, Hun-Hunahpu.

The owls returned with the gourd to the father of Ixquic.

"Is everything concluded," Cuchumaquic asked the four messengers.

"Yes," they replied.

"Well let me see now," said Cuchumaquic, taking the heart of resin from the gourd. The sap-blood began pouring out. "Good. Now arouse the sacred fire, for I will burn the heart of my daughter to purify it forever from this disgrace."

At the moment he threw the heart in the fire, a divine fragrance invaded the whole space with the sweetest smell ever, rising straight up to the heart of the heavens. While the father and his counselors were pondering this, the owls, now unconditional servants of Ixquic, flew up to the heart of the upper realms. This is the story of how the lords of Xibalba were defeated by the young maiden. She fooled them all.

To this day, the Maya people say that, when they burn the copal incense, the divine smoke reaches the heart of the heavens. It is a way to send the prayers of humans to the Upperworlds.

THE HEART
OF THE HEAVENS

The world of the ancient Maya is a world of beauty and divine symbols of sacredness. Their everyday life is unquestionably enriched by the magical associations of their common objects in relation to the greater significance of the creation of the cosmos. For them, what is on Earth is also in the sky. The Maya, by their perception of the universe, inhabit a world where symbols of fertility and of death are woven together in a most subtle manner, complex, yet remarkably simple and pure.

Rain, the sacred water falling from the heart of the sky, is associated with all the natural excretions of the body—tears, blood, sweat, woman's milk from the breasts of the Earth, sperm, urine, and saliva. All these great symbols intertwine magically with the mucus of nature, the morning dew, flower nectar, the sap of the copal tree, the crystalline water of a spring, and melted bee's wax, in one unique and poignant meaning. For them, all these substances are the cosmic sap and contain the very essence of the gods themselves, symbolizing the blessed rain from the heavens. The sustenance for the gods is said to be *Itz*, or the cosmic sap that sustains their essence. Even solidified lava, the slime of the Earth, is venerated on altars dedicated to the great fluid essence of the Earth Goddess.

In a natural mind, one that recognizes the light inherent to all things and beings, the world cannot be one of distinctive objects. It cannot be made just of this and that, as the contemporary mind has been trained to see. For a magical mind, all is interrelated, all is interdependent, from the large comes the small, and vice versa. The near and far are in direct relation to each other, as the visible is a manifestation of the invisible.

In the ancient Maya myths of the origin of the universe, the heart of the heavens was created by three thunderbolts. This also explains why most Maya rituals are based on the Chacs, the rain gods. In order to grasp the importance of rain in their cosmic vision, it is important to understand that the Maya were and are a sedentary people, unlike the northern tribes who were nomads and primarily hunters, although they, too, have been corn growers. The Maya, living on one of the most fertile soils on this planet, are essentially an agricultural people, their subsistence based on growing corn, beans, and squash (the three sacred sisters). This dependence on the cultivation of the corn makes rain vital. The Chacs, therefore, were constantly called upon to assure the vital liquid would be available to the people. In this region of the world, where there is a long dry season after a heavy rainy season, this sacred necessity is even greater.

Even today, May 3rd is celebrated among the Maya as the *Dia de Santa Cruz* (Day of the Holy Cross). This occurs just before the rainy season begins, to ensure abundance. Beautiful ceremonies are performed on this day. Everyone is invited to walk many miles to the natural spring of the community, guided by the holy drummers and flute players. Men and women hike in procession through the mountains, forests, and jungles, carrying tropical fruits and flowers of all sorts to be placed at the three blue-green crosses by the spring, where an altar of candles and incense venerates the spirits of the water. The Santa Cruz is a representation of the ancient cross of fertility, and, as we have previously seen, also symbolizes the four Chacs of the four directions who horizontally sustain the Upperworlds in the form of a cross of the four winds. The frog spirit is the main animal that mediates with the Chacs to call the rain for the next six months. Therefore, all the frog spirits are considered to be the sons of the Chac's wives, and, traditionally, the younger boys of the village embody the frog spirits, croaking and chirping to implore the Chacs during the ceremonies. The Chacs are depicted as pouring water out of their large gourds or calabashes, while riding their roaring horses (clouds) causing the thunder, and blowing the four winds in each direction (the breath of the Chacs). They also hold their *machetes* in one hand, symbolizing the lightning. It is said that, when they urinate, rain falls between their legs.

After the Conquest, when the Maya were forced by the Spaniards to adopt the new Christian religion, the Sun god, *AhKin,* was transposed into the Christ, and *Ixchel,* the Moon goddess, became the Virgin Morena of Guadalupe. The Chacs, in turn, were transmuted into the four horsemen of the Apocalypse. The symbol of the crosses was already existent in pre-Columbian times. These were named the sacred crosses of the jaguar house and first-tree-precious crosses, and represent a cult that talked to spirits, a rite that is still practiced in some regions of the Maya land. The rain tree crosses are associated with water and the primordial cosmic sea raised into the sky. The sky itself is laid onto the Earth in a pure act of love. By virtue of the fact that all women own the waters of the Earth, the rain rituals to the Chacs are feminine in essence, due to their properties of fertility.

For this reason, the Chacs are seen as great nurturers and protectors. They are the bearers of the edge of the world, but they can also act as destroyers, announcing their masculine power through thunder and lightning.

The frog spirits were named smoking frogs, since clouds and smoke are seen as the same. The term "smoking frogs" refers to an extremely ancient practice of burning the *milpas* (corn fields) filled with dry corn stalks just before the rainy season. When people burn their fields, they often shout to the turtle spirit so she will go to a safe place. Burning himself, the Corn God returns as smoke to Hurracan, the heart of the heavens, interceding on behalf of humans to the Chacs themselves to call the rain. Since the four Chacs love to smoke tobacco, this offering of smoke pleases them very much! This is when the rainy season starts.

While the ancient Chacs carried the tobacco on their backs along with their rain gourds, other ancient deities, such as the Corn God and the death lords, were also depicted as smokers. For the Maya people, as for all natives of the three Americas, tobacco is one of the oldest protectors, holding exceptional power. Old Maya natives may tell you that tobacco heals everything, for it is endowed with powerful medicinal virtues. Traditionally, tobacco smoke is used in prayer and blown to the four directions to call the blessing of the rain. This power plant may induce a light trance, helping the spiritual smoker to meet the higher spirit. The tobacco plant is considered a male plant, as opposed to the copal spirit and sage, that are of a more female nature. Tobacco is unquestionably a spirit being that feels, possessing an unfailing and consistent active force. For this reason, it is a strong shield for those who petition directly to this spirit for rain.

The symbolism of the rain gods is without a doubt a rich one among the Maya people. They are the "Chacs, who place the light in the sky," the "Chacs, who sweep the sky." Furthermore, the Maya have names for every type of rain. This makes perfect sense, for I have never seen so many different types of rain as exist in Chiapas—jaguar rain, rabbit rain, the blessing rains of the magical dwarfs, rain that ruins the crops, and so forth.

In addition to the frog, the turtle is also allied with the Chacs. When there is much smoke in the burning fields, her eyes are filled with rain, and it is said that the Chacs are then listening to our prayers. The tears of humans also make her cry during the dry season and this attracts the rain. The turtle is also associated with Earth, for she holds the rain cross on her chest.

She is turtle star, *Ak Ek* or *Turtle Orion*. Orion's belt of three stars, which she holds on her back in the night sky, is also the three stones of the hearth, the center of every Maya home, signifying the three stones of creation and sustenance of the people. The three stones of the hearth form a place where Maya women sit most of the day to prepare the food and the tortillas to feed their people.

Turtle Orion is the turtle of rebirth. Not only does she hold the three blue-water crosses on her chest (as the three stars of Orion), she carries on her shell the maize tree, the first tree precious, along with the thirteen Maya moons for the year's cycle. She is the precious shell first mother, keeper of the white flower souls, *Nichimal Vinik*, the souls of the Maya people. The turtle shell is a symbol at the center of Earth and ocean, directly associated with the smoke shell of the Chacs, their very souls. It is represented as the abalone shell (or the ocean turtle shell) used to burn the copal incense, sent as smoke to the Chacs.

Now that the Chacs have been implored to bring the sacred blessing rain, nature is once more growing, more luscious and exuberant than ever, green as the jade, shimmering like the quetzal feathers and the hummingbird's iridescence. The rattlesnakes rejoice in this rejuvenating bath, iguanas do not seek the shadows anymore. Jade is the skin of the serpents that brings the new jungle rain. The emerald jade is associated with the quetzal, the king bird of the jungle. All the trees now bear exotic fruits of the most divine tastes, such as the red flesh of *mamey* fruits, the sacred *nanchis*, the *zapotes,* the milky *guanabanas.* The delicate flavor of vanilla, the lively taste of cacao, the precious smell of copal can now be offered in acknowledgment to the gods, in a pure act of veneration. In this devouring and prolific nature, where everything that dies is almost immediately brought to life again, the Maya mind can only be permeated with a supernal sense of enchantment.

The world of the ancient Maya has not been lost, contrary to what anthropologists may say. The Mayas today may have abandoned their pyramids and their ancient ceremonial centers, but their world, their way of envisioning the cosmos, is still impregnated with the beauty and magic of these conceptions. When you travel to the Maya land, what you may see of the indigenous world is an impoverished, conquered people striving to survive. But if you scratch a little deeper, you will find treasures of inspiration. I have discovered, through the great knowledge of my Maya *compañero*, Eliberto, that the ancient ones are not gone. They are here, and not only in the ancient sites. Their ancient visions have transpired through millennial forms of rituals and practices. The women's embroidery of their *huipils* still depicts all the ancient fecundity symbols of rain and serpents. Their disguised form of practicing the imposed Christian religion is filled with hundreds of important rituals of ancient times. Furthermore, despite the apparent machismo brought to this land by the Spaniards, people still practice matriarchy in many places in the jungle, as in the times of the ancient civilization. This people has preserved many of their ancient ways. Even forms of traditional trade were practiced not so long ago. My compañero has told me that, when he was a child, his grandmother would send him with a few cacaos to buy sugar cane at the local store. She had some pesos hidden in a clay jar by her bed mat, but throughout his childhood and even up to the late 70s, he only saw her pulling pesos from her jar three times. They always traded for what they needed. These ways have done much to ensure the preservation of the genuine perception of the Maya, even up to the present day.

THE GREAT COSMIC CORD

Many of the ancient legends of creation depict the fight between the upper and Under gods, the eternal combat between light and darkness. The Maya cosmic vision includes the creation of the cosmos and the ordering of the world and humanity, always suggesting the triumph of the forces of life over the forces of death.

As the divine fragrance of the copal incense conveys the prayers to the heart of the heavens, the ancient Maya priests saw that Earth was connected to the heart of the universe by an energetic cord traversing the various layers of the cosmos and connecting humanity to the gods. This life-sustaining cord from the heart of the universe is the very source of existence for all beings on this planet. The celestial umbilical cord is believed to be maintained by the offerings and the prayers of humans, which open the heavenly portal at the core of the Upperworlds. For it is only by unveiling this portal, that we, humanity, will open our third eye and increase our spiritual awareness. This portal separates the human world from the spirit world, often called the glory hole, referring to spiritual enlightenment. This gateway at the heart of the sky is seen as a black void, a star field that is also aligned with the emergence hole of the tree, at the heart of the Earth (of Xibalba).

The divine portal between the Upperworlds and the Underworlds holds thirteen gourds or thirteen suspended clay bowls that represent the thirteen constellations of the Maya cosmos. It is said that only through the galactic cord can we enter the thirteen heavens. We can tap into this cosmic fiber or cord from the various thirteen medicine centers of our bodies (as described below and throughout this book). I have explained earlier that we have a cord attaching our dream body to our physical body (the silver cord). But there is also a cosmic cord attaching, in its turn, our dream body to the cosmic dream body of the universe. It is only through this cord of great extent that we can receive the greater spiritual teachings and find our sacred inner dreams and our true vision as humans.

For each of the thirteen suspended bowls, there is one of thirteen Upperworlds or heavens, representing the thirteen branches of the cosmic tree rising up to the sky. As in the Underworlds, each Upperworld has a corresponding god. Although it is important always to keep the link clear with this cord reaching the higher spheres, it seems that the gods of the Upperworlds are more passive than those of the Underworlds. The Xibalba lords may send us illness and destruction if we are not aligned with our cosmic tree, but they are also far greater protectors of our human nature when implored than the upper gods. The gods of the Underworlds are the ones to whom we must pray directly for all our Earthly matters, for they are bound to humans by blood ties, having a form of organization similar to humans.

The Upperworld gods, however, are not interested in our Earthly affairs and rarely interfere, as they inhabit the higher realms of the sky, but they can become a great source of inspiration and illumination for humans. They can guide us to the higher awareness of our human consciousness.

The Upperworld gods grant their help primarily to shamans, priests, and true warriors in the ascension rites of resurrection after the small death passage of the Underworlds. Because we have manifested our true will to light, we will be granted the assistance of the upper gods. All these gods have died themselves into the lower regions before becoming true masters. For the ancient Maya, the great consciousness of these celestial gods resides in a high frequency that is beyond human language and all petitions of a mundane nature. Usually, these spirit gods emit a certain note or rate of vibration that can be heard by very spiritually developed people. To attune to this tone of primordial music is to become increasingly aware of energy in all its dimensions.

Each time warriors conquer one of the obstacles in the Lower roots, they automatically climb one Upperworld branch, for everything below is reflected in the upper levels. In other words, each time warriors pass a lower level by conquering a major fear through authentic detachment, they can become aware of the frequency of the corresponding upper branch.

All the gods in the upper realms are, without a doubt, the gods of creation of the universe. Thus, we owe them life and veneration. In the Upperworlds, as in the Underworlds, all the gods have their feminine counterpart and reign as partners on their particular frequency. It is also interesting to observe that many of the Underworld gods are represented in the Upperworlds as well. It is important to understand that, for the Mayas, the gods and goddesses of death and of creation are not only spiritual entities, separate from us. They each live within our thirteen inward spiritual centers, also called the thirteen gourds within. These are in direct relation to thirteen constellations in the cosmos.

The owl messengers (sent by Ixquic out of the lower regions) also travel through all levels of awareness, both in Xibalba and in the heavens, carrying messages and knowledge to all the gods and goddesses, linking their consciousness to ours. In the end, for the ancient Mayas, Xibalba and the heavens are not separate or independent realms. Both dwell within the sacred tree inside each one of us—our inner roots as challenges and power, and our branches as accomplishments and realization.

My attempt to briefly describe the thirteen Upperworlds is primarily based on the number attributed to each god, as found in the old codices and glyphs of the ceremonial pyramids. It is important for the reader to understand that many of these ancient teachings have been hidden or lost for eons, but years of recompilation and careful observation of these ancient teachings has provided me with some clarity of this ancient knowledge.

The thirteen regions of the heavens represent thirteen accomplishments or detachments. These accomplishments are powers received after the conquest of the lower obstacles inherent in our human condition. In order for spiritual warriors to conquer an apparently invincible obstacle, they must undergo a deep sacrifice toward true detachment, a letting go, a death toward rebirth. In the Upperworlds, the reward is the power of the soul and the expansion of their essence. The thirteen powers received are connected to the thirteen spiritual centers of the body. Each of these energetic healing centers will then bloom with greater light, conferring on the seeker an expanding consciousness. The attainment of full awareness through the opening of the inner centers is all that the warriors may own, having detached themselves entirely from all other external needs and personal concerns. The thirteen spiritual centers are unity, life, intuition, will, discernment, wisdom, power, silence, imagination, trust, higher consciousness, divine order, and cosmic totality (see figure 7, page 186).

THE FIRST BRANCH: Here, Ixchel, the Moon Goddess, after her death passage in the Lowerworlds during the day, is reborn every evening in the East, entering the Upperworlds. She is associated with the constellation of the Hare (Tzub) and the body center of intuition at the navel where our dream body is attached. This center is activated when we overcome the fear of depths.

THE SECOND BRANCH: Here we find the gods and goddesses of ancestors, holding the tree of humans and lineage. These are the gods invoked in oracle or divination rites. They are associated with the constellation of the Owl (Moan). The body center of life at the first sexual center is reached when the fear of death (and pain) is conquered.

THE THIRD BRANCH: Here we find the old gods of creation (Bacabs) who hold the whole universe at the four corners and are linked with the guardian constellation of the Dog (Pek'). The center of spiritual will located at the kidneys is opposed to willfulness, beyond the fear of being (or body).

THE FOURTH BRANCH: This branch is attributed to the Sun serpent god, named *Ahkin*, during his celestial resurrection into the fourth upper region and Balanke (jaguar, Sun God) in the fourth house of Xibalba. The Sun God is connected to the constellation Kan, the Serpent. This level corresponds to the center of discernment, at the solar plexus, when we are free from the fear of soul.

THE FIFTH BRANCH: Here we encounter the gods of cosmic winds that connect us with the center of spiritual power, the higher intellect center of the throat and the constellation of the Hawk (Coz). Silence as a great center is activated when the fear of truth is overcome.

THE SIXTH BRANCH: Home of the Chacs, the gods of the cardinal directions of this plane, associated with Kutz, the Turkey, constellation for the fertility symbol. Here the inner center of trust (or faith) of the great forces at the pineal gland reaches its full potential beyond the fear of expansion.

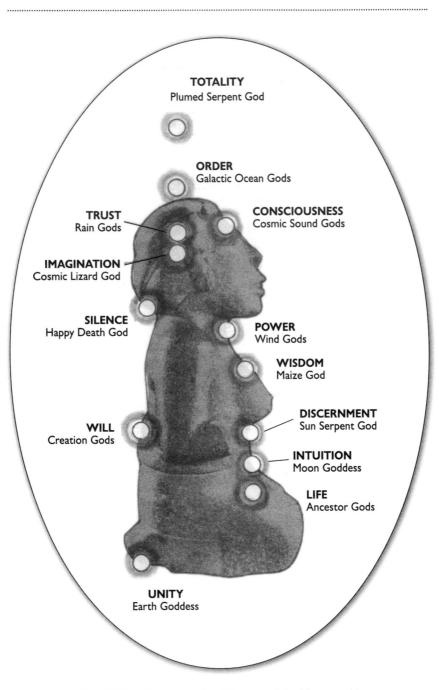

Figure 7. The Thirteen Spiritual Centers of the Upperworlds.

THE SEVENTH BRANCH: Herein dwell Itzamna (cosmic lizard) and his wife, at the constellation of the Scorpion (Dzec), connected to the mind center of imagination, at the pituitary gland. The god of fire, Itzam, the iguana, is one of the most ancient gods, the principal god of creation who sustains the entire world. He was substituted for the god of the Christians after the conquest. The imagination center is strongly energized when the fear of dreaming is overcome.

THE EIGHTH BRANCH: Associated with the Maize God, god of creation, who has given his substance and flesh to create humanity, the souls and the bodies of the Maya, and of all people. This god is related to the constellation of the Mono (Batz Kimil, monkey) and the heart center of wisdom that opens when the fear of love is defeated.

THE NINTH BRANCH: Dedicated to the Snake Earth Goddess, Ix Pic Tzab, by the ancient Maya (Coatlicue, by the Aztecs) associated with the higher spiritual center of unity at the feet, and the Turtle constellation (Aak). The Earth Goddess in Xibalba is close to human prayers and, in the upper realm, is seen as an inaccessible being of divine beauty. She was transposed after the Spanish conquest into the Black Madonna of Guadalape. Wisdom must be conquered beyond the fear of knowing.

THE TENTH BRANCH: The house of the happy God of Death, the ultimate liberation. Here is the celestial seat to which warriors dead in combat, pregnant women, and babies dead in childbirth proceed directly. This heaven is connected to the spiritual center of silence at the medulla, associated with the constellation of the Bat (Tzootz), symbol of death and rebirth. In order to awake this center, we must conquer the fear of void.

THE ELEVENTH BRANCH: The level of the gods and goddesses of cosmic music, associated with the spiritual center consciousness, at the third eye, and the constellation of the Deer (Keh). Divine order in this spiritual center awakes when the fear of light is mastered.

THE TWELFTH BRANCH: Occupied by the gods and goddesses of galactic oceans, the world of pure feelings that emerge from the universe. It is the divine order at the crown center, and is associated with the constellation of the Fish (Xibkay). You can connect to the greater divine order found at this center when the fear of merging is overcome.

THE THIRTEENTH BRANCH: Here we find the highest seat of the upper world, the reign of the god Kukulcan, the divine plumed serpent of the morning star (Venus). He represents the center of higher totality at the star center. This is where the rattlesnake god (Kan) transcends his condition to merge with the king bird of the jungle, the quetzal. From this mating, the plumed serpent can then extend to the highest level of consciousness reachable in the Under- and Upperworlds. In his cycle, the evening star, Venus, undergoes a death passage in Xibalba, to be reborn in the upper spheres as the morning star. It is the greatest symbol of feminine and masculine synergy for the Mayas. This level is associated with the Jaguar constellation (Balam). What prevents this center of cosmic totality from awakening, is the fear of infinity.

For the Mayas, numbers were not just numbers, but pulsating frequencies of awareness. All their gods have numbers attributed to them, and these numbers are directly linked to the myth of origins. For the priests, the number thirteen (Kukulcan) symbolizes the highest manifestation of the thirteen heavens. This number is envisioned as the highest resonance, the one that *sustains* the entire universe. Many of their astronomical cycles end with thirteen, the number of death and rebirth. It is the harmonic number of perfectly pure and all-pervading love, translated as the hope to ascend the superior planes, to attain the place of no doubt in the totality of being. It is also believed to be the energetic number of the speed of light. The number thirteen is the realm of perfect clarity and reason in the endlessly spiraling time and space of the cosmos.

THE VISION RATTLESNAKE

In our further exploration of the Maya cosmos, we cannot omit talking about the Rattlesnake clan, the highest and most recognized cast among the nobles, as opposed to the Jaguar clan of priests representing the night of Xibalba. The clan was named after Chic-Kan, or the Precious Serpent of Jade. Due to the nature of the rattlesnake itself, this clan was a solar cult, as well as an earth and rain cult. Serpent medicine is one of the richest symbols in the Maya world. The Rattlesnake cult is therefore an important totem for artists, a symbol of solar beauty and order of the Upperworlds. In the magical natural land where the Maya lived, the rattlesnake was also seen as the great master of the rain forest, along with Balam, the jaguar. The prevalent rite consisted of the priests shape-shifting into rattlesnakes. The worship of this animal was so strong that the priests carved their teeth to resemble the serpents' and considered naturally crossed eyes, like those of the snake, to be a divine mark of beauty.

The rattlesnake, due to its lack of legs, is the animal who lives and moves closest to the earth. Because of this, its totem was an important teacher of authentic humility, of the imperative requirement for all spiritual leaders to stay close to their people. Thus the rattlesnake totem is a crucial one. Not only does rattlesnake crawl close to the earth, it is also considered a great giver of light because of its inborn connection to the Sun god. It is known that the golden disc is the home of the rattlesnake, the place of its origin. The rattlesnake is believed to be the terrestrial incarnation of the Sun. The Maya Rattlesnake clan initiated its warriors and priests into the Upper realms, as well as meeting death in the Underworlds, for although the Sun is the primary source of life, it can also kill through overexposure. The same is true of the rattlesnake. Its rattles are symbols of new life, but its bite carries a deadly venom.

The rattlesnake is venerated as a powerful totem of rain. When the Chacs are pouring the rains from their calabashes, the serpent bathes and is said to confer the color of its jade skin on the luscious, green foliage of nature. The age of the rattlesnake can be determined by the number of rattles it grows, reaching maturity after seven years. Thus the serpent cult marked the passage of the solar year, and of time in general. Each rattle usually has the shape of a heart and represents the fourth center at the heart level. Another amazing association that the Mayas made was to see the rhombus on the back of the rattlesnake as a representation of the four doors of the medicine wheel. They also observed that, when resting, the body of the rattlesnake forms four loops, marking the four seasons that follow the equinoxes and solstices. Therefore, the rattlesnake was strongly linked with the number four, and constituted an essential symbol of the wheel of solstices and equinoxes. In addition, Venus, as the morning and evening star, is the plumed rattlesnake, depicted as the twin serpents, and marking the solstices and equinoxes that were magically associated with this star's two cycles. The twin aspect of the serpent is also symbolized by the descent of Venus into Xibalba as the evening star and its ascent as the morning star into the upper spheres.

Another interesting correlation with the Sun God, AhKin, was that the rattlesnake often rests in a circular position, like a solar disc. This circle, marking 360 degrees, can also be seen in the yearly cycle of their solar or civil calendar, which consisted of 18 months of 20 days each, equal to 360 days, or kins, plus five unfavorable days (Uyaeb) to complete the year. Moreover, since the serpent coils just as the sun coils around the Earth (forming the solstices and equinoxes), the Chic-Kan clan developed into an astronomical and mathematical clan, observing the progression of Venus, and of the Sun from Earth.

Another interesting observation about the plumed serpent is that rattlesnake babies are born in mid-July, coinciding with the Sun's zenith on the Maya latitudes on July 16. The ancient Maya New Year is July 16, which also coincides with the time that the quetzal birds hatch their eggs. All these transcendental symbols convinced the Mayas that they were sons and daughters of the great celestial rattlesnake. While Itzamna, the great iguana, the principal god of creation, first dreamed the universe, the rattlesnake and the jaguar were the two great animals who helped in this creation, shaping it by their movements as they both fought and played together. The rattlesnake as the day (masculine), and jaguar as the night (feminine) together portrayed a perfectly balanced and magnificent power. In fact, the rattlesnake is the only Earth animal that the jaguar will not dare hunt. Even today, despite the Catholic infiltration of their religion, the Tzotzil-speaking people still chant the Bolon Chon (Balam Kan/jaguar-serpent), an old prayer-song illustrating the creation of the universe by the jaguar and the rattlesnake.

The native people know deeply that their body is made of the flesh of the Maize God, as told by the following ancient myth. The maize tree on the foliated cross is a myth of origin that tells the legend of how humanity was created through the sacrifice and rebirth of the Maize God. Directly associated with the Sun God, the Maize God was said to be the first father, who went into the Underworld where he was killed in Xibalba by the lords of death. The twin sons of Ixquic, Hunahpu and Ixbalamque, went to Xibalba to defeat the lords of death, avenge their father, and bring the Maize God back from death to the Earth. Resurrected from death, and through a pure act of love, the Corn God created us, humanity, from his blood, sperm, and the sacred copal sap. Our human flesh is shaped from the Maize God, who created the receptacle for the flower souls of true humans to be born.

After his descent into Xibalba, the Maize God flew to the Upperworlds. This long journey into the cosmos was made in a canoe, lead by various animals. This travel to the Upperworlds signaled his resurrection from death, when he was brought in his sacred canoe to the source of all creation. The Milky Way is his divine canoe, and those who paddled it were the jaguar, macaw, and monkey. These animals formed some of the constellations in the galactic sky as they pursued their travel. Nevertheless, the celestial canoe, caught in the endless spiral of cosmic eternity, sank, and the Maize God fell and fell into the endless void of the star field. In his descent into the emptiness, the Maize God dropped one of the gourds in which he kept his corn kernels. This is how the seven star-seeds of the Pleiades were created. The seven sister-stars, or *Tzab*, were magically formed by the seven rattles of the cosmic rattlesnake, coiling and spiraling in the universe. The Milky Way depicts the body of the great serpent. In this endless falling, the Maize God eventually emerged from the mouth of the vision rattlesnake, as from a birth canal, in the primordial galactic sea that is the entire cosmos. This is the passage of the resurrection of the god.

The Maize God is attached to the silver-eyed, turquoise-toothed vision serpent, by the snake cord, made of jade. It is said that the cosmic cord emerges into the world from the very navel of the Maize God and that we humans are indivisibly linked to this sacred sidereal cord. The navel of the god, where the cord is attached, is a divine portal leading to time and space of the other worlds. Each time the vision rattlesnake opens its jaw, it conveys gods, ancestors, and humanity into the land of living. This is the ecstatic experience of the cosmic serpent, one of a most transcendental nature. For the ancient Mayas, the word "sacrifice" also means to "open mouth," the mouth and words of truth. In the birthing trance of the serpent, the Maize God is being given birth, as is humanity. And this birthing of truth establishes the road to cosmic communication. This notion of sacrifice as open mouth reminds me of the conception of the twins of Ixquic, the skull head spitting saliva into her hand symbolizing the word of truth and of birth.

This birthing of the gods through pain and suffering is very comparable to a delivering woman. In her journey, she paddles alone in her canoe. She gives her blood, which, in turn, gives new souls. In the Maya understanding, to "sacrifice" also means to "harvest," in relation to the sacrifice of the Corn God, who gave the gift of corn to humans, as in the new harvest of a birthing child. Birth and sacrifice are thus intimately linked. So the sacrifice of blood is the mindful expression of power, equal to the expression of divine energy in the natural world around. It is said that this sacrifice of blood sustains the cycle of all our human souls and the heart of all-pervading love, throughout eternity.

This understanding of the act of love and the necessity for the pure detachment and sacrifice involved in reaching all thirteen levels of consciousness is what the pre-Columbian sacrifices exemplified. In the early times of this great civilization, the sacrifices of blood were not like the massive ones of the decadent times after the Mayas were conquered by the Aztecs, when thousands of virgins were sacrificed in ceremonies to the entire pantheon of gods. What was involved in the earlier times was an equitable offering of the spiritual warriors' own blood to the gods, as a way to demonstrate the deep commitment, demonstrating that they were ready to give all that was needed to earn true knowledge from the depths of their souls. This giving of one's own blood was the willing act of these warriors and warrioresses to the gods. The warrior, with an obsidian blade, would cut certain parts of the body, for instance, the testicles, and the blood was deposited in a white cloth, then burnt in an offering to the gods to ensure the continuity of the race. The obsidian knife symbolized the willingness for the warrior to defeat all the mirrors of shadows.

Since blood is the sole essence that is passed from one generation to another, this symbolic act of sacrifice, of shedding blood, always involves a death and a rebirth. This is essential to the journey of every one of us to be born from the mouth of the great serpent, to be born to our spirit. What is being born in this sacrificial act is our soul, in its whole frequency, beyond the many false ways that the personality-ego has created to impede this emergence into the true Self.

Many people are shy or timid about fully embracing the power of their souls, being bound by what others may say or think of them. This timidity is created by fear, and keeps them from moving to a higher frequency by instilling an apprehension that they may be discriminated against. This is very culture-oriented and is instilled from a very early age in many cultures around the planet. As we reach the end of the millennium, however, and enter a great cycle of spirit, as we will see in the next chapter, it is timely for people to break free of their old conditioned forms of being. In order to liberate ourselves from the chains of our human condition and these impediments that block us from meeting our inherent spirit, this authentic sense of sacrifice must be realized at all levels. Spirit cannot be earned if we have not shed the blood of our spirits. Many may say that enough blood has been shed on the planet and that the simple thought of shedding blood, even symbolically, is odd. I can understand this, but I truly know that, if every human were truly guided through the shedding of the blood of their spirit, there would be no more war and no more shedding of actual human blood, for this act of humility is the real teacher of genuine brotherhood.

This is the true meaning of Indian sacrifice in all the cultures of the Americas, which gives us the power to uncover our sacred vision. It does not reflect the shedding of our own blood, in the literal Christian sense of mortification and patterns of martyrdom that many people usually display even in their simple acts of life. The martyrdom that people "practice" on a daily basis is not true sacrifice, but is largely based on false pity, expectations of others, resignation, deception, and passivity, all reflecting the fear of truly giving away your own Self. On the contrary, the genuine sacrifice of the blood of your spirit imbues you with a tremendous sense of connectedness, higher purpose, and a great inner serenity throughout all the challenges on your path. What I mean here relates to the true sacrifice of the Christ (and many other great spiritual leaders). His crucifixion was an act of pure *spiritual passion*, not of fatality. The Christ of the Bird Tribes, high incarnation of the Sun, the most advanced soul ever incarnated on this planet, chose to teach us through his death, a privilege granted only to great warriors. The Christ's death was the teaching. He chose to give himself completely and fully for all of humanity. In the shedding of his blood, he removed the karmic chains of his humanity and planted the seeds for a major event that could only take place two thousand years after his death. These chains are soon to be removed for us, as we will see in the next chapter.

We are all born in this sacrifice of the gods, of the higher spirits—every one of us. The very thought of this should infuse us with a deep appreciation for life and an undisturbed gratefulness at every instant. This sacrifice is inherent in our human condition. Why is it that, in all the animal kingdom, only human gestation is so long and births are so laborious and painful, both for the mother and for the child? It is because we are given, as humans, a special spirit that we must earn as we are being given life. The Maya people knew this well, for their most ancient birth ritual is one of the most sacred and meaningful.

The umbilical cord of the child represents the rattlesnake cord and is attached from the new soul to the cosmic navel of the Maize God. Soon after birth, the cord is cut with an obsidian blade on a dried corn cob. This symbolic act repeats the birth of the Maize God, being delivered to the cosmos from the mouth of the serpent. In the same way the child is delivered from the vagina of the mother, a symbol of the serpent mouth. The red corn grains, now covered with the blood of the infant, are planted in the soil during the rainy season. This new life and growth is a remembrance of the human's origin, made of the corn flesh of the god. The first one to eat the corn grown from the blooded grains is this child. From birth, one blooded corn grain is also attached to him, so his soul will not be stolen when he is alone. The corn spirit thus guards the child forever, even into adulthood.

The corn harvested and produced from the sacred kernels is then replanted each season, and forever. It is said that this is the same corn, from the same Maize God plant, that was planted to feed his children. And, amazingly, it is upon this same corn, of the lineage of ancestors from remote times, that the cord of this small one is now being severed.

The love for the corn for the Indian has a truly mystical connotation, for the corn spirit is a symbol of fecundity and fertility. The corn spirit and the Indian are both allied, indivisibly linked, through sperm, blood, and the flesh of both, each one needing the other for its respective existence. The Maize God hears and touches the heart of his brothers and sisters by conferring on them sustenance and abundance. The native peasants show their gratitude by planting, giving life, and revering the sacred corn plant. This is the story of the *maiz eterno*, "the eternal maize," and it is a story that has no end.

THE SPIRAL
WHEEL OF TIME

To understand the importance of the Maya wheel of time, we must first understand the perspective that their mind has adopted and the notable place of the zero in their conception of the spiral, in both their cosmic and daily awareness. Everything begins with a movement that is the very nature of the human mind: spiraling. Any attempt to over-rationalize, as in linear thinking, thus keeps us from our true Self. The very essence of our minds is an endless spiral. There is a point of order, however, in that apparently chaotic spiral: the moment that is *now*, here, in the present, in the perfect silence, glimpsing the vast world of immediate knowledge. This is the zero, the center of the wheel. This is the point of true reason within the spiral, encompassing the past and future, and beyond. In the Maya perspective, true reason is far from rationalizing, but is an essential, natural alignment, given from the sidereal cord attaching us to the heavens and rooted into our hearts.

The ancient Maya priests taught humans how to have their heads full of stars and their feet well buried into the red clay of Earth. The true foundation of spiritual reason begins with this understanding. They fathomed that our minds are the cosmic serpent, spiraling in the universe, like the Milky Way. In addition to their incredible astronomical and mathematical minds, they had an accurate magical intelligence. This is what made their world one of the most advanced and complete the Earth has ever seen. They were futurists and visionaries, looking far beyond our present scientific advancements. Their knowledge is so vast and complete, yet so intrinsically connected to the small through its spiritual expression of the universe, that it goes beyond any imaginable attempt to describe it.

The great perfection of their ways of perceiving results from the complexity of their understanding of the great cycles and, at the same time, the simplicity of the basic principles through which they articulated their discovery of the cosmic laws. For example, the numbers of their mathematical system were represented with only three symbols, but they could calculate to the infinite in a most precise way. A seashell represents zero. The seashell is the symbol of the cosmic sea.

A small pebble represented the number 1, the number of unity, and the symbol of the egg of birth. A stick or a branch gave the number 5, symbol where all axes converge with the zenith and the four cardinal directions.

The seashell, as the number zero, is a transcendental symbol that represented far more than the 0 we use. For them, it is the great center of the spiral, where all other numbers are born and where they return. It is a divine frequency, a note expressing the great void, the great orgasm of the cosmic ocean, the beginning and end of all life, death and rebirth. Within the symbol zero is contained the whole universe and the true way of being. The zero shell is the seashell, the turtle shell, the Moon shell, and the womb shell of the universe, symbol of all women, the creators of humanity.

Zero is the mouth of the serpent, giving birth to its vision, our origins, and our sacred vision as well. We, as humans, are attached to the cosmic cord of the zero womb of the universe from which we come. Our souls hold the portal of the thirteen suspended gourds into our thirteen inward centers (chakras).

Zero is named *UH* in ancient Maya. UH is the suspension before breathing, the silence before the creation of life. The suspension before breathing is the moment when the heart almost detains itself, the moment of the exact embrace of love, when infinity is felt. The moment when you feel this is absolutely "breath-taking." The universe was created in that moment of suspension, just before the breath of wind and of movement, for UH is the glorious sigh of the universe . . . *Uhhhh*.

If you observe a seashell, you may see the universe spiraling in its form. If you listen to the seashell, you hear the sea, the UH before the breath. It is no coincidence that the human ear, one of our most delicate organs, is mysteriously shaped like a spiral, like the coiling fetus. Hearing is the last sense to die. For hearing is touching. It is to give ear to the heart of the cosmos and hear the sigh of the universe that is within our breathing, the great healing sound.

UH is the order within the chaos. It is the germ of all that exists within the womb and void. And this is when *hope* is born. UH absorbs all that exists, creating the light within the black hole, the light at the end of the tunnel. The end of the birth canal, where the child emerges into light, symbolizes the creation of the vision serpent. UH is the zero for all the dreams, for all the seeds that become true to the great cosmic vision. For this, the galactic spiral is the foremost and original manifestation of the cosmic dream in which we live.

To understand the Maya mind fully, we must reach the truth they have found and unveil their tremendous knowledge, these incredible gifts they have given humanity. The gifts of their great spiritual awareness are coming back to us. To grasp this significance, we must first understand the simple symbol of the zero, the shell, and the spiral. Their whole world was based on this awareness. By returning to the spiral, we return to the circles of the Self within. For they saw the medicine wheel in the whole cosmos.

To spiral means to go inward and never end, to travel forever to the center, but never entirely reach it. This is how our galaxy evolves, inwardly, reflecting our original nature. As soon as you try to go counter-spiral in your lives, when you try spiraling outward, you lose contact with your center and you lose touch with your inner self. You become superficial, always grasping for something external, more materialistic, and more empty. Many people have experienced this already. When the thunderbirds or the Chacs strike them, they realize they are going outward from their nature. This leads to the death of the spirit. So they change gears in the spiral and start seeking inward for spirit and meaning in their lives. Identification with the material plane is what keeps you from your source. This moment of reverse, of changing direction on the spiral, is the UH, it is the zero time from which the true movement of your life is born. The center of the spiral is the place in the great mystery from which we come. It is also the place to which you must return: *the vanishing void*. The entire universe has evolved this way, and will continue so forever.

For the Mayas, the spiral is the greatest expression of the universe. It is also how time moves and how music meets the macrocosm. UH is the potential of all the sounds, notes and octaves, tones and overtones, that exist in the universe. Our ears can only hear a very diminutive portion of this. The sound of the universe holds the very purpose for which we live as humans, to attune ourselves to hear what we can of the great harmonic composition of the cosmos in our little lives.

The priests used to blow on a large seashell, made into a musical instrument by cutting a small hole in it. It was believed that the sound of the shell was synchronous with the sound of the universe. It was linked to the no-sound of time, the passage of stars, and the manifestation of life toward immortality. Still today, I have seen, in some remote Maya communities, the shell being blown to convoke those natives living far off to the council meeting of that day. I also witnessed this same practice among Mongolian shamans, blowing their seashells in unison before performing oracles and certain ceremonies. When the shell is blown, it is calling out to the sky for the great spirits of these ancient traditions.

Another important aspect of the spiral is that the zero, symbol of the spiral, is also connected to Venus, the morning star, the soul of Kukulcan, the plumed serpent. For the ancients, Mars represented the past, Earth, the present, and Venus, the future, the hope of humans. The plumed serpent coiling in the Milky Way undulates like the waves of the galactic ocean. The Milky Way is thus the road to the zero, a transmutation of the birthing vision. He is the symbol of the serpent, coiling and biting its tail in eternal return, symbol of the transformation of matter into pure light energy. The serpent bites its tail, open mouthed, and gives birth to itself.

The entire galaxy actually revolves around the seven rattles, the Pleiades. The Milky Way is the white road of the flower souls into this plane, the birth canal through which true humans enter this world. Not only does the body of the serpent coil and spiral as the Milky Way, the flight of the quetzal is also associated with the spiraling shell. The Mayas observed that the luscious green quetzal was the only bird that makes its flight in an upward spiral, an expression of the higher spirit. Thus, Kukulcan, the feathered serpent, became one of the most grandiose symbols of this manifestation. Quetzal and the serpent made a sacred pact to merge and the vision serpent transcended into a greater revelation.

In this coalescing emergence, the spiral becomes the gateway to pure innocence. The zero is a powerful teacher, helping us conquer all illusions, to unite all duality and paradoxes. The zero reveals that contradictions exist only in the mind of the ego. In the zero consciousness, there can be only agreement of oppositions in perfect integration. This is the zero wheel of the universe and is very similar in vision to the Chinese Tao. In the center of the spiral, the mind finds freedom and totality in a primordial state of *neutrality.*

The spiraling cycle was fundamental to the Maya worldview. Anything that occurred in the celestial roof had its counterpart in humans, as well as in the environment. This was observed with great care and constancy, in order to determine the relationship between their calendars and the natural cycles. The ancient Maya priests found that there are determinate patterns of time, energy, and space. They could ascertain the precise day in the cycles when some of the cosmic manifestations, over a hundred thousand years, would occur and converge. They saw how all the wheels, as great calendars moved within each other, as toothed wheels. Their tremendous understanding of time rendered their most ancient prophecies true, proving to be most accurate in relation to the greater cycles. To reach this awareness, they studied the great wheel of the cosmos as did no other civilization on Earth.

It is important to see how interconnected all their universal cycles are. The study of their vision of the cycles can only help us to enlarge our spiritual perspective, now conditioned by a linear scientific conception. I do not presume here to explain all the great calendars—a subject far too complex and extensive for the focus of this study. I seek only to demonstrate briefly how all these cycles were connected in a way that made it impossible to examine them entirely separately, as scientists of today often do.

The solar system is not composed of planets, nor of spheres composed of gas, of cosmic "debris," as scientists say. For the Mayas, the planets don't exist. They are contemplated as stars, as our brothers and sisters, as advanced souls who often have incarnated among us, yet as powerful teachers with the greatest consciousness of their celestial bodies. In those times, the Maya third eyes, the energy center of consciousness, were developed to such an exceptional proportion that they could embrace the larger, greater vision of the universe. With the third eye fully opened, this far-reaching consciousness could see beyond time, thereby making astonishing predictions.

In the observation of the cycles, the ancient priests always searched for the exact points of convergence between the cycles of Kukulcan, or Venus, Ixchel, the Moon, Ahkin, the Sun, Jupiter, Mars, and the hawk-star, Mercury, seeing these beings in relation to their history and the destiny of humans. The greater transcendental meaning resides in these points of star convergence when considered as the meeting of the god stars themselves, their crucial council meetings, from which they projected their major teachings to the solar systems, to the Earth, and to us, over the millennium. Because of this colossal understanding, the ancient ones could predict, clairvoyantly, prophecies that relate to our times, from the great distance of antiquity.

10
DISCERNMENT

CONVERGENCE
OF GREAT CYCLES

We are living in incredible times. We find ourselves at what has been announced as the dawn of a new order of ages, a golden era. This "new becoming" consists of a growing awareness of the inherent spirit within each one of us. Nevertheless, it appears to many people that the whole planet resides in a boiling condition, seemingly crumbling under massive problems. It looks as if the planetary situation dwells in a more terrible conjuncture than ever, hardly unfolding naturally and painlessly toward a new dawn. In reality, we now "just" have to make up for an eon of a counter-spinning cycle. Clearly, the task is major. To a certain degree, I would say that we all ought to be quite realistic when witnessing the world's situation, for Earth's balance is so precarious that anyone with a minimum of consciousness can easily discern the problems. Increasing racism and the tyranny of control by many groups and governments is progressively strangling people at all levels. The unleashing on the planet of all the winds from the house of vices and the underworlds makes us question whether humanity, being so permeable, is doomed never to blossom spiritually.

Ancient prophecies affirm, however, that humanity has gone through the worst. There is no doubt of this. The Bird Tribes tell of the terrible clashes of hate that have always existed, everywhere, between the forces of darkness and the forces of love, fomented by greed and ancestral feelings of racial superiority. This is not something new. What is distinct now is that the abuses of the dark forces, some hidden for thousands of years, are being brought to the polished surface of the international mirror for all of us to see, to feel the indignation, to witness thousands of daily violations of humanity made visible to the light of our souls and hopefully to be healed all together.

These events are manifest illusions, reflected in this amplified mirror, nightmarishly distorted, but nevertheless real. The only hint of optimism we can hold, however, is the hope that this might be the maturation of a human disease process. Every good healer can say that, in any healing process, there is a cathartic point at which the disease grows more purulent than ever, when the pain becomes unbearable. This is when the illness begins to leave the body, at last transmuted. Humanity has now reached this point, because a consciousness *beyond* the cultural obscurantism of the last thousand years is now available to anyone who chooses to open to it. This is the good news.

Since the Harmonic Convergence in 1987, the Earth, along with our entire solar system, has begun the ascent into the cosmic tree of life, after its interminable descent into the realms of Xibalba, into the insensibility of our human ignorance. Today, any attempt to make positive change creates a good and direct repercussion on the planet, even on a small scale. While, centuries ago, many good deeds done for the benefit of all races were suppressed by the coercive classes and shut down forever, today, the energies of cause and effect prevail in a most direct cosmic alignment. This new state is given by the shift of eras and the cosmic laws. What took centuries to reap, for good or for evil, is now almost immediate. The dark forces may still try to resist a positive action, but the decisive movement of love is now engaged among humans, and it is only a matter of time before its irreversible effect prevails on a large scale. The obscure powers may continue their old, frightening tactics of repression, but there is today a boomerang counter-effect that turns these acts into clear self-sabotage. In consequence, the dark forces are drowning in their own bath of madness everywhere on the globe. Meanwhile, decent-hearted humans all over understand that, within this apparently disconnected world imposed upon us, we must keep our consciousness intact. Right now, thousands of people from all races and classes dream of a better world, the exact same one of which you dream. This is a reality, not an evasion. In this dream dwells our future, our *morning star*. In a time when the global swelling of the empire of money is at its fragile pinnacle, only faith and conscious action based on a planetary awareness can be the remedy. This is all part of a necessary process through which the organic body of Earth expels any deep and rotten afflictions.

The majority of ancient prophecies around the world speak of the shifting eras at the end of the 20th century. Some present a more apocalyptic picture than others, yet all of them refer to a major transformation we are about to live, if we are not living it already. Some predictions announce that half of the population will perish and Earth will undergo catastrophic alterations. Clearly, Earth is already enduring adverse changes. We can concentrate exclusively on the negative aspects of these prognostications, but the growing and positive awareness of humanity is actually in correspondence with the intensifying forces of love around the planet. When there is an important natural disaster on Earth, the international community mobilizes to bring aid. In some countries, it has been the civilians and the international community that have stopped wars and genocide—for instance, the war declared by the Zapatistas in 1994 against the Mexican Federal Army and government, and the politics of terror exercised against these natives in 1995, 1998, and still today.

In an attempt to acquire a deeper understanding of world events, I have closely explored the ancient prophecies, at first as a form of diversion, almost like reading a horoscope. Later, however, as my own frustration grew at the lack of clarity and hope I found in the world, I began to immerse myself in these prophecies as a way to envision the larger lines and cycles beyond our meager human awareness, seeing them as authentic maps of guidance in the vastness of this postmodern human jungle. What exactly were the ancient shamans and priests seeing of us when they recorded their accurate perceptions, thousands of years ago? In looking at their remarkable foretellings, I realized there were incredible, reappearing correlations between the Maya, Mongolian, and Iroquois prophecies, seers from all three traditions discerning our times for us with their great gifts of divination. They had probably perceived that we would not be endowed with the ability to envision the larger wheels of cycles in our own present season of great shifts, in the midst of the international turmoil through which we are living.

THE FIFTH SUN

The ancient Maya people possessed an enlightened understanding of the universe that they expressed through the creation of their calendars. In their study of the galaxy, they recorded the passage of time in the smaller counts, or minor cycles, as well as in the large counts of the great Baktuns. These major cycles are the progressive wheels of the great eras.

In order to grasp the great Maya prophecies, we must examine the larger *wheel of Baktuns*. Every one of us is connected to the galaxy through the dreaming cord of higher consciousness. Therefore, we can refine our awareness, to the extent of harmonizing all aspects of our life to these cosmic movements. This thread of consciousness is attached to the Earth, the Sun, Venus, and the Pleiades at the very core of the galaxy, and is the passageway for these entities to teach us into our being. We saw how our zenith is determined by the passage of the Pleiades in the sky. This also represents the height of inner consciousness. So the inner centers of the Earth and Sun are aligned with the cosmic zenith (of the Pleiades), just as the shamans are in the Tree of Life teachings. These wheels of star systems exist within much larger wheels and are moving at their own rhythm, at the pace of their own heartbeat, in an eternal circular pulse synchronized with this greater galactic breathing. All the various cosmic wheels cross at different specific points in time where the energies meet, creating a loom of vertical and horizontal threads very similar to the Mongol cosmic vision I will share here. At the crossroads of the threads, where stars meet in the larger loom, the shamans determine the convergence of the cycles and uncover great truth by estimating the movement of eras in the great wheels of time and space.

In the ancient Maya calendar, what is called the large count clearly exposes the vision of the great cycles, as well as the prophecies of this changing era. For them, cycles of time are moving and spiraling in clockwise and counterclockwise motions at the same time, the currents of energy of the tonal and the nahual axes penetrating each other. In their view, the galaxy is an immense being, breathing in us as we breathe, that transcends consciously to a magnitude we cannot even imagine. In their infinite concept of time, time itself cannot be seen as linear, for it is not a single continuum. Time is circular, moving inward and outward at this very moment. In the vast mystery, there is a vast consciousness, an intelligence of the pure divine order in which time is a converging gyroscope, flowing within and without along the serpent cord. The ability to perceive that time revolves clockwise and counterclockwise at the same time confers a wholeness on this discernment. Our current linear perception of time merely conceives of time as a line that goes away, in a progression of moments we are leaving and ones that we are heading toward. This is the countermovement of time. Only shamans are trained to experience the clockwise current of time, the one that comes toward us, the one that holds the past in our future, the future in our past, neutralizing the pure illusions of past and future movements of time. For a shaman, seeds of past and future are in the exact present, in the meeting place of these two opposite movements, in the *now*. What we can understand here is that, although in our perception time may appear to move in a clockwise manner, in fact we are also counter-rotating with this linear concept. If humanity could adopt this new vision of time, clockwise and counterclockwise at the same time, we would have no need of making or holding onto human history. Our societies would be perpetually stable and centered. This is the magical mind that has grounded the most stable tribal and shamanic societies that have ever existed, some of them for many thousands of years.

Among the Maya astronomers, the large count calculates cycles in relation to the great *Baktuns*. The basic unity in all their complex calculations is the Tun of 360 days (or 360 kins). The Maya year is composed of 360 kins, plus a five-day period of bad omens, named the Uyaeb, at the end of the year, for a total of 365 days a year. *Kin* is the Sun and represents the unity of one day, each day being considered as notes or tones that determine its very frequency. One Baktun lasts 400 Tuns (or 394.2 of our solar years). This is then sub-divided into 20 minor cycles. The Mayas determined that a larger cycle ruling our galaxy was composed of thirteen harmonic Baktuns, symbolized as the large tunnel of the vision serpent, its actual body. Thirteen Baktuns last 13 x 400 Tuns, a total of 5,200 Maya years of 360 days (or 5,125 solar years). This means that the vision serpent requires thirteen Baktuns for its digestion process in order to manifest all its incredible visions of the cosmos. Another way of looking at this is to see the main canal of the serpent as having a diameter of 5,200 years, or thirteen Baktuns in time. Each Baktun emits an organic intonation, each represented by one of the under or upper gods. In even a larger view, they observed that there are effectively thirteen great cycles of thirteen Baktuns within this greater cycle, and that the consciousness of thirteen is the frequency that radiates its awareness in all directions at once, permeating the universe with the knowledge of the great galactic serpent.

The thirteen Baktuns in the great wheel of time are called the Ahau Cycle. They last 5,200 Maya years. This cycle repeats itself endlessly and forever, from one to thirteen and then thirteen to one, in a clockwise and counterclockwise count. Every Ahau Cycle of thirteen Baktuns is considered an important wave of teachings for the entire galaxy and, more specifically, for the solar system. With this system, they could calculate all the great eras, far behind and far ahead, throughout billions of years. And these cycles encompass the life of our solar system and the entire galaxy.

The first Baktun of the Ahau Cycle that we are in now started on August 11, 3113 B.C. and ended in approximately 2718 B.C. The last of the thirteen Baktuns, the one we are presently completing, started in 1618 and will end on January 11, 2013. The predictions affirm that these particular Baktuns of our present cycle symbolized the coming of the nine lower lords and the descent into Xibalba, reaching the ninth house of death in this thirteenth and final Baktun. Therefore, the last 5,200 years were ruled by the nine lords of shadows and death. This cycle we are leaving is said to be a counter-gyration to the clockwise revolution of the galaxy.

The Maya prophecy affirms that, at the end of Baktun Thirteen, we will start our ascent to the thirteen upper spheres, when the new cycle begins in 2013. We have only reached the year 2000, the end of a long millennium according to the Gregorian calendar, we have entered the Aquarian age (at the end of the 1950s), and, according to the Mayas, we are also ending this much larger cycle of thirteen Baktuns.

These thirteen Baktuns of 5,200 Maya years (or 5,125 solar years) is the life of one Maya Sun. As we reach the end of this larger cycle, the Maya priests hold the knowledge that we are leaving the fourth Sun and will soon set foot in the fifth Sun. The various eras of the Sun are of great importance. They understood that the Sun exists as our major channel to the knowledge and intelligence transmitted by the galactic navel of the serpent, through other stars. The supersensory information flowing through the great cord of the heart of the universe is transmitted from one galaxy to another, one star system to another, until it reaches our solar system. This form of cosmic communication occurs through the divine intercourse of energies and knowledge that occurs through rays, threads of energy, waves of sound, and filaments of higher forms of light. Once the Sun, as a perfect receptacle, receives the cosmic knowledge, its beacon provides each of its children-planets with a life-path of teachings. To move from the fourth Sun to the fifth therefore implies that our solar system has been permeated by all of the thirteen Baktuns. This change signifies that a new digestive phase of the great rattlesnake is about to begin:

dreaming, envisioning, teaching, and integrating. We have thus apparently entered the dreaming phase, the beginning of this new process. This connection also corresponds, in the human body, to our solar plexus that holds the light of the Sun and is directly connected to it by a thread. This medicine center is named *discernment*, or the power of discrimination, knowing, and natural justice. The solar plexus is also the seat of memory in the body.

So the cosmic serpent is about to give birth to the emerging fifth Sun through its mouth, in the same way it gave birth to the great vision of the Maize God for the survival of humanity. In this dreaming phase of the birthing, the Sun originates emissions of higher teachings and energies that may gradually change the Earth. As we reach this extraordinary transition into the fifth Sun, however, the Earth

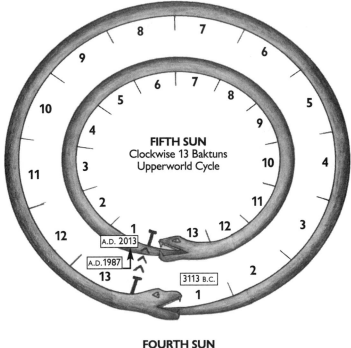

FOURTH SUN
Counterclockwise 13 Baktuns
Lowerworld Cycle

Figure 8. The Maya Ahau Cycles.

definitively suffers a colossal compression of energy in the natural overlapping of the cycles. It is important to understand that cycles do not end on one specific day, but overlap in a transformation period, the one ending being severed counterclockwise and the new one increasing clockwise. This simultaneous occurrence creates a period of solar compression that lasts twenty-five years and began at the Harmonic Convergence on August 16 and 17, 1987 (see figure 8).

Since this date, Earth, due to this enhanced compression, has reached a very high vibratory level of perturbation in her core in trying to adapt to the new changes of the Sun, now showering us with the radiation of a new consciousness from the core of the galaxy. The twenty-five years of overlapping is called the period of purification, being the initiation of this critical burst of energy. For all these reasons, the dawn of the fifth Sun is believed to be of unparalleled magnitude.

The Mayas also prophesied that at the closing of Baktun thirteen (in A.D. 2013), all the degenerated people would perish. The transition into the fifth Sun is symbolized in the ancient predictions as a fight between the arrogant and the humble man, a struggle in which true humility vanquishes arrogance, and survives as the ultimate winner. This heralds the end of pyramidal societies and the establishment of egalitarian societies, a great return to the ancient native Council Ways as the model of life for all the people.

The prophecies emphasize that a period of sixty hours of darkness between the shift of the two suns in A.D. 2013 may fall upon us as the very first sign of the renewal of all people toward the great brotherhoods.

The Christ, being the thirteenth of his twelve disciples, came during Baktun Seven to remove the karmic protection of this planet for the year A.D. 2000, or more precisely, A.D. 2013. Until now, this supposed protection has kept humans from harvesting the consequences of their actions (positive or negative) in the same lifetime. These consequences have been felt through a slow process and over many lives. Now that this protection is removed from humanity, we are all bound to cause and effect in a most direct manner. Sometimes actions and their consequences appear only weeks apart. In other words, we all must purify our past life-actions in this ending cycle, for we are now facing their immediate repercussions in the entrance into the fifth

Sun. This is the speeding up process that has been predicted for thousands of year by seers. The Christ, the Sun God, came to announce that the last judgment will occur 2,000 years after his death, that the degenerated souls who have not chosen light will be forever forbidden entrance into future incarnations on Earth. Without this occurrence, humanity will never be capable of a true purification toward an authentic evolution, being constantly enticed to the lowering of spirit by degraded and corrupt souls. In the terms of a possible *last judgment,* we have to understand this as something different from a castigation process. It is rather a major purification of humanity.

The great density on Earth over the last few thousand years, translated into the materialistic greed from which the Earth has suffered under the reign of the nine lords of the Underworlds, has kept humanity from lifting its awareness to perceive the higher harmony of the universe and achieve lasting brotherhoods. The trial of the last thirteen Baktuns consisted of looking into the shadow mirror and conquering the fears of death in Xibalba. Those souls, especially infants and young souls, who have not conquered their fears of death and shadows in their previous incarnations in this long cycle, must be born now to meet this trial in their own inner Xibalba. Before the critical mass is reached in A.D. 2013, everyone's fears must be mastered, for we cannot enter into the new Sun with the encumbrance of our human density (physical, emotional, or psychic). Since the Harmonic Convergence, the majority of new souls being born to this plane consists mostly of old souls with higher wisdom who will be ready, in A.D. 2013, to take their place in order to establish the peace governments and the true ways of living among the people. Up to now, we have been predominantly ruled by young souls striving to fight for power positions, out of greed and corruption.

But what exactly is the Harmonic Convergence?

The Harmonic Convergence is a most exalted gateway at the end of Baktun Thirteen and the entrance of the new cycle (in 2013), the gateway to a new cycle that will last 67,600 Maya years, or 66,625 of our solar years. In the great perspective that we have seen, the priests witnessed that there is an even larger cycle of thirteen cycles of thirteen Baktuns (13 x 5,200 = 67,600 years) that represents the perfect cosmic evolution, or the movement from light to shadows and shadows to light (1 to 13 and 13 to 1). As we end this tremendous cycle, thirteen cycles of thirteen Baktuns, the Harmonic Convergence launches us to the very point of concentration between each cycle. The doorway was August 16 and 17, 1987. It is said that, in the twenty-five-year period of purification, old fixed and static structures will be challenged by the new intensity of the expanding awareness that we are receiving through an increased flow in the medicine field of the solar system. In the consonant adjustment of Earth with the zenith of our cosmos cord, the Harmonic Convergence announced a drastic reversal in the chaos and discords that the Earth has suffered up to now. This is a tangible alignment toward global harmonization through the cords that link us with the Sun, Venus, and the Pleiades. In shamanic terms, this is a *pure alignment*, an increased awareness of our responsibility to Earth, as her core aligns sensitively and slowly to the cosmic core. The entrance into the Harmonic Convergence, therefore, involves the overcoming of all antagonistic forces when entering this higher frequency. Even if the overthrow of the dark forces called Dark Mentalists is announced cosmically, we, as humans, still have to manifest our will, our positive action, and our alliance to combat these negative forces.

The twenty-five years of purification are irrevocably the end of the counterclockwise wind, or the dissonant wheel. In A.D. 2013, the clockwise movement toward the ascent in our tree will lead us to adjust and disengage from our human history. The clockwise return will allow us to realize how badly we have been counter-spinning and how far we have gone from our original essence. From our egocentric navels, we must now open to the astounding navel of the galaxy and start dreaming this original connection, its existence, substance, and very laws.

In these times, many native prophecies affirm that the thunderbirds may strike massively, or may already be striking. Apparently, all our personal lessons are increasing and this is happening through gentle cosmic compression when seen from a larger perspective. Yet it is surely intense for every one of us on a human level. The necessary personal and world crisis that precedes the true transmutation is of utmost importance. The crisis may be felt at all levels, from spiritual and psychological to technological. Our old Mother Earth is undergoing a major *shamanic rite of passage* for twenty-five years, into the small death passage before the rebirth. For this, the purpose of the Harmonic

Convergence is to convey the new Sun's vision of her birth through the mouth of the cosmic snake. As with every birth, there are waves of painful contractions, times of opening and struggle, the breaking loose from antiquated, inflexible systems, the timeless activation of memories and reminiscences of ancient archetypes, all energies descending from the thirteen heavens and awakening the deepest reservoirs of Earth. This period of energetic condensation leads us irremediably beyond our limited sense of self and into a new way of life, a new order of being. The Harmonic Convergence, as the gateway into the twenty-five years of purification, is the zero point, the entrance into the portal, bringing into the midst of apparent planetary chaos a definite line of order with which we must align. It is the return to the center of the spiral, to our original nature as humans. We are therefore falling into the void of the very zero for twenty-five years and there is nothing we can hang onto, absolutely nothing, until we land on the authentic dreaming of our humanity, of being together, for this next period and Baktun.

The Mayas knew that the return to the clockwise cycle propels us toward the complete transmutation of the dominant male mind that has ruled us for centuries—an old skin about to be shed, the shedding of the decayed skin of the cosmic snake. Based on scientific materialism, the thought that the Earth is dead matter, the notion of the superiority of humankind's mind, must suffer a tremendous and sudden shift. We have seen that in the Medicine Wheel practice, when we move counterclockwise around the wheel, it sends energy into the Earth, releasing inner negativity. On the other hand, the clockwise walk lifts energy from the Earth to the sky. This understanding of the law of gravity versus the law of levity and of light is seen in the Maya great cycles.

The counter-spinning cycle that belonged to the West direction of the cosmic wheel bound us to materialism in the dense law of gravity ruled by the lower lords and the fear of death. We are now being born into the East, seeing, at last, the light at the end of the tunnel. This birth takes twenty-five years. As we emerge from the tunnel, we are merging with the East, ruled by the law of light and levity. The warriors of fear, of greed, and of wars are about to be superseded by the warriors of the East, seeking the new light of truth. We are definitively entering into the reign of the Rainbow Warrior. We must not, however, forget the lesson we have (or have not) learned in the last 5,200 years, because the lessons of shadows are the very roots of the tree for the great Rainbow Warrior. The transformation of the old, the passage from history to post-historic civilization, will not just happen, but will require a *"revolution by and for the Earth."*[1] This is the conscious memory of the warrior. Outside of this, history is useless. In this transformation, levity does not mean being weightless, floating in the ether (or our ozone holes!), but rather the enlarging of our human tree of consciousness. For this, we decisively need strong roots. This is what has been called the Maya Return.

THE RETURN OF KUKULCAN

Oh, Kukulcan, morning star, you are the pure light of our hope, of our consciousness.
Oh, Kukulcan, evening star, you are the most profound reality of our hidden dreams.

These are the times when the return of Kukulcan, the plumed serpent, the feathered jaguar serpent is imminent. The return of the plumed serpent is the entrance into the highest consciousness of the thirteen heavens that is descending upon us into the medicine field of our Sun and our Earth. In the Maya predictions, this return signals the eradication of the Dark Mentalists, or negative forces, from the Earth. According to these predictions, the signs are already here.

Kukulcan is a bearer of light, precursor of our consciousness, the highest symbol of spiritual transformation representing the union of heaven and Earth, of male and female. The Venus consciousness is resurrecting from the Underworlds as the dawn of the morning star, as the cosmic intelligence, the spiral force that rules the movements of all things.

In ancient Maya language, *Kuc* means "wave," *Kukul,* "undulation," and *Kan* "serpent"—the serpent that undulates in waves, or the flying serpent. As we have seen, its symbol is the earthly serpent crawling from the lower regions and climbing the Ceiba tree of life toward the thirteen Upperworlds. This also represents the passage from the last Baktun into this new one. To achieve this, the rattlesnake grew

---

[1] José Argüelles, *The Mayan Factor: Path Beyond Technology* (Santa Fe: Bear & Co., 1987), p. 164.

quetzal feathers and returned to the very source, the great navel of the universal dreaming cord.

Kukulcan is more commonly known as *Quetzacoatl* in Nahuatl, the ancient language of the Aztecs. During the Aztec invasion, before the decline of the Maya civilization, the priests stole many of the Maya oral traditions. Kukulcan, a highly important incarnation of the Bird Tribes, was a prominant priest who probably incarnated among the Maya in A.D. 435, a phase of great harmony and awakening of humanity's third eye. With other extremely knowledgeable priests, he created the basis for one of the most refined cultures, one of the greatest eras of peace and prosperity, the Earth has seen. It was said that he came mysteriously from the eastern sea, his consciousness descending from Venus, the morning star. He was white and bearded, generous and wise. He taught all the universal laws, the mathematical, astronomical and agricultural calendars, as well as the larger counts, the cycles of the Sun, the Moon, Venus, and the Pleiades. He taught the Maya people to record their writings by carving them in stone and shared the teachings of healing stones and much more. Under his reign, everyone reached great spiritual advancement. He forbade the taking of human life and animal sacrifices, then commonly practiced in other nearby cultures. For this, he was respected as the great master of truth.

A priest of the Aztec culture named *Tezcatlipoca*, or Dark Smoking Mirror, challenged this high priest leading him to his defeat. The actual challenge is a little vague, historically, but some legends say that he was invited by the Aztec priests to their region for a great "intercontinental" meeting. The custom in those times was for guests to offer gifts to their hosts. The Aztec priest expected to receive Maya virgins to sacrifice in his honor. Instead, Kukulcan offered only flowers, butterflies, and quetzal feathers. Tezcatlipoca, furious at this, declared war on the Maya priest, out of envy and greed and his desire to obtain this flourishing culture for himself. Another version tells that Tezcatlipoca showed Kukulcan the mirror of illusions. They first made sure the high priest was drunk with *pulque* (maguey alcohol), so he lost himself in the distressing mirror and was irremediably defeated. After this, the Aztecs declared war and invaded the Maya land, bringing a reign of terror and the decadence of human sacrifices to the people. Fear had made its entry into this beautiful culture. Since

Kukulcan held to the principle of nonviolence, he had no alternative other then to abandon his beloved land. This began the decline of the Maya flowering tree. The great priest went to the Caribbean Sea, on the coast of Yucatan, probably at Tulum, and, on the beach, he proclaimed his last predictions: that he would perish in the sea from which he came to Earth but would resurrect from the Underworlds after eight days and return for all to see him as the morning star, the spiritual home of his soul. He departed on the eastern sea in a small boat, wearing his quetzal headdress, holding his turquoise mask, and wrapped in a jaguar skin. He probably died soon after, eight days before Venus returned to its morning position, symbolizing his resurrection. Another version of his death says that he built a big fire by the ocean, jumped into it, and burned himself alive. According to this version, before he resurrected as the morning star, his heart was retrieved from the ashes intact, for he was the master of truth. His consciousness is now the star Venus and the third eye of the serpent, his plumed body coils spiraled into the cosmos as the Milky Way and the rattles of his tail are the seven sister stars of the Pleiades. This is why, for the ancient Mayas, the celebration of the first ray of light at the return of each morning star, once every 584 days, holds great significance. The effect of the first ray is believed to be most prodigious and vital to the health of the human soul.

Kukulcan also prophesied that one day he would come back to reestablish his reign in his beloved land and, once and for all, overcome his terrible enemy, Tezcatlipoca, the dark obsidian mirror. He said that, on the day of his return, his very consciousness, the light of Venus, would be engendered from deep within the Earth, as a serpent rising from the ashes, shaking and shedding the old inflexible paradigms, the human decayed skin, and rising in shining newness in all the regions of the turtle continent of the three Americas, North to South. The plumed-serpent consciousness, emerging from the depths of the Earth, will then live inside each one of us. The date of this numinous return, August 16, 1987, marked the descent of the spiral of the serpent's tail onto the Maya land.

During the Aztec invasions of the Maya regions, the rulers used the legend of Quetzacoatl to control the Maya more easily. The prophecy was taken back from their land to the Aztec world in central Mexico in a form of domination, a false hope engendered in the subjugated people. It is well-known that, when Hernán Cortés arrived on his "high" horse from Spain in the 16th century, in the Empire City of the Great Tenochtitlan (now Mexico City), he was mistakenly confused with Quetzacoatl, for he arrived from the eastern ocean and appeared before them white and bearded. This created a very advantageous situation for the Spaniards, making it relatively easy for them to settle and conquer the entire pre-Columbian world.

The return of the impressive consciousness of the real Kukulcan, by and from the Earth herself, is in complete accordance with the return of the rainbow warrior. Venus inspires the pure wakefulness of love, the male warrior consciousness of love that incarnates the deepest presence of feminine compassion, enduring beyond the fear of death—the love that does not fear dying, but that embraces the shadows to be shed and transmuted. The immensity of this primordial love and feeling from the Earth consciousness will be more easily accessed and deeply understood by the masses in the year 2013 than it is now, for this is when we begin our ascent into the first Upperworld, although countless seeds are already burgeoning within the consciousness of many.

This is the Maya return. The Maya return doesn't imply a romantic view of the restoration of the ancient gods and their knowledge, but rather "a revolution without guns, it is a revolution by and for the Earth."[2] The events of the uprising of Chiapas in January 1994 are not without significance with respect to the prophecies of the Maya return. What is happening on the Maya land today involves a major call to humanity for consciousness. On the surface, the revolution in Chiapas may appear to be a revolution with guns, yet there were thousands of *campesinos* marching, holding their wooden rifles adorned with white flags at the National Democratic Convention in Aguascalientes, Chiapas, in August, 1994. At this gathering, 7000 people from all over the world proved, in a great rainbow bridge, that this was not the case. As sub-commander Marcos said, these peasants, in fact, carried "weapons that only aspired to be useless."[3] This was definitely not a revolution of guns, not the usual war of religious or ethnic conflict. It is not without

---

2 Argüelles, *The Mayan Factor*, p. 164.
3 Marcos, in a speech given at the National Democratic Convention, 1994.

importance that the third eye center of America is at Palenque, Chiapas, the ancient Maya astronomical site where the descent of the serpent-consciousness was predicted to occur. It is also not without significance that the Zapatista revolution of 20,000 Maya in Chiapas was not a revolution for political power, and surely not only for food, but rather a movement toward truth and dignity. Its distinction lies in its being primarily, and above all, *a spiritual revolution*.

The opening of the third eye of the Americas has reached the whole state of Chiapas, and now all of Mexico, increasing after the news of the massacre at Acteal, Chiapas (December, 1997), that so deeply moved the international community. The third eye is now powerfully pulsating to the universe, comparable to a throbbing of light and shadows as a center of consciousness in Central America. It is boiling and vulnerable in all its strata—politically, socially, economically, and spiritually. True transmutation and the shedding of all skins always results in a time of utmost sensibility and pain for the birthing rattlesnake. Conflicts, inflicted at all levels, by the dark smoking mirror in this country and ruling since ancient times, are now ready to be purged, once and for all. This is a revolution in which the Mayas sent their calls to all humans to participate in the overthrowing of the obscure smoking forces, not only in Chiapas, but in the whole world, and in every human heart. Herein lies the uniqueness of this social and spiritual transformation that has been foretold.

THE RESTITUTION OF THE ERA OF WOMAN

The great cycles of the universe were known, not only by the Maya, but by the Mongolian shamans as well. Both possess an incredible understanding of the great cycles that the universe traverses, and share much of the same clarity of vision with reference to the great Baktuns. The Mongolian vision may be not as sophisticated as the Maya in terms of transcendent symbols, but it is, nonetheless, as accurate and, I must say, as powerful.

The Mongolian cycles are peculiar in that they take their source directly from the medicine wheel, bringing a greater understanding that the wheel itself not only opens us to the singularity of our human existence, but also includes the awareness of the vastness of which we are a part.

In the same way, the Mongolian shamans and priests have grasped the great cosmic movements, a knowledge still passed down in a direct line and still very alive today. This wisdom offers a convincing view of our human evolution in an unbroken relation to the medicine wheel. Mongol erudition was prevalent throughout America a long time ago when the sharing of knowledge between Central Asia, Siberia, and North America was widespread. Since the sacred wheel provides a reflection of all that exists in the universe, the Mongolian shamans experienced the great cycles as a daily reality—the wheel adapted to enlarge their vision of the world. It is astounding to see that these transcendant prophecies held a centered and pragmatic reality for these very down-to-earth shamans, who diligently practiced a daily understanding that the microcosm lives within the macrocosm.

Their medicine wheel, like all universal wheels, holds the five major directions (the center being the fifth), as well as the four doors, representing the solstices and equinoxes. Each door of the four major directions represents, for them, a larger era. Each era lasts 5,400 years and is half of a larger cycle of 10,800 years. These cycles, or eras, are respectively named after each door of the wheel. Within their medicine wheel are found the eras of the Southeast, door of Earth (profoundity), the Northwest, Door of Sky (intelligence), the Southwest, Door of Man (truth), and the Northeast, door of Woman (silence).

These four major eras of 5,400 years each total 21,600 years and are called, respectively, the Era of Earth, the Era of Sky, the Era of Man, and the Era of Woman. These eras succeed themselves in the cycle of time in an exact pattern, but in an opposite way around the wheel. Earth opposed to sky, and man opposed to woman, form a cosmic cross on which is found the zenith of the shaman tree. Our planet and our solar system, as a single organic living being, traverses these eras, that repeat themselves endlessly, one after the other, forming a circling spiral of primordial energy.

Each era has its respective gateway. Each gateway to the larger eras of 5,400 years is effectuated through a door-transition of also approximately twenty-five years, leading up to the actual entrance into the era itself. This occurs when the energy overlaps, at the end of the large-cycle era and the beginning of the new one. A cycle of 10,800 years is completed in a horizontal plane when two eras of 5,400 years each have concluded, corresponding to two opposite doors in the medicine wheel—for example, the Era of Earth and the Era of Sky (with their respective gateways). Once this cycle is consummated, we move to the other horizontal cycle, the Era of Man and the Era of Woman, that continues this movement.

According to these prophecies, we are naturally entering into the second half of a 10,800-year cycle, leaving the Era of Man to initiate the Era of Woman. In the Mongolian understanding, the Era of Man refers to a predominance of the cosmic masculine forces within the cycle, and the Era of Woman to a prevalence of the universal feminine forces. The ancient prophecy also tells that before the Era of Man (3415 B.C. until A.D. 1985), humanity was in the Era of Sky (8815 B.C. to 3415 B.C.) and before this, in the Era of Earth (14215 B.C. to 8815 B.C.). This elucidates much about the passage of history in terms of the great human civilizations. In the Era of Man, we have seen the proliferation of patriarchal societies and their dominance in all forms. In the previous Era of Sky, great enlightened and spiritual civilizations flourished, taking their roots in Lemuria and Atlantis, societies known as the Children of Ones. These societies were governed by light-seekers who had great interest in teaching spirituality to the masses, and became the inspiration for other later civilizations, as in China, India, Egypt, and the land of the Maya. Prior to the Era of Sky, the Era of Earth was predominantly led by huge communal and matriarchal societies, inclined to worship a pantheon of fertility goddesses. In this era, Earth was seen as fertile, the womb of Earth was magically associated with the womb of women (see figure 9, page 220).

Even if the great eras are named for the doors in the medicine wheel, they also refer to the powers of each of the four directions. As we have seen with the medicine wheel, the Door of Earth gives entrance into the purifying South, the Door of Man into the dreaming West, the Door of Sky into the wisdom of the North, and the Door of Woman in the Northeast gives passage into the illuminating East.

The major lessons that humanity had to learn in exiting the Era of Man belonged to the West—lessons of humility, introspection, and a veritable sense of earthly power, the West being the Earth-passage into the Lowerworlds. The positive aspect of the Era of Man represents the capacity to unveil truth and the dream of the Earth, qualities

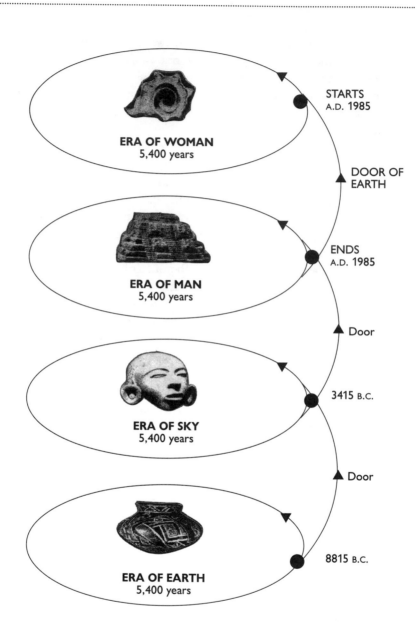

Figure 9. The Mongolian Cycles.

inherent to the Door of Man. The dream of the Earth is also translated into a capacity for inventions and creation of earthly materiality, scientific awareness, and prodigious inspired art in all its forms. This is what has been expressed in the Era of Man, which has given birth to some of the greatest artists, inspired people, and geniuses that humanity has ever seen. Also involved in the universal masculine forces is a great capacity for courage in the meeting of inner shadows.

Whether humanity has completely learned these lessons or not is independent of the passage from one era to the next. But we must now move beyond the Era of Man, in view of this great cosmic and earthly transition. How well we have attuned to the great teachings of a particular era determines the way we will handle the next cycle. The shadow, or negative side, of the West and the Era of Man refers to a lack of humility, to self-importance, an improper notion of power, and the incapacity to full introspection. The good news, however, is that we are now "cosmically" leaving these antiquated patriarchal forms of human behavior and that we are irreversibly inaugurating our voyage into the Era of Woman. Since many of our human assignments were obviously not accomplished in these past 5,400 years of the Era of Man, and since the authentic humility of the West has not been a cultural virtue practiced by the most dominant autocracies, the task here is daunting, to say the least. We have, first, to *unearth* the dream of this planet within all of us, as part of the west passage we are leaving, and then to dispose ourselves to be prepared for our entrance into the luminous East. This is clearly similar to the Maya predictions.

In the Mongol prophecies, the actual middle point between the Era of Man and the forthcoming Era of Woman was the year 1985. The entrance into this new era was announced by the journey into a gateway that began in 1985. In this moment, and for this particular concurrence, we are transiting through the door of Earth for twenty-five years. For the Mongols, the new era has already begun, but it takes the length of the Door of Earth to propel us fully into the Era of Women. And now, a little less than 5,400 years into the Era of Woman, this awaits us.

It is through the Earth door that we will depart from the Era of Man, through the Earth door that we will loom into the Era of Woman. Through this Earth avenue, through the death and rebirth of our renewed spirit, through the under roots, we will reach the upper tree of the Mongol shamans. In the Door of Earth, the shamans affirm that everything is possible—humanity can take the wind of this door in many ways. In this gateway, there are two possible paths: we can deeply receive from the Earth the consciousness and awakening of this new era, if we attune with a pure and simple soul, or, on the other hand, if we miss the point, we can be trapped forever in one of her Underworlds, in spiritual death and madness. For the Mongols, one of the major reasons why humanity is undergoing greater ego impulses, sexual perversions, vices, and material grasping than ever before in human history, is due to our negative consciousness, entailed in the shadow side of the Door of Earth.

The guardians of the ancestors and old memories also dwell in the Door of Earth. Meeting and confronting these guardians becomes our challenge as humans, for as we have seen earlier, we cannot resist the winds of a door. The rendezvous with our ancestors is imminent. We all have to meet the wall of our races, for twenty-five years. As the wind takes us in the ways of this door, ancient memories and hard lessons confront us, lessons we do not want to consider and lessons our own ancestors could not face, though they may have created the chains. On the other hand, ancient archetypes are induced within us, lost and hidden wisdom is recalled and sent to us from the core of the galaxy through the Earth and our dream body. It is through the Earth that we are given back these ancient dreams, just as she is dreaming us.

As we leave the 5,400 years of intensely patriarchal ways of the Era of Man, women will be restored to their original power by the very cosmic movements of the universe, restored to their natural way of being in the entrance into the dawn of this era, not only for women, but for all the cosmic feminine forces that will be restored in the universe and our solar system.

Here we can observe that the relationship between the Maya and the Mongol prophecies, though continents apart, are remarkably similar. The 5,400 years of each era are, without a doubt, very close to the 5,200 years of the thirteen Baktuns. One may say there is a 200-year difference between the cycles of the two traditions that, at the end of four eras, makes a total of 800 years. This is surely a big difference. I cannot speak for these shamans with regard to these specifics, but the fact remains that the two cycles, Maya and Mongol, reach *the same exact point* after many millennia, and this "coincidence" is really astounding. The Harmonic Convergence and the Door of Earth stand only two years apart! Taking into consideration the significance of this similarity and the magnitude of these broad cycles, this difference appears quite insignificant in light of these great messages.

THE MONGOL REVELATION

In February, 1985, the time of the Mongol New Year, I was invited by the Mongol shamans to one of their momentous ceremonies. On that day, the atmosphere was especially "electrified" with a sense of power and greatness, a feeling that something was going to happen or be revealed for the first time ever. None of the fifty guests and apprentices invited knew what the true purpose of this meeting was. In the exquisitely decorated round room, Eastern incense filled the air and, guided by the shamans, we started with what seemed to me an interminable, yet inspiring, medicine wheel meditation. We proceeded with extremely ancient Mongol rituals of breathing and chanting. Then came the teachings. Male and female shamans, clothed in their traditional Mongolian garments, sat in front of us. Behind them hung an immense silk banner, covered with another fine embroidery cloth. They began talking of the major eras according to their oldest calendars. They told us that this very day was the time of physical entrance into the Door of Earth. They shared their knowledge of the gigantic cosmic movements, of the evolution of the female aspect throughout the Earth consciousness, through all the wombs of women and the awakening of the female side within each man. After they drummed for a while, they raised the fine cloth that covered the banner. We could now see their symbol of the "Restitution of Woman."

I was stunned. I had dreamed, a month ago, of this same esoteric symbol which I had never seen before. I had dreamed of my Canadian aunt, who passed away that night, while I was several thousands of miles away. I could not have known of her actual death. I dreamed that she was a floating white light, visiting me. From this, I knew she had passed away. The most interesting part of the dream, however, was that she handed me this same restitution symbol in the form of a clay object. She told me that it had come from her mother, and her mother's mother, and that it had come to the North from the Inuit mothers, far back in our lineage. She also said that I was ready to receive this symbol of the women's restitution. And now, there it was, in the beautiful silken banner behind the shaman women.

For the whole evening afterward, as we feasted, the leading teacher man spoke of the restitution into the Era of Woman. He said, in their own terms, that the cosmic movements of this very important restitution were then to be seen all over the planet, increasing everywhere like a natural *inner consensus*, as something women feel somewhere inside. Women are rising everywhere from the dust, they said, even in countries where male supremacy is still strongly predominant and the claws of patriarchy had yet to loosen up. Women are organizing everywhere, taking steps and awakening from a long, lethargic, oppressive dream, and from a disastrous slumber into passivity that had lasted several thousand years. It was predicted that, in this restitution of the feminine forces within us all, women and men would join in a determined walk to humanity's prosperity.

These two consecutive eras, the one we leave and the one we enter, relate to the nahual axis—West and East. After meeting with the Crazy Woman of the West for 5,400 years, turning us upside down, dealing with our lowest passions, Rainbow Woman of the East now awaits us, the inspiring muse, seeker of peace, order, and new birth. The East tells of awesome visions of new life, of new order, though we must be cautious not to be blinded by this new light, just as we had to be careful not to succumb to our crazy egotism in the West passage. Not to be blinded by the light will become humanity's challenge for the next 5,400 years, just as conquering our fear of death was our challenge for the last 5,400 years. Maintaining reciprocity with the Earth will be the panacea to this exalted blindness, through recalling where we came from and what have we gone through—the very depths of the Underworlds.

Exiting the Era of Man, on the other hand, involves shaking all the male structures of patriarchy everywhere, even in the points of greatest resistance on the planet. According to these shamans, where patriarchy is ready to be peeled off it will undergo a clear metamorphosis into a true democracy in which woman will, at last, embrace the place and responsibility that belongs to her. As we depart from the Era of Man, we will slowly relinquish the appalling spell of materialism that has hypnotized us for so long, and that still does.

"Dominated by a white, male, Neoprotestant priesthood defending its scientific objectivity,"[4] humanity created deadly belief systems to defend its own trap—scientific materialism and its holy objectivity. In the name of this, humanity has made many wars and caused much bloodshed. This reflected our counter-spinning, which has been slowly declining yet is abruptly breaking down, in the same way as a vehicle that must halt in order to take another turn. More than ever, we can thus see all the contradictions inherent to matter reflected in this mirror of changing eras.

For women, this era, our era, implies overcoming 5,400 years of ingrained passivity, suppression, and the inherited illusion of being dependent. For so long, we have restricted ourselves to the rigid role of being mothers. The more dominant the patriarchy, the more we were confined to this exclusive position, through all the last centuries. The gentle restitution of our feminine forces means taking responsibility for the role given us by the cosmic forces, for our true active place among our societies at all levels of life.

The Mongols teach that, in a naturally centered society, the women's clans reside at the center of the circle, and the men's clans at the outward ring, encircling the women. This is a natural law observed by every species. In the universe, the feminine forces are protected by the masculine forces, in the same way that fertilized eggs are protected by the nest, and in the same way that the Earth is surrounded by the sky. "The sole purpose of all about this universe that is masculine is to serve the feminine through the celebration and animation of the beauty that lies in her heart."[5] In this truth is found the female inspiration of the universe, for the reproductive virtues that hold the principle of natural economy. In light of this, the Mongolian shamans said that, in all societies, economy should naturally belong to the women's clans. For everything in the universe is based on this natural economy—except for humans, who, until now, have lived in the Era of Man, in the inverted circles of Western cultures, placing the men's clans at the center of society and isolating the women's, not even truly clans anymore, in the outward ring.

----

4 Argüelles, *The Mayan Factor*.
5 Ken Carey, *Return of the Bird Tribes* (San Francisco: HarperSanFrancisco, 1991), p. 189.

5,400 years of patriarchy have reversed our inherent circles, seriously and dramatically jeopardizing the fragile balance of humanity. The world economy at the center ring is in the hands of many unconscious and unspirited men—your money, ours, the fruits of our own sweat. The capital of the world's people is in the hands of financial powers who control our lives, who decide how we should live and what we should consume, which wars and death will produce economy, which people should be left to die of hunger. This elitist circle of men resides at the very center of society, while the women's lodge is isolated at the external ring.

The Mongol shaman emphasized the urgency that we undo this damaging, inverted wheel. He gave us an illustration—simplistic, but nonetheless quite convincing—that, if all the women were to simultaneously seize in their hands all the money of the planet, at this very moment the world would manifest tremendous and visible enhancement. The majority of women on this planet would never invest in the weapons, implements of wars (even less, Star Wars) that jeopardize the lives of our children, because natural distribution is the feminine principle of economy that every woman owns in her womb. We are the model; we are the natural teachers of the Earth. *Women are the Earth.*

For centuries, many intelligent women of all colors and races who attempted to bring about real change were excluded or burned. The restitution of the Era of Women implicates that, now, we can create and authenticate the seed of changes of which we have dreamed. These can have an unstoppable and lasting effect. Not to fear this natural power is to embrace it as a glorious fetus within our wombs, to feel its power forthcoming from the Earth, and to start walking again. As women, we may slip and make mistakes, and we must be disposed to withstand some blows. We shall, however, rise again with great pride and love.

Now, I can "hear" men reading these words, asking themselves what this restitution may involve for them! For a man, the changing of eras must resonate within his own fears and cast out the shadows of his ego. Men must not be afraid to allow women to induce and provoke the reversal of our circles in the world. To step back from always being the focus of humanity's affairs involves a great deal of abnegation. If he is willing to share equally, however, he may find, at last, great peace and inspiration. In this, he must unburden himself of the heavy responsibility of being the unique provider of humanity. He must unload the backpack of 5,400 years of greed, internecine wars, against humanity and himself. At last, he must surrender, not defeated, nor conqueror, but *just as himself*, as ugly and beautiful as he is, in tears and in laughter standing at the side of women. He must be open to woman teaching him, showing him that he may not always be right. He must allow his soul to rest, at last, from the intense competition he has imposed on himself and his brothers, this useless seeking of false pride. He must give up the need to be always great and in control, for now he must kneel to Earth in true humility. This is his true power from the West. It will give him a great freedom. This is what the restitution means for all of us.

Rejoice now, both men and women, for this Era of Woman symbolizes a celebration of the feminine forces of the universe. We can now start envisioning a true form of global balance between men and women. We can begin dreaming the true models of councils that may one day be seen among all people. Once the visions are sown, once the seeds sprout and take root, they will precipitate our true birth as humanity. But we cannot simply subsist within the present mirage. We do not have 5,400 years ahead of us in which to accomplish this. If we do not make a beginning we may just destroy our Mother Earth long before the coming of the new age.

The task is considerable. We must relinquish our resistance, our conditioned passivity, our spiritual lethargy and find true courage. Why fight against each other? Why fear the search in your womb? Why resist deserting the old structures? All of this simply gives rise to further hardship and makes our birth even more painful.

THE GREAT MEDICINE FIELD OF THE PLEIADES

In light of these great ancient prophecies, it is important to talk of the most recent astronomical findings. Seven years ago, I came across an old book on Egyptian prophecies written by a Mexican, Rudolfo Benavides.[6] Benavides commented concisely on the findings of a German author, Paul Otto Hesse, on a phenomenon called the

---

[6] Rodolfo Benavides, *Dramaticas Profecias de la Gran Piramide* (Mexico City: Editores Mexicanos Unidos, SA, 1987), pp. 200–202.

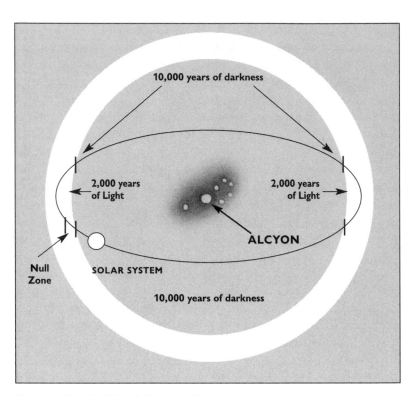

Figure 10. The Medicine Field of the Pleiades.

"Photon Belt." Just by chance a few years ago, I received, through the mail, an article describing this same cosmic phenomenon. I embarked on a number of studies to discover more about this occurrence and its transcendental meaning.

To grasp the meaning and significance of the Photon Belt, a phenomenon I have come to call the medicine field of the Pleiades, we must consider the location of our solar system and its relation to that of the Pleiades. The Mayas certainly perceived the importance of the Pleiades in relation to Earth and our solar system. As we know, the Pleiades are a cluster of seven young stars at the very heart of our galaxy that includes Alcyon, the center star of the galaxy. Six star-satellites rotate around Alcyon, forming the Pleiades. Our Sun is the seventh closest star to Alcyon.

The precession of the equinoxes (so-called by the scientists) reflects the gyroscopic movement of the Earth. It creates the solstices and equinoxes, which also bear a direct relation to the Pleiades. This particular movement of the Earth can be compared to the balancing movement of a twisting top. The polar axis of this spinning top points in different directions, taking 25,827 years to come back to the exact same point. In this process, our planet, as it spins, creates a 72-degree arc around the center of the galaxy, a process that carries the same numerical value as the normal rate of beats per minute of the human heart. By virtue of this phenomenon, we are intimately linked to the Pleiades in a much deeper way than we may think. Our relation to the Pleiades, in fact, attaches us to the dreaming umbilical cord of the universe, a cosmic rhythm parallel to our own vital rhythm.

According to Otto Hesse, our solar system is orbiting around the Pleiades and, more specifically, around Alcyon at the core of the galaxy, in a revolution that takes approximately 24,000 years, a period divided in two cycles of 12,000 years each. Manifested within each of these two cycles is a 2,000-year cycle of light and a 10,000-year cycle of darkness. This passage from dark to light and light to dark is explained by the gigantic ring around Alcyon, similar to Saturn's ring, but one so immense that it reaches an energetic expansion of many years' light. Our Sun takes 2,000 years to cross this radiation field, situated in a plane that runs transverse to its orbit. We are supposed, now, to be ending 10,000 years of obscurity and entering 2,000 years of light (see figure 10).

Since the late 60s, American scientists and astrophysicists, in their increased studies of outer space, have perceived invisible waves of unknown energy reaching our solar system. From what they have observed, this radiation is composed of split electrons, called photons, that had been totally unknown on Earth until now. Some pilots have even reported new forms of lightning that go up instead of down, exploding as fans of colors in the atmosphere, and all sorts of other new manifestations in the Earth's field. Their latest discovery with regard to these photons confirms that, when the solar system and our Earth are penetrated by this radiation field, all molecules become excited and the atoms of all matter and living creatures undergo a transformation of great magnitude.

This radiation appears to be of a form superior to light, unknown until now—*a light without heat and shadow*, a light that reveals itself beyond the physical expression of the light we know, a light that cannot be seen with the naked eye, but that is definitively saturating the solar system and impregnating all particles of matter. Our solar system is thus, right now, being "bombarded" with this unknown appearance of radiation that permeates us at this very moment. The Earth has apparently started to enter again into the field of the Pleiades, after 10,000 years of darkness in outerspace.

The entrance into the 2,000 years of light is manifested by first traversing *a null zone* for a number of decades. This zone can be compared to a veil of fine mist, much like the mist that comes before a rain. Our entrance into the null zone is already occurring. We can easily associate all these discoveries with an entrance into the medicine field of Alcyon, with the closure of Baktun Thirteen, and with the gateway into the Harmonic Convergence, the Door of Earth, and an entrance into the fifth Sun. Having made this correlation, I am positive that the ancient Mayas truly knew about the Photon Belt.

The fact that the solar system takes 24,000 years to revolve around the Pleiades, however, still has to be studied. In the precise Maya astronomical cycles, the Harmonic Convergence surely represents the entrance into the null zone of this 2,000 years of light. As one Ahau cycle of thirteen Baktuns is 5,200 Maya years (5125 of our solar years) long, this phenomenon may well occur every two Baktuns, or every 10,400 Maya years (10,250 solar years). Four cycles of thirteen Baktuns (5,200 each) equals 20,800 Maya years (or 20,500 of our solar years). This may be a truer calculation for our solar revolution around Alcyon than the 24,000 years of Otto Hesse. The same can be said of the Mongolian cycle: two larger cycles of 10,800 years, equaling 21,600 years of orbit around Alcyon may be another possibility to take into consideration in estimating this revolution of the Sun around Alcyon. All of these great cycles, that not even the scientists have yet discovered, surely need to be studied more closely. The amazing fact remains that, according to three of these cosmic perspectives, we are definitively entering an era of light in the same time frame as these great cycles.

The null zone of this gigantic medicine field refers, without a doubt, to the entrance into the zero-womb of twenty-five years of purification already mentioned. It is an astounding comparison. The scientists assert that the null zone contains a region of incredible energy compression, a place where magnetic fields are so tightly strung together that it is impossible for any type of third dimension to pass through it without being altered. In this way, the medicine fields of Earth and Sun may suffer substantial transformation, moving into a new type of "interdimensional magnetism." The scientists affirm that we can expect increased changes in the Earth's electrical, magnetic, and gravitational fields, some of which have already begun. The polar axis has already shifted a number of degrees, and an increasing pressure is felt on the Earth's atmosphere, causing more seismic activities and volcanic eruptions, dramatic changes in our planetary weather patterns, terrible floods, hurricanes and more hurricanes, unexpected droughts, and ozone holes, not to mention alterations in our Sun, such as the dark spots.

As we penetrate further into the null zone of the great cosmic cloud of light of the Pleiades, the Earth has to make serious adjustments to this new and higher frequency. If the Harmonic Convergence of the Maya signaled the entrance into this medicine field, it can also be considered as the date of no return into the zero-womb that is, significantly, the null zone and the great zero within. From a cosmic perspective, the passage of the Earth into the zero-womb of these times is occurring in a very gentle manner, although, from our perspective, it unfortunately affects millions of people through natural disasters. Another interesting theory deriving from this scientific prognostication affirms that 110 hours of darkness may occur at some point in the null zone, much the same as the sixty hours of obscurity announced by the Maya priests. Of course, I am not here trying to predict the future, but simply sharing this information and pointing out some relationships.

Much speculation flows from this enticing panorama of information. All of this coincides with the Aquarian Age, as well as with the Christ prophecies of the uplifting of the protection of human karma. It means we are ready to face ourselves and that the entrance into the 2,000 years of light may bring an era of perpetual internal enlightenment. This enlightenment surely does not refer to blatant illumination, but to knowledge and erudition based on spiritual edification—an acknowledgment that this *light beyond light* will illuminate all things from inside out, that this special radiation may allow all beings to experience a higher degree of spiritual refinement, that this *light beyond light* is casting out all our shadows, to be reflected in the great mirror of our consciousness. In this field of consciousness, there is no place for hidden fears, no more space for the reigns of terror that have governed humanity until now. The dark forces are resisting, as ever, knowing it will not have any entrance into the next cycle. It is still up to us to defeat it, once and for all—a task that could not have been accomplished fully before now.

At this moment, your very cells are showered with this subtle, yet positive, radiation. This gentle pressure permeates everything. This cosmic pull is very strong. The more you resist this new form of light, the more strenuous your individual lives become. You are asked to take position, asked whether you will hide forever in the darkness of your unconscious traumas, or whether you will take responsibility for the bright future that may lie ahead of us. All negativity surfaces in your own disguises. The nature of this higher form of light is penetrating everywhere, in the most clandestine corners of your soul, to show the mirror of truth.

You must cast away your inner dismay, your dormant, passive self. Attune to your creative spirit. Wake up. Take responsibility for originating a world that is in alignment. Cleanse every region of your life. Cleansing means purging, purgation, ablution, catharsis. All that is not aligned can no longer exist. The fever from which the Earth is suffering amplifies our own human dissonance. Since the aggrieved Earth now must adjust, a new diapason must be reached in order to stabilize the human cacophony. The Earth's alignment takes place at the full power of this compression, to awaken your consciousness toward a collective attunement, when you will acknowledge your full responsibility to the Earth. As the patriarchal paradigms are shed, the light of consciousness slowly emerges. This is the planetary menstruation we must go through all together. This is the Earth's baptism. Through this rite of passage, where fear can no longer exist, an awakening from "cultural trance" leads us to "the mobilization of social energy."[7]

And for this you must access your inner, untroubled power and breathe within the integrity of each moment of your existence.

---

[7] Argüelles, *The Mayan Factor*, pp. 173 and 176.

RETURN OF THE IROQUOIS CONFEDERACY

There is an ancient Mohawk prophecy that affirms that, after the dark times, after the termination of Indians, the red tree will grow its root, blossoming again. In those times that hopefully are soon to come, the Iroquois League of Peace will become the perfect model of government for people living in community. The predictions mention that the Iroquois form of councils will reach all Americas, as a perfect inspiration to all the people. This ancient form of native government perfectly affiliates both communal and true democratic tendencies, holding the vote of women in this matriarchal society as sacred and most important. For women are always in the majority, representing the children as well. The League of Peace has survived many wars and more than one conquest. It is the only Indian, matriarchal government that exists entirely intact today, as it did before the conquest, in all the Americas. When the prophecy is fulfilled, this will be the return of the true council ways among all the people.

To a certain degree, this has already been occurring in recent decades. We can observe seeds of discontentment and anger all over. The ruling governments are not aligned with the peoples' inner ideals. Individuals strive harder every day just to survive. It is exhausting to live in Western society, especially for the poor, lower, and middle classes. The systems that rule our lives are constantly competing, outrageously complicating the lives of the common people and suffocating everyone with incomprehensible and arbitrary laws. Actual politics are a dead end. Most governments stand as puppets in the hands of big financial powers, never consulting us for what we, the people, have to say. Our nervous systems try to subsist, constantly under the pressure of all the taxes we have to pay, the world "services" of revenue that are, most often, spying regimes of terror to get the money of the contributors. The insurance companies literally strangle their customers, instead of protecting them, not to mention the constant inflation that plagues many countries, the violence that is everywhere, and weather disasters, to name but a few of humanity's hardships. On top of all this, the exasperating computerized phone "attendants," the bad temper of most people, unkind looks at all times, not to mention the tremendous pressure imposed on us by the end of the Baktun and the photons bombarding us and asking us to grow!! The picture is quite enticing, don't you think?

In view of all this, it is obvious that the shift from the old dissonant frequency into new ways of being, and the imperative to align to the new cosmic harmonics of the Earth, could be much more easily achieved if we could align our ways of living together to these natural forces. With such disconnection between some of the marionettes who "rule" us, those who have the "power," and those who try to simply live a human life, however, the result can only be massive and pathetic depression, expressed in the collective incapacity to breathe freely (and not only because of air pollution!). In the first-world countries, where the majority of people live isolated, with no moral resources other than heading to the psychotherapist, subsisting as individuals and robotized into a constant pushing of external buttons (never the true internal ones), we are made passive by a "what's-the-use" mentality imposed by cultural thinking, ensuring that no one will ever create a real revolution, even in their own lives. In the third world, the extreme misery imposed by the ruling powers, and the moral abandonment, attempts to ensure the same.

In the end, the Earth will have *the last word*, expressed through those who follow her powerful voice. This is when true changes will befall, when the social modification will unify the duality of darkness and light in our daily lives, starting at the trivial levels of our lives. This is the return toward dreaming the ancient forms of councils, councils so well adapted to the true ways of being human among humans, of showing the way to self-government. This is timely. We must create energetic openings to allow these perfect wheels to return as our form of living. This can only result from our internal and irremediable frustrations, because these are the major triggers within us to make the true changes.

The Iroquois prophecy is already being fulfilled. The return of our ancient form of government to all Americas has begun. Twenty thousand Zapatista Indians, living in what they have claimed as their liberated territory of southern Chiapas, have organized themselves, at the end of the 20th century, based on the most ancient democratic and communal form of government. Their communal laws for their autonomous government, their own form of constitution stated in their Five Declarations of the Lacandon Jungle, their women's rights, their own legal army (based on Geneva Treaties), and their war laws to protect the people from the illegal abuses of a dark government and, as said by Marcos, to ensure that their own commanders "command by obeying the people," all proclaim the fulfilling of this Iroquois prophecy.

Why have they organized themselves this way, when these Maya people were not unified in this way a few decades ago? Beecause, as children of the corn, born of the Earth, kept naked on the Earth with absolutely nothing given by the rulers in power, having to strive to barely survive, their sustenance being always and only from the Earth, the Zapatistas have already gone a long way toward leading humanity into the Earth door. They have already met the guardian ancestors of this door in this new coming era, and these brothers and sisters are now remembering the true ways. They have heard the call from the very Earth and they are themselves the living prophecies.

~~~

Without anyone telling him anything, the Indian knows many things. The Indian reads with his piercing, sad eyes what the stars write when fleeing, what is hidden in the woods, what is engraved in the soil. The Indian hears what the wise birds sing when the sun comes down, what the trees whisper in the silence of the night and what the stones may glimpse at dawn.

No one taught him these things, or tutored him in the great mysteries, but he knows. He knows and doesn't say a word. The Indian talks only to shadows when he dreams. And when he awakens, he will know more than before. The Indian walks with his eyes fixed on the flesh of the Earth, and feels the sun on his back. At night, he stares at the stars falling into his eyes and, deep in his chest, becomes filled with light.

If you ever look deep in his eyes, you will see hidden a spark bright as the evening star, constantly burning inside his darkness. This light is his faith, his hope. It shows him the way. Wrapped in his sadness, he walks the land and witnesses. He sees what others do not see, and something more. Do not ask him what, for he will not tell you. The wind of sunset and the breeze of night talk to the heart of the Indian, as echoes of voices that only he understands. When he lays down on the Earth, he hears the sweetest voice, the music of a song of a mother bringing her child to sleep. He knows the sacred land that has heard him cry for so long. He knows how it was before. He remembers.

The love that exists when the Indian embraces the Earth as he sleeps, covered by a blanket of stars, is what he knows. There are so many things—so rich, so immense, and so good—that are only for him, gifts of the universe to him.

And without these, he has nothing.[8]

---

[8] Inspired by Antonio Mediz Bolio, *Tierra del Faisan y del venado* (Merida, Yucatan, Mexico: Produccion Editorial Dante, S. A., 1989), pp. 21-23.

11

TRUST

CELEBRATING MEN'S AND
WOMEN'S TWINNESS

The tree of life holds a very ancient teaching on the foundation circles of men and women. This teaching describes the Moon Lodge as the roots and the Sun Lodge as the flourishing branches of the tree. It provides a model for humanity to live with accordance to the natural cosmic laws. The ancient prophecies state that, in these times, we must return to the true ancient Earth ways of living on this planet. It is, therefore, essential that we understand the reciprocity basic to the hoops of being a man and woman, as well as our respective circles in the society. To understand the principal impediments that have kept humanity from reaching full balance on our Earth walk is, necessarily, to ask questions about the Moon and Sun Lodges.

Women are born in the Moon Lodge, men in the Sun Lodge. These are our first natural and basic hoops as we come into this plane. Because the Earth dreams of the Moon, women are also said to be coming from the Earth, and because the sky dreams of the Sun, men are said to be coming from the sky onto this plane. Women are the Earth-Moon circle, the first hoop of this plane. We must, therefore, hold the center circle in the Council of People, and the men's Sun circle must revolve outside, protecting the universal female forces.

Basic universal laws, throughout the entire galaxy, contain this primordial principle. We can observe how the procreative forces remain the most important and at the same time, the most vulnerable within the inward circle. Yet this vulnerability of the forces of pro-creation holds the greatest power of the universe. Every gestation celebrates an inward process that requires a protective circle that is externally attentive. Pistils, as female forces, are gently protected by the circle of petals, in the same way that male animals often watch over their females during gestation and feeding. That the female forces bear and raise the progeny validates an innate knowledge of natural economy, by providing the species with a connection to its roots within the great law of survival. Every part of nature is imbued with this inner intelligence of natural economy and respect. That is why nature inspires us with such majesty when we blend with her mystery.

THE COSMIC FOUNDATION CIRCLES

The *first principle* in the Council of People reinforces that both men and women must be introduced into the Earth-Moon Lodge, for we are all born of this lodge. To accomplish this, women must embrace the Earth authority in the center of the community and hold with their sisters, the Earth circle, with all the power that this lodge requires. The first precept dictates that all women are, and must be, *the real teachers* of the Earth laws on this plane. Unfortunately, many women, mostly in Western societies, have forgotten and become disconnected from the first hoop, their Moon Lodge, and their roots. They cannot, therefore, be proper teachers, anymore than men can learn the true ways of living on Earth. The result is that men really never enter into the Earth-Moon Lodge during the Era of Man and have rather created a Sky-Sun Lodge on Earth. Needless to say, humanity desperately needs to restore the roots of the Moon Lodge, before our tree of humans dies from lack of sap to feed its roots and being.

It is essential to be clear on what natural authority for a woman may involve in her Earth circle. Power and true influence, for a woman, must abide at the center of her world. By externally seeking authority within the Sun (men's) circle, she may simply emulate the men's lodge, denying her true self. On a long-term basis, this is erroneous and destructive to her, because she will disengage seriously from her true feminine circle and start fighting against her own Moon Lodge, as well as the male Sun Lodge. Natural authority, for a woman, is not outside in the world. It resides at the seat of her womb, in creating her own circle in the center of her being. From there, she must live and create all the movements of her life in pursuing her vision in the world.

Because natural economy belongs to the female principle, the first step to freedom for a woman is through her economic independence. She may have developed moral and spiritual freedom, but, if she still depends on a man for her survival, she will never be a truly free woman. This is the first step toward her natural autonomy. Once a woman has taken her inward authority, she declares her existence as a free and fluid being, not afraid to fight for her truth. She can move mountains, rejecting the limitations of being a female in a male society. Through this, she originates a true inward revolution, helping to shift the wheel of her own circle. Since 5,400 B.C., her wheel has become quite rusty, so the task is not easy. When she does this, she can assert her own feminine difference, not by fighting the male world, by making the changes in the basis of her own life and making the space for her own ways.

Once she reaches her center ring, no longer perceiving herself as an outsider trying to emulate the men's lodge, once she conceives of herself at the center of the creation, she finds herself linked with all the other women of her own circle. She then feels connected with all the women in her womb and is not isolated anymore.

Once a woman lives again in her inner hoop, a powerful metamorphosis occurs in both the male and female circles. The circles find their proper places. In this very principle resides the stability of every society. A woman must be willing to penetrate into the Earth cave of the nine Underworlds, walk with her fears, plunge into the unknown. She must own this immense obligation, for after all, this is our lodge of women. We must not be afraid to get to know our great Mother. If woman fears Earth's secret labyrinths, how can a man ever meet her and learn how to live in balance on Earth. Every woman must show the way into Earth. By emancipating herself from her too-often confining vanity, by overcoming her narcissism and emotional distress, she sees beyond her self-doubts and stops seeing herself reflected in the eyes of all others, especially of men. By liberating herself from the constant search for approval, she opens the eyes of her womb, finding true purpose and direction based on her most intimate knowledge of the Earth, no longer guided by what the society asks her to become, but by what her spirit tells her to be.

Many women still stand empty in their own inner wombs, however. The reflected image of the society represents superficial ways of being a woman. On the day that we cease to observe thousands of man-made, sexual-power advertisements showing half-naked women lying on cars to sell a product (an undeniable offense to a woman's dignity), on that day the lesson will be learned. Hopefully, one day, women will refuse to play this game any longer. Power, for a woman, is expressed from within the Earth (not on cars!). It is not easy to embrace or affirm the Earth within each of us, but, when we do, we receive tremendous courage and great inward balance.

Once a woman reaches the balance of her own inner authority from the Earth, she is no longer a prey. She becomes *a true jaguar huntress*, owning a veritable spiritual purpose. Before this, she has nothing, no true vision. She just wanders in life. Even when she "plays" the game of the society, thinking she is hunting there, she can also be prey to her own emulation. A woman can only be happy when, with a renewed vision from the Moon Lodge, she participates actively in the growth of a society. In the Era of Man, woman, confined to the role of child-rearing, was not really happy, for it was not enough to encourage her self-realization. Conceiving a child cannot be considered a true, personal creation. It is primarily a biological function, for the child is created by universal forces. So a woman must seek to conceive and birth her own vision from within. She will then understand her place in society and how her world fits in it—how, as a true natural educator, she contributes to the balancing of these two natural circles.

In these times, the patriarchal paradigms must be completely overcome, and this begins with an understanding of what they are. In all patriarchies, based fundamentally on possession of private land, the defense of men's estates has become a real issue. All during the Era of Man, men have possessed the land, the soil, the Earth, and, at the same time, woman, who is the very Earth. With the end of most nomadic societies, the sacredness and mystery attributed to fertility no longer had a place. In the Era of Man, men plowed the Earth. Her fruits were seen as his creations. The feminine principle was thus irrevocably displaced outside the inner circle. Women's domain of economy, agriculture, education of the people and children, sacred ceremonies and healing practices, her powers, land, and ascendancy, were all passed under his hegemony. Women were limited only to child rearing and to nursing and curing men from their adventures in their own quest for power. Because men now owned the Earth, they became quite concerned about their own mortality, hence the extreme importance given to sons, the future heirs, and the diminished importance given to the birth of daughters.

During the Era of Man, the positive archetypes in Western societies of how to live in balance within the inherent specifics of that era were not assimilated in most areas of the planet. The positive archetypes would have shown men how to help women fight for higher spiritual ideals alongside them. Instead, women gave away their Earth power to men. As a result, they were no longer free, and men took advantage. Why not? They allowed the institution of marriage to become a suffocating burden, because they needed to ensure the paternity of their children. Abortion became illegal, adultery and divorce severely restricted. If women appeared too smart or too loquacious, they were criticized and burned. At all costs, women must not be allowed to disturb man's "consecrated" plans!

I remember once giving this same speech and being told by a woman, "Ohky, this may still happen in third-world countries, but surely not in our post-modern society, least of all in the United States, where the emancipation of women has been the motto in these last four decades." I simply replied that we all might be quite surprised to see how many unspoken frustrations women still contain within themselves, as the result of not being truly heard by their men at home. Well, of course, this opened the circle to a very long talk that night about the frustrations of the attending women. Women all need to think of this; to observe how men still rule or impose on their world, starting from those in government, right down to our jobs or our households.

In actuality, a common modern, and supposedly emancipated, woman, striving to pursue a career, often carries an exhausting load— much more than what is expected of a man. She always has so much on her hands. She must now work for her living, and also because she wants to. She must fulfill her busy agenda, take care of her children, help them with their homework at night. She must attend school meetings, do all the errands, be sure that the refrigerator is always full, that her husband's shirts are ironed, maintain a nice, well-decorated house. Her own clothes must be presentable for the next day at work and, on top of this, this consumed and worn-out woman, who oversees all this and thinks for everyone in the most diminutive details, must never turn old or wrinkled. She must remain young and attractive to her husband as long as she can to fulfill the image of the perfect *femme fatale*!! Besides this, she often ignores her own genuine sexual, sentimental yearnings, not to mention the small offenses with which she lives every day, often being put down or not fully appreciated. She must never be angry or sad, for, besides the fact that this creates more wrinkles on her face, it may destabilize her marriage or her family. For all these reasons, she also becomes the target of a large consumer market of cosmetics and beauty products, as well as modern appliances that will supposedly ease her domestic burdens and keep her beautiful. Moreover, she must inspire, as a gentle smiling muse (though often a bitter one), speaking only words of understanding, nursing the whole world around her, men and children. More recently, she must pursue demanding educational programs to make sure she still fits in the society somewhere. In brief, what is expected of her is basically inhuman. And this anonymous woman may end her days in a psychiatric ward, hysterical, neurotic, and desperately lost, rejected by the people she thought loved her. For her, this life has no meaning, and rightly so!

After all the consuming palliatives she may try to adopt in an attempt to give meaning to her life, this woman still has no real vision of her own, one that awakens her in the morning with a great feeling of wanting to change the whole world, starting with her own. When she was young, she could handle all of it and stay attractive, but her body, as she turns 40, confirms that Mother Nature may deliberately be the vanquisher. In the end, out of pure exhaustion, if she is not already dead, she simply gives up and renounces this adopted modern and artificial ideal of the perfect woman.

She rests for a while on the Earth, her great Mother, and calls for her help. Reposing, half dead, on her belly and womb, she may then receive a vision, a true one, a glimpse of the powerful warrioress within her, *the vision huntress*. And this time, it is genuine. This is the emergence into her true walking toward her authentic feminine Moon Lodge, one that is entirely adapted to her ways. From now on, she will have the courage to fight for a new world—her own—and to accomplish great revolutions within herself and, then, in the world. She will see herself expanding to the larger horizon, where the Earth merges with the sky, and find true happiness. But this cannot be achieved without great changes in her life.

Once a woman has achieved the restitution of her inner lodge, she is prepared to receive men in her circle. This is *the second principle*, which states that a man must be introduced into the Moon Lodge in the Earth, to birth alongside her, in the sweet ways of living on Earth. The way of true democracy in the Medicine Wheel ways teaches that men must be humble enough to reach the Earth-Woman Lodge, to learn primarily from women, with respect and consciousness. From the sky, they come onto the Earth plane. It is here that women can educate them about the skill of true organization, Earth timing, ways of respect of all natural things on this planet, Earth economy, ecology, veneration of the sacred and feminine laws of this plane. Many times, however, women go in his lodge first. This creates an imbalance, for it is men who must come into our lodge first.

What does it mean for a man to enter with his feminine self into the Earth realm? When does this occur? Usually, in a traditional and balanced matriarchal society, the mother teaches a young boy about the respect and veneration for the woman's lodge. Then, when, as a man, the warrior is disposed to fulfill his vision in the world, he must always return to the Moon Lodge, the feminine lodge living within and without him. For him, entering the Earth Lodge with humbleness also signifies his integrity as a man, as a warrior, and his willingness to comprehend his feminine side and to put himself in a woman's moccasins. This task is quite difficult for most men.

In exchange, women must honor the reflection of their warrior within. They must respect his coming into their lodge and stop resenting and fighting him. Women must be open to men with all their love. Many women hold much anger toward men. They must understand, however, that, within all men, there is a reflection of their own warrioress, in this instance, themselves. Women must not think of themselves as being separate from men. And men cannot think of themselves as separate from women. The internal reflection of *being twins* is given by the universal archetype of creation. Men and women both belong to the same reflection in the waters of the Moon and the fire of the Sun. Both live within all men and women. Deep within a woman's *inner voice of truth*, she will find a warrior. Deep within a man's *inner vision of beauty*, he will find a warrioress. Both are linked in our dream bodies, in the great dream of the cosmic serpent.

The entrance into the Era of Woman does not entail a reversal of the patriarchal ways, or establishing a simplistic view of matriarchy that will restrict men in the same way women were denied their ways. It doesn't consist of taking revenge by striving to repress men and inflict our own fate upon them. Both men and women have something to teach each other in order to reach true partnership. I have observed that, in many ancient and actual matriarchies, men are well respected in their freedom and their voice, holding influential positions within the society. The major difference dwells in the fact that the domain of women is also well founded, their voices being considered sacred. In this way, matriarchy allows both circles to live freely and equally in their differences. More important, matriarchy ensures that womens' voices will never be silenced, as has so often been the case.

Many intelligent and concerned men have often asked me, "What becomes of my role as provider if the economy must be in womens' hands and women no longer need us anymore as providers? How can I live with a strong and powerful woman, taking her power from the Earth? How can I resolve my own anger about my relationship to a dominant repressive mother, and, now, a fierce independent wife? How can I reconcile with the female principle within me?"

Of course, my answer to all these important questions is that these can only be reflected and answered in the woman's Earth lodge. When a man realizes that he will not give up any more than his own enchaining confirmation of a false sense of "power," and that, at the worst, he must abandon his false pride, bound to an often restricting machismo, he may encounter himself naked. That is the worst that can happen to him. Naked, he must realize that he will be infinitely more connected to his spirit than he has ever been until now. Free, he will then thirst for his true spirit warrior. Beyond desperately needing to constantly show that he is male, he will simply find the true inspiration to merge with the Earth, to make love to her, to the sacred Mother, in purity and beauty. He will discover the forgotten ancestral dream of her essence. Nakedness, however, is primordial. It is imperative for him not to be afraid of his vulnerability.

Once a man has learned from the Earth-Moon hoop and lives a true balance on this plane, a woman may fulfill, along with him, *the third foundation principle* —the responsibility for a woman to meet man in his Sun-Man Lodge and learn the sky laws. With her warrioress, she must learn about his ways of hunting. This he can easily teach her. She must be willing, in turn, to integrate the male principle and to learn the mental laws of the cosmos. It is in the sky law that she will find her true vision, based on the seed of her Moon within.

Many women already live in the Sun Lodge, but they have severely disconnected from their Moon roots. They have forgotten their inner Earth laws. Their visions are not real, but rather vain illusions. Many women, although trapped in the man's lodge, fear it. The reason for this is simple. They have not taken root in their own circle first. They must go beyond this and assume the power of their own lodge. Women must be courageous, for then, and only then, will they be unafraid to lose themselves in the Sky Lodge. I must say here, however, that, when men apply the first principle of meeting the Earth circle, their lodge will be very welcoming to our ways. They will teach women in the Sun Lodge how to meet the external world, the realm in which women can creatively consummate their visions. The Sun Lodge will then not be a frightening, disconnected, or hard circle in which to live, as it is now, but rather one filled with the beauty of walking tall, as *Ongwhe Onwhe*, the true noble man and the true dignified woman, unfolding their visions together toward a distinct society.

IXCHEL—MOON GODDESS, AND AHKIN—SUN GOD

An old Maya legend tells how, a long time ago, the Moon Goddess, Ixchel, shone as brightly as the Sun God, Kin. She was so radiant in her immaculate silvery purity that the Sun longed to charm her. He shrewdly disguised himself as a precious hummingbird and threw himself into the great immensity of the sky. As he fell, he collided with the mirror of the Moon's resplendent and shimmering face and landed, wounded, at her feet. Seeing this, she felt so sorry for the emerald bird that she immediately adopted him, for she is the goddess of all medicines. After she had carefully healed the small bird from all his injuries, he revealed himself to her in all his magnificent, flaming glory. She fell in love with him at once. He embraced her ardently and they fled together to his realm, into the heart of the heavens. In their passage around the sky, the Sun God, Ahkin, began to show signs of jealousy and to hold her more tightly. He became more and more possessive as days went by, desperate to control her by all means. He became extremely suspicious of vultures and eagles who flew close to her silver skirts. He tried to enchain her with his powerful rays. The Moon began to realize that her husband was becoming too overpowering for her subtle nature, and she felt eclipsed by his radiant nature. She began to look pale by his side. One day, as Kin was dozing in his own warmth, she gracefully escaped from her prison. She took refuge in the nights of the Underworlds, where she hid, catching her breath, free at last. She died in the regions of Xibalba and was resuscitated after thirteen days and nights. Her journey there represents each one of her thirteen moons during the year's cycle. In the fourth house of Xibalba, she made love with Venus, the evening star, before his return as the morning star.

The obstinate Sun concluded that the matter could not remain like this, for his honor and self-pride were irreparably hurt. He commenced an interminable chase after the resplendent silver goddess. By passing through all nine houses in the Underworlds and conquering the lords of death, however, she was given a special place in Xibalba, where the Sun couldn't find her, even during his own passage into the lower regions at night. In this way, she learned how to have him respect her instead of eclipsing her, for she had discovered that she could not live in his gleaming realm. She possessed a kingdom of her own. It is said that the Sun is still endlessly pursuing her to this day in their rotations, never really able to capture her. After an eternity, however, he is not pursuing her because of his jealous rage anymore, but rather because he wants to apologize and learn truly from her way. He has now learned to follow her awesome dreams and to celebrate her noble beauty.

After she resurrected from the Underworlds, Ixchel gave birth to her daughter, Spider Woman, who is named *Ix Chebel Yax*. Who the father was, whether the Sun, Venus, or the vulture, the story doesn't tell. I wonder, however, it might be that there is no father. That Ixchel simply conceived herself and gave birth to her own vision. Whatever the case, Ixchel has been, for many Maya women in need, the all-knowing goddess of the night realm. She is the true priestess for us. She inspires the Moon rites of passage and the Moon Lodge ceremonies, in which all women's blood must return to the inner water of their sacred dream. The shadow side of Ixchel's being reveals our deep-rooted feminine dreams. She mirrors the reflection of our fears, and leads all of us to find courage and power.

A woman is Moon in essence, being born from the scintillating beams of her womb lodge, while a man is born into the Sun's brilliance. In the Moon Lodge, the fears of being a woman are mirrored, and in the Sun Lodge, the fears of being a man are brought to the surface. In their respective inherent natures, men and women must conquer their fears, so that they may reach their opposite external hoops.

As we are emerging into the Era of Woman and the door of Earth, the inescapable exigency for both men and women to understand their relation to the Earth-Moon Lodge is pressing, in order that they may attune to the greater movements of this coming era.

For a woman, the Moon embodies the ancient Maya goddess of birthing and of all the waters, shimmering reflections of her silver disc. Pregnant women invoke her as a significant fertility symbol, as do those who wish to conceive. Ixchel is the most ancient midwife, the goddess of all healing medicines. It is believed that she also comforts babies and small children. She regulates the Moon cycle of women, causing the waters of women to flow every month and she also causes the high and low tides of the ocean. Ixchel is said to be the first woman of this world. Being a warrior-goddess herself, she teaches of the becoming into true womanhood, of being a mother, a lover. She enlightens our quest toward our vision. Eagles are associated with her during the night and are messengers of her Moon essence to the Sun Lodge during the day. For this, she is called Moon Eagle Spirit Woman. Her internal Moon organs are formed from deer antlers, embodying the gentleness and delicacy of the South, but she is also the West, as she reflects the fears in our inner womb.

To learn from her Earth-Moon womb, a woman must hold fast to the vessel of *perfect intuition* with which she is endowed from birth. Moon essence essentially unveils her nature as *gentle and receptive*. This has often been viewed by the patriarchal mind as emotional feebleness and lack of intelligence. On the contrary, in the sweet Medicine ways, the sensitive ways of the Moon Lodge, transform all the dream potential into Earth powers. Therefore the Moon Lodge manifests the profundity of the feeling realms, and makes the invisible perceptible through the opening of the womb's eye within. In other words, a woman in the Moon learns to see with *her womb's eye*.

When, out of fear, a woman disconnects from her Earth-Moon Lodge, she hopelessly isolates herself from her circle of women, her sisters. A woman may erroneously imagine that, in order to be equal to a man, she must obtain the same opportunities that he enjoys. To some extent, this opinion is justified. A woman may even try to become a man to realize this principle, totally adopting the ways of the Sun Lodge. The result is that she removes herself further and further from her Moon roots, irremediably leading her to give away her true power. This is the death of her spirit. Her womb will hurt and she will suffer severe emotional disorders.

This is the fate of more than one modern woman. Modern women have abandoned their Moon womb for the sake of their minds and heads, and live exclusively in the Sun Lodge. Each day, they become more and more involved in pursuing a career, most of the time having to cut themselves off from their woman's lodge by entering the man's world. Of course, there is nothing wrong with a woman pursuing a career. This reflects an essential and healthy motivation to participate in the community. Women must develop an awareness, however, that, in being in a society formerly based on patriarchy, they inevitably participate in the competitiveness of men's rationality. This often holds the potential of exhaustion and collapse, as we saw. In order to reach equal opportunities in a man's world, a woman may deny her true femininity, adopting superficial ways of being a woman. The reason for being a true woman is then forever buried, unless she can revive her Moon womb within. In her disconnected sense of femininity, she dresses like a man, she talks, moves, and shapes her body like a man. She thinks like a man either to prove she can do it or be heard and respected. She may even compete as brutally as a man (if not more so). She strives to do all that he can do, in this way only repressing the true feeling of her internal dream river. She may find herself with all sorts of womb problems or uterine cancer. She begins drying up like a dead tree after years of this regime she imposed on herself. This is the reality of millions of women. They want to claim their rights in a society that is predominantly male. This can be viewed as a very noble cause, but in the culture they challenge, there is no real place for women and even less for their truly special ways of being graciously themselves–their Moon time, their pregnancies, nursing their babies, and their time of menopause. Male society (first-world and third-world both) has not been reformed in its deepest foundations for 5,400 years. This is women's task, to achieve this reform in the door of this changing era. All together.

The dreadful drama of this woman-man-made dilemma leads this woman to one day awaken completely alone, sterile, with no other women at her side to understand and support her, for all her sisters are absorbed in the same disconnection. Moreover, there are no men to truly share with her what a Moon world could be. She has inevitably cut herself off from her Moon and will never be fully part of man's Sun world. That is only an illusion she has made up.

To think that a woman can ever be equal to a man is absurd. The contrary is also true, however. A man can never be equal to a woman. The eternal touchy topic between men and women must not revolve around equality for women, but rather in soundly assuming our own *distinctiveness* as receptacles for the universal forces. Only then can women create a world sensible to their ways, one that will confer on them the space and privilege they need to be fully themselves.

Another type of woman—less fierce, perhaps, but one who has also denied her Moon realm—can be called the "Barbie type." This is the type we find lying on cars. This woman may not dress or shape herself as a man, but she also competes with herself, creating all sorts of synthetic manners of being a woman. She rejects her womb, essentially out of her puerile fear to embrace life, preferring to stay a woman-child forever, spiritually and emotionally under-developed, denying the responsibility inherent to being a natural and powerful woman. Her passivity disempowers her. She only emulates the external ways of being a woman. Trapped in the apprehensive shadow side of the Moon, she fears losing herself in the great void of being. She is an empty receptacle, waiting to be filled up, completely emotionally dependent on others, especially men. Expectations of all sorts prevail as the only motivations of her life. She grasps at people and external values around her as the only way to ensure that she will be alive somehow. She is also dead, however, dead to her internal life. This occurs when she becomes extremely possessive herself, trying to hold onto everything and everyone around to fill her emptiness. She makes her life and the lives of her loved ones a real nightmare.

The great truth about being a woman is that we must never leave our own womb within and the truth that we are creators of the universe. This is how we can successfully make our dreams come through in our Sun Lodge. If we desire to join the Sun's world of a man, it must be with our most intimate and intrinsic ways, the ones that marks us as true goddesses of the Earth, true Ixchels, as authentic feminine warriors and full women.

We must greet with open arms the 180-degree shift within ourselves. We must desire the internal revolution toward creating our own world, one where we will not deny our Moon Lodge anymore, where our peculiar and fertile ways grow as our internal strength, translated into the consciousness of the world, a circle that welcomes man to converge at the Moon's dreaming of the Earth. How will man ever learn not to fear his most tender and compassionate side if a woman does not hold the Moon mirror, so that he may glimpse and meet his own principle of fertility? How will he ever untangle the confusion of how to be in his feminine self without denying his manhood? And above all, how will he ever understand women?

For without the Moon inspiring his Sun vision, man may just burn himself. There exists no virgin soil in the Sun into which his luminous spirit can be seeded, no place for anything to grow, because there are no roots there. Without the Moon, there are no dreams to nourish his ingenious Sun visions, however illumined they may be. If humanity has the responsibility to transform the unbalanced world, this can only take place within and through the womens' lodge first. To dream together in the Moon Lodge is the first parameter for a spirited people to live in harmony. Without the true dreaming heard from the core of Earth, humanity's mind will only juggle with the rationality of cold numbers and an avidity toward more inhuman computations ruling the world. And the world will remain indifferent, conflicted, hard, wounded, and out of balance, with many children dying of hunger in many places.

In the Moon Lodge, woman not only gives birth to children and to herself, she gives birth to man. In her, man gives birth to himself. He learns from his Moon goddess within the true inspiration that animates his greater vision. Woman learns that she holds inside the most important dream of the universe, one that invokes the greatest power on Earth, power that allows her, ultimately, to consummate the greatest realization of her Sun vision.

Genuine transformations in the world primarily manifest from women. Women raise our young boys, our future men. We are the only ones who can teach them that a woman stands higher than anyone else in the hoops of nations, for she is the source of all on this Earth plane. Through our blood and suffering, all existing souls are born. And this unique truth should be our real motivation and teaching.

In many women's wombs there exists more than one ancestral fear and humiliation. These must be exorcised at all costs. Only through embracing her own trustworthiness, holding her womb fully with her arms, will she stop being violated, ripped and cut open by everyone around. It is because she has left her womb empty that she is violated in many ways.

Once I had a spirited argument with a lady who had been raped and was refusing to hear the principles that I was teaching within a circle of women: *What you fear, you will attract.* If a woman fears a man in the assumption of his supposed physical power over her, he has already won a tremendous advantage and this woman may even be doomed to be raped. Of course, this is not to be misinterpreted as what some doctors or judges have claimed—that a woman is raped because she wants it somewhere inside. No. A woman has tremendous womb power, however, that she needs to discover in order to become the vanquisher. This arguing lady was so caught in her own suffering and previous trauma, that she was convinced that, once you face a man with a knife whose intentions are already set, there is nothing you can do but submit, be raped, or be killed.

I do not agree at all, for I was also violated once and I understand this very law. I know how my own fear impelled and attracted the rapist and I also know what I have to do in the future if the situation should arise again.

When I realized that my own fear attracted this irreversible act of molestation, I cleared any emotional pain attached to the fact of having had to submit to such a terrible offense. There was no point in falling into self-pity. I took the path to strength. Therefore, I took the positive responsibility to stand on my feet again and pursue my path without limitations. Inevitably, one day, I found myself facing almost the exact same situation. Four repulsive men appeared out of the blue, cornered a girlfriend and myself in a solitary passageway of a dark city street. It became evident that life itself was asking me to really prove that I knew the lesson. In the midst of my friend's panic, I instinctively placed my power animal in front of me, as I saw the four men reaching for her. I showed no fear. It was quite clear and amazing to observe that none of them had touched me yet, but that her fear was a real magnet to them. The more she panicked, the more they pursued her. I stood there, totally free to run if I wanted, but obviously I could not leave her this way. I uttered something. Two of the men were about to approach me, moving to "get" me. The most amazing thing happened. I saw how my own *energized* animal field stopped them in the act. I was surprised that I had no fear, and they looked mesmerized. They were unable to move further into my field. I urged them to leave us in peace. The calm yet forceful voice that came out of my throat did not appear to be mine. They all stood back at hearing "this" voice and left us, before anything unfortunate happened to my friend. Since then, I have traveled all over the planet, often sleeping alone in wild and, I must say, dangerous surroundings, and I have never been molested again. This inner sense of confidence that a woman can develop is her most powerful shield. The type of man who thinks of desecrating a woman really fears the true Earth shield of woman and will not dare to approach her, however physically frail she may be. No man's physical strength, however great, can overpower the womb shield of *a decided woman*. This is the very law of the Earth Lodge.

On the other hand the Sun Lodge, for a man, exemplifies the outward emergence of life, of what is seen, and what is awake, in contrast to the Moon's ways. It is *the East vision*, opposite to the West Moon-Earth Lodge of inner shadows. The children of Ahkin Sun, in the ancient Maya rituals, represented the Rattlesnake clan as a way into life. They had rituals for complete physical rejuvenation and spiritual regeneration, as well as ascension rituals to the great star. Their ancient practices were mainly composed of ceremonies of healing and contemplation of the red Sun. Thousands of years ago, these Sun clans modeled some of the greatest brotherhoods that the Americas have ever known, from North to South. Most of pre-Columbian pyramids were built in the Era of Man as altars honoring the Sun, using the rattlesnake as a totem. (The same is true for the pyramids built in Egypt in the Era of Man with their altars to the Sun God, Ra.)

For the Maya, the Sun vision inspires a pure celebration of life, an absolute triumph over the fear of death. Ahkin is the greatest warrior-hunter of all, the golden disc being his bow and the rays, his arrows. The Sun teaches the hunting ways of clear strategies. He teaches about fearlessness in hunting and killing our true vision on Earth.

As the husband of Ixchel, goddess of medicine, Ahkin also holds an important place as a powerful healer and as the greatest protector of light against any dark forces. Since the Sun also merges into the Underworlds at every twilight, he is considered a master teacher, revealing the penumbras of our soul, helping us to find the light and freedom of our spirit. The Sun, however, can captivate us with its illusion of ardent light, causing total blindness and ungrounded spiritual exultation. This is why the Sun apprentices, men or women, know the vital responsibility to cast out all illusions. Living very intensively at each moment, they glow with inner light, knowing the secrets of conserving vital energy at its maximum potential. For all these reasons, the Sun Lodge of the tree of life represents a model for society. When the root Moon Lodge is strong, the Sun teachings motivate toward organization of a society based on universal order. This is how the Sun makes his connection with Earth, how his higher vision of the cosmos may be generated here, through us.

Man is born in the Sun essence. He naturally possesses a strong activity of the mind. For example a woman, when entering a room, is much more sensitive to the general atmosphere, how it feels. A man will look at the specifics of the same room, how the furniture is made or arranged, with a mind that is seemingly never at rest. Accordingly, the Sun Lodge imparts the knowledge on the proper use of mental energy and the tremendous *power of thoughts*. Every thought, good or bad, is immutably bound to manifest on the Earth's physical plane. This is one of the basic laws of the Sun Lodge. Moreover, the Sun teaches us not to be fearful of burning ourselves in the fire of life—to burn our shyness, false prudence, personal attachments, and ego grasping. The Sun's power of transmutation is the pure light of love, for he confers the seeker with great energy to manifest beyond the self for the sake of another being. This is true brotherhood.

A man can be easily trapped in the fascinating power of his Sun-mind, however, just as a woman can lose herself in the passive void of her Moon. Because the Sun-mind conceives itself as essentially self-sufficient, it can be quite controlling when not accompanied with the depth of perception of the Moon. A man can go so far as to dominate and enslave the world. This mind can become severely destructive. The cure for a man so misled is for him to pursue and meet the Moon Lodge, just as in the old Maya legend. Just as a woman must not leave her Moon as she enters the Sun Lodge, so a man must not fully leave his Sun Lodge. A man who cuts himself off from his Sun roots when entering the Moon circle will become very passive, as if hypnotized and obsessed, even victimized, letting himself be dominated by external people and things.

For a woman well in her Moon, the Sun totem gives her great inspiration, *her realized dreaming.* A woman, with the potential of her intuition within, must create her world in awe of the Sun. In the Sun Lodge of the East, both man and woman, with the West Earth Lodge, will encounter the spirit fire of being brothers and sisters, in full consciousness and responsibility.

In the total wakefulness of the dawn of the fifth Sun, the children of the Sun are returning, elevating their higher self toward the red Sun of the Maya, contemplating with the absolute flame of mind, and more than ever ready to meet the depth of Earth and engage the responsibility to create a new world.

THE TWINS OF CONSCIOUSNESS

The female principle sustains to create. This is the inner circle. *The male principle creates to sustain.* This is the outer circle. When these two principles are aligned and at peace, they can merge in perfect harmony. If humanity is to return to the ancient Council ways, it is important that we examine the kinship between man and woman at every stratum of life and society. This step must induce into dreaming the eventual prospect of the true way of living together. Dreaming is essential, for we can no longer base our ways of living on imposed or adopted external models. In this time, in this new opening, they must spring forth from within, from every one of us, from this inward recognition in our deepest core.

It is time both men and women start dreaming together with their dream bodies. Dreaming the Moon into the Earth, the Sun into the Earth—this is *the real marriage* of our inner warrior and warrioress. This gives the awareness that we are joined in unison within the Earth's womb. This dreaming is a prerequisite, as well as a discipline and responsibility, and can only happen in the inner meeting of the inherent warrior, for a man, and the warrioress, for a woman.

For this, the Sun Lodge must first enter the female lodge in the Earth, thus inseminating the Moon, so that both lodges may conceive through dreaming into the Earth. It is interesting to observe that, in the ancient matriarchal societies of many American Indian tribes, the symbol of the mother clan was the Sun, while the symbol of the Moon represented the male chief's lodge, connecting the opposite counterparts. In this way, all the circles blended together in complete inclusiveness, the Moon in the Sun and the Sun in the Moon, as the perfect equality of the democratic tree of life, as the true marriage of *Ongwhe Onwhe* whose voices are the language of spirit and Earth.

This true union between the high warrior and the powerful warrioress within is far different from the common concept of marriage. Most people, when they marry, begin living a third life, called the common life. Most of the time, this form of marriage leads to an irremediable dead end, where spirit no longer has a place. Both may give up certain dreams and purposeful inner visions in order to pursue this common life, with all its heavy requirements of everyday responsibilities. The true meaning of this union is, therefore, never realized. Most of the time, each one expects the other to fulfill everything for which they have longed. They demand that their companion satisfy their spiritual or sentimental needs, because of a fear that they cannot do it themselves. This is usually fatal, and can end in simple divorces or, worse, co-dependency relationships.

The real image of true partnership is of a man and a woman walking on parallel paths and building bridges along the path to meet, each maintaining their respective vision, yet shouldering responsibility for the daily task of living together. These rainbow bridges are rooted in mutual inspiration, in the sharing of what can be common in the personal vision. Often, however, people join their lives together because of a fear of being alone and of assuming their real purpose. Instead of maturing within the relationship, the spirit of each partner becomes dull, bored, and caught in conformities of all kinds. Eroticism between them contents itself with being based primarily on genital and sexual satisfaction, lacking the romanticism of their initial meeting. In such a conformist union, sexual love is never really seen as a spiritual fusion of their deepest sentiments. The dreaming of being true twins will never happen.

To reach full harmony, the Sun of a woman must dream with the Moon of a man. A perfect society, rooted in the great tree of love, first carries the Sun into the Moon, so man and woman may carry out the consummated dream on Earth. In the end, it is the Moon who fecundates the Sun. Before we all reach this beautiful, yet abstract, concept, however, we must travel a long and difficult path. There are still plenty of handicaps for both men and women to meet in their daily lives.

The following does not intend to expose them all, but I hope will give some clues about what needs to be healed to live together in parallel canoes and meet on the rainbow bridge.

FOR HER: A great obstacle for a woman resides in the powerful misconception that, when a woman creates a common life with a partner, everything will be easier, and that, conversely, the lack of a partner will make her life harder, materially and sentimentally. This makes her extremely passive and resentful. A true woman, a spiritual warrioress never depends on *anyone*, but only on her Earth Lodge and her instinct. Even when she apparently relies on others for the fulfillment of her vision, she is not expecting anything of anyone. For no human has the right to depend on someone else out of expectation.

There exists very deep within a woman a long-lasting anticipation of the validation of her beauty and her intelligence by her partner. This is another important obstacle. When this is not forthcoming, she often becomes depressed. She pushes herself too hard to be perfect all the time. She asks too much of herself, which, of course, keeps her from relaxing. Stressed and tense, she is not entirely herself.

Another complex impediment to meeting a man fully resides in her inability to feel real passion, caught, as she is, in external futile things. She may work all day. She may even pursue a career. But she doesn't hold a spiritual fire of her own, nourishing her spiritual fervor. Often caught in an antiquated Puritanism, she fears risk and her prudery may keep her from developing courage and leaping into the unknown. A woman must have a real passion of her own. She must fight the tendency to dream other people's visions, although this is what has been expected of her or what her man may expect. In the past, she has often gone as far as forsaking her own path for his. This, in the end, leads her to resentment and anger toward him. This is a millennial pattern. Only if she holds a true vision can she help her partner with his.

Even the most emancipated woman may be caught in egoistic contemplation often expressed in vain and shy activities. This occurs most often out of sentimentalism: unnecessary friendships, superfluous objects, redundant ways of being, empty self-admiration. I am generalizing, of course, in order to help you understand that it is not easy for a woman to be a true warrioress. Most of the time, she may not have received an education that provided her with this sort of self-esteem. As a little girl, she may have been protected and limited in many ways that may become an impediment later on in her life as a young woman. In womanhood, she will have all sorts of fanciful fears and pretexts not to pursue her true power. She just refuses to admit to herself that she is often bored to death with her life. In order to survive the 5,400 years of the Era of Man, women often became expert in lying about their true feelings.

A woman who seeks to realize herself in all her potentiality will frequently enter into a direct war with man, at home or at work. Even if she has to scream to be heard (generally, she has no other option) this will not really lead to what she wishes to attain, but may aggravate the problem. If she is more subtle, she invents all sorts of strategems to humiliate men. This makes her feel that she has taken some revenge and may rejoice. She may attempt to hold a man through caprices of all sorts, inventing intricate ways of how he should please her. This is often intended to thwart his plans, out of anger. She thinks, erroneously, that this is how she can manifest her woman's power. Unfortunately, this woman has cut herself off more and more from her real way of being and from a true partnership.

FOR HIM: The major impediment for a man to meeting a woman fully resides in his own false pride. It is very hard for a man to accept humiliation, for it triggers a reaction of fear and even violence. What could be an opportunity to grow is taken as a humiliation or as a direct attack on his self-esteem. Having been educated to have a self-proving and validating instinct, he is entrapped in his vanity, which is then translated into his own need for achievement and exploit. The whole Westernized culture presents a model of hero and/or anti-hero that keep men from simply being themselves. It is hard for a man to abandon the need for validation and desist from seeking to be always admired. To counter this, he must learn to listen more to women and simply surrender in a natural way. He must completely give up his own value system, one based on competition and controlling behavior.

All the fallacious dreams that a man projects onto a woman are rarely fulfilled, of course, and often become the deception of his life. He projects his own illusions onto her and, thus deceived, he backs off when he realizes that the dream of love was not what he had expected. This can cause great pain to a woman. His education has misled him to think that he is born to guide a woman and to be her consciousness. This is firmly ingrained in him, infiltrated in many small ways into his being. This need for control in his marital life and career may result in an expressed distress and a direct ego war with his female partner. This war of sex is traduced into the confrontation of expectations against projections. He must understand, with complete and certain abnegation, that she irremediably seeks her freedom, and that it is not given easily to her. He must also desist from always seeing her as an erotic object to fulfill his own desire. Once he achieves this, the first requirement toward their true spiritual meeting will be in place. He must grasp woman's basic need for space, which is not something as easily conferred on her as it is on him. He must genuinely encourage her on her own path of decision, thus manifesting true love for her. Unfortunately, many men unconsciously try to inculcate an inferiority complex in women through small gestures, spoiling their effort toward true reconciliation. If, in gratitude and appreciation, he can support her in all her ways and her tremendous work, understanding her opposite voice, a major battle is at last won.

FOR BOTH MAN AND WOMAN: Together, they must demystify all these mutual false projections and forgive each other, meeting at the true dreaming place of pure respect and sensible equality in their differences. Man and woman, however liberated they may appear at the end of the millennium, still suffer within these predominant cultural patterns. Even after forty years, these models, though challenged, survive. Most people become partners for the wrong reasons: sexual needs, a longing to share, fear of loneliness, economic reasons, or first-sight sexual attraction. Very rarely do we meet the true soul companion willing to share the great vision of being on Earth.

Most men and women still bear their little child shield in front of them. Societal values do not encourage the transition to warrior or warrioress. In native traditional cultures when we were children, we carried our children shield in front. Placing our warrior shields in the front and moving the child shield behind us must occur in our teenage years, traditionally at the time of the Vision Quest. In the poor societies of the third world, this shift often happens at too young an age. There, children usually cannot be children, but, at a very young age, must be responsible for hard labor with their parents during the day. Such people become emotionally ripe and aged long before adulthood. In the modern societies of abundance, the contrary happens. Many times, this crucial shift is never made. In adulthood, a man still carries his boy shield in front and a woman carries her girl shield. These child shields are simply not equipped to meet the strong winds of life's adversities. It is interesting to observe how, in modern society, most women transport their babies in a cart, in front of them, representing their own child shield, while in traditional societies, women carry their small infants on their backs, in a shawl or a little cradle, protecting them with the inner warrioress in front. Because so many men and women in the modern Western world try to protect themselves with their child shields, when they marry, it is often these children who marry, not the true lover-warriors. And this marriage of children results in mutual projected expectations. He expects her to be in charge emotionally and she expects him to take care of her sentimentally. This is disastrous. This is why there are so many divorces these days. The child shield is not emotionally capable of making judicious choices regarding the strategies of life. The consequence is blame, resentment, and a permanent frustration toward the opposite sex.

For a man and for a woman, holding the warrior and the warrioress shield forward consists of recognizing, emotionally, physically, and spiritually, the responsibility, first to the self, and then to the partnership, in accordance with the great vision of life. If the warrior has a family to care for, it is also part of their inner dream that nourishes every second of life and, therefore, can never be seen as a burden to inner liberty. To reach a balanced society, it is essential for adults to shift the child to the rear and the warrior/ess to the front. Only when a man and a woman assist each other toward transcending the emotional patterns of childish hurts will they endure life together in a powerful way. Then the dreams of the collective vision of humanity may emerge fully. This can only happen when the man evolves to the point of embracing a woman's dreams through his, and when a woman stops resenting upholding a man in his quest. Once each shoulders the other, then marriage may lead to respective freedom and love. It can hold the freedom of choosing and following the calling path, with the mutual respect it must engender.

True love must be a source of inspiration, joy, and strength, although this means striving to overcome internal dissension. Reciprocal deference is a far deeper expression of love and maturity than any external demonstration of sentimentalism. Sentimentalism is the greatest obstacle to true mating. It creates a destructive mental game that keeps people from truly knowing each other. For no one can ask anyone else to be their exclusive and primary reason for living. It is imperative, therefore, for women to drop their desire to be seduced and dominated by men in sex, and for men to give up seducing and dominating women in sex. This reflection stands at the core of this crucial understanding. They must both realize that, when they have intercourse, a more transcendental channel opens, allowing the great dream of the cosmos, united with the Earth, to make love within them, sustaining their respective and shared life's vision in a consummate embrace.

Both partners must truly see and enjoy each other's opposite movements of freedom. Without this, profound separation will necessarily occur. *Trust* for each other is of absolute importance. This is an energy center located at the pineal gland within the brain that translates as mutual understanding. The freedom of one should be the inspiration of the other. They must be warriors, capable of losing themselves in spirit, while retaining all their integrity and sincerity. Times of loneliness for both are, therefore, a crucial requirement of regeneration toward an authentic sharing that will endure beyond the daily strain. The great warrior and the powerful warrioress will then converge in the great womb, emerging jointly onto the Earth, at last recognized by each other in a united vision of the world.

12

ORDER

MANIFESTING THE ANCIENT COUNCIL WAYS

The Woman's Lodge and the Man's Lodge give birth to the Council ways that stand as the perfect hoop and create the most powerful shield for people to live in harmony, based on the Medicine Wheel ways. These ways offer a matchless model for all the tendencies of a society, both democratic and communal, toward a united government ruled by the people themselves. These ancient and important archetypes are now reemerging as the true ways of people and as one of the only balanced approach to relating to one another in a larger planetary sense.

The primary teaching of the medicine wheel resides in the learning and integration of the spiritual rainbow warrior, known among the Maya as *Nichimal Vinik*, the flowering humans, and among the Mohawk people as *Ongwhe Onhwe*, or the true people. This knowledge teaches a way to self- respect, inner dignity, and loyalty to the spirit of the community, regardless of individual status in the society. The precepts of the Council ways always seek the conciliation of differences that can only come when a deep love for sacred Mother Earth is commonly expressed in the inclusiveness of diversified community ways.

Most people in the individualistic societies that assail us today have not retained an awareness of relating to the larger circles of people. So the medicine wheel is a major guide that consolidates the meeting of our brothers and sisters in the circle of this world. For this, the Council way is the oldest form of relation within a community. A long time ago, all the ancient, balanced confederate governments were profiled and governed under the awareness of truly wise people, unlike today.

There are inherent laws essential to a collective awareness that can eventuate on the wheel, beyond any particular and individual differences. Because the majority of our problems always come when we have to deal with others, whether in institutions or as individuals, a sensitive knowledge and a sound disposition when relating to others is imperative. This is true whether we talk of the destiny of a nation, or of the relationship with our neighbors. It requires first, a personal connection to our soul. This is what the wheel has to offer. The touching and the meeting of people on a deeper level confers a true sense of sisterhood or brotherhood. This has apparently been lost in the genetic memory of humanity, after an era that evinced thousands of wars. Many people have lost contact with their true souls.

On a smaller scale, individuals often cannot meet in the wheel of people because they are unaware that they even stand in one, having no understanding of their single perspective on the circle of people. Competition and struggles in relating to others begin when you are unable to open to other viewpoints as part of the same wheel. You may see contradictions, when there is only natural opposition—simply not seeing that they hold a natural opposition. This occurs mostly when your ego is the ruler of your own impulses, causing discord instead of clarity. Then you lose the awareness of the larger circle. Conquering your ego requires much abnegation, something most people do not have. But true abnegation leads to a neutrality of emotions, nobility of the heart, and a capacity to stand tall with your inner truth, beyond personal reactions, that is essential in learning to relate to the wheel of people.

One of the afflictions of the modern world results from the great difficulty that people have in learning *impersonality*, collectively and individually. This is the principal motivation of the genuine *Ongwhe Onwhe*. Impersonality means natural objectivity, a capacity to achieve a proper distance from emotions and ego. We natives are usually raised to think of our community first and how our actions will affect the larger wheel. When facing a problem, however, the general tendency of individuals in Western societies is first to get involved on a personal level, perceiving through the ego's eyes. This is when the collective mess begins and when the heart simply closes. Blame, confusion, distress, offenses, are all created by the anguishing grasping of ego, incapable of recognizing a greater wisdom beyond the little self. We then confuse true humility with self-humiliation. This is wrong. Our hearts and our minds are just refusing to learn.

The Medicine Wheel ways offer a natural ground for solving internal and external conflicts among all people, for avoiding hostile separation. Although, sometimes the resolution may conclude with a strategic withdrawal from conflict, this occurs through a natural understanding, not due to a human inadequacy to resolve it in the circle.

My statements on the ancient Council ways do not refer to a romantic vision of a perfect society. This is not a Utopia. This natural model, based on the balance of Earth and sky paths, leads men and women to a great point of balance. It really exists and is at hand, even though it may take another era to develop completely on a planetary scale! The true Council ways unite all ideologies from the right to the left (or up and down), as long as every mind is willing to meet, share, and respect every position at the center, symbolized as the fire of people, a self-responsibility to the larger circle. In the end, even the most rigid tendencies of the extreme right of the mind are recuperated by the larger wheel. One day or another, discerning confrontations will become the only mirror of purgation and spiritual advancement for all tendencies to accept each other, as long as the wheel laws are observed, as outlined in the Hau De No Sau Nee Address to the Western World (Iroquois Nations):

> *The majority of the world does not find its roots in Western culture or traditions. The majority of the world finds its roots in the Natural World and its traditions . . . which must prevail if we are to develop truly free and egalitarian societies. . . . The people who are living on this planet need to break with the narrow concept of human liberation, and begin to see liberation as something which needs to be extended to the whole world of the Natural World. What is needed is the liberation of all the things that support life, the airs, the waters, the trees, all the things which support the sacred web of life.*[1]

The Iroquois Confederacy League of Six Nations, also called the Great Council of Thirteen Fires, constitutes one of the most balanced governments that has existed for over 800 years. Based on the model of this perfect circle, it survived the conquest intact. The Confederacy creates within its constitution "the oldest living, participatory democracy on Earth," as the Hau De No Sau Nee League of Peace calls it.

The great tree of peace is the greatest symbol of unity among the Iroquois. It is the perfect model for unifying nations beyond threats of dissension. The Great White Pine of Freedom is guarded by the bald Eagle, symbol of the great spirit, always perched at the crest of the tree. Over eight hundred years ago, the peace tree was planted by the Iroquois people, who buried their trivial weapons of war at the foot of

---

[1] "The Hau De No Sau Nee Address to the Western World," in *Basic Call to Consciousness*, ed. by *Akwesasne Notes* (Summertown, TN: Book Publishing Company, 1978), pp. 77–78.

266

this tree. Through this meaningful act, the wars among people were transformed by the Earth herself into unity, power, and love. This set the ground for the Council ways to be established.

The strong foundation of this model distributes responsibilities between the male Chief Clans and the Clan Mothers. Each clan (usually a totem-animal clan) within each nation sits at the long house with their representatives or chiefs. For example, the male Turtle Clan and the Turtle Clan of Mothers are in direct relation, yet opposed in the long house. The men of this clan sit on one side with their Turtle chief, and the women sit with their Mother representative on the other side. This is true for every totem clan of every nation. Each nation has three or more animal clans, depending on the structure of their traditional councils. When a problem occurs among the people, each male clan gathers with their representatives, talks over a resolution, and then meets with the women of their respective clan. If the Mother clan accepts the men's resolution, the chiefs meet at the Hau De No Sau Nee Council (or League of Peace), where all other nations who have previously undergone a similar process join to discuss the larger perspective of the question and its possible solution. If an alternative resolution is brought up, all chiefs must return to their respective inward circles to consult again with all the clans. This can be a long process. Because the communities have used this form of government for many centuries, however, the process can also be prompt. Often, not much is discussed. Everyone agrees upon an unmediated solution. The results show that, when people live in a *true community of minds*, what is just and clear is seen by all.

Democratic impartiality resides within the law that allows the Mother clan to have the last word on every decision. This is basic democracy. Representing the children, women are in a majority within any group. Most countries that state that they have a democratic regime do not, in our view, because to think of a democracy without applying this natural view of the women's circle is only a mirage. Giving women the last word in decisions by their government is not a very common practice.

The American constitution was based on the spiritual inspiration that Thomas Jefferson and his group gained from the Iroquois government. They drew out of it what they thought was a democratic tendency. On the other hand, Karl Marx, apparently inspired by the

Iroquois government, wrote *Das Kapital* mostly by drawing on its communal or socialist tendency. In both cases, however, these thinkers omitted the most essential element of the Iroquois League of Peace, the Mother clans and their right, to hold the last word in decisions. If a majority of women do not agree with a decision of the men chiefs, the men may not proceed. The omission of this apparently diminutive "detail" (that accounts for more than half the population) significantly contributed to the fact that these supposedly democratic and communist systems have been and are both crumbling, some abruptly, some slowly.

In the Iroquois Confederacy, the men are never allowed to elect the chiefs. This is a privilege strictly reserved to the mothers. Their inherent wisdom recognizes in their sons who is born a chief and who is humble enough to balance their position of power. Traditionally, chiefs and tribal leaders have stood as spiritual "politicians," but often have not had the power to elect or vote. For no law can be above anyone, and no one can be above any law. This is how they compensate for their positions of power. Chiefs must show great wisdom and exemplary moral strength. Leaders must embody the law, must uphold its application and its understanding, because the laws primarily belong to the people. They must hear the will and decision of their respective clans and find ways, as powerful orators, to express this. They must know how to touch the heart of the people. In this resides an important precept understood by many Indians: *that spiritual consciousness is the highest form of politics.* A chief's role must be a neutral one, although he must always advocate and take action for the humblest members of the community. This surely doesn't seem to be the case with most of today's politicians! To prove their modesty, the Chiefs must display a vehement, yet centered, power. They must pledge their lives to the people they represent and be a proper channel for their views. They must sacrifice their own personal ambition as an inward prerequisite, in exchange for their high position. In this way, the law is observed and everybody is truly equal. No one can be above another, as in a pyramidal system. This is the foundation of every circle.

In the natural return to the Council ways given by the changes of eras, no one will be able to be above the others. Our leaders must "command by obeying" the will and decision of the people. It is imperative that we undo this ingrained pyramidal mind-set of the Era of Man. Only at the "lowest" circle of people can we truly start creating the Council ways. At the bottom circle, we can hear the voice of the poorest people of this planet, the ones closest to the Earth. We must understand their reality and attend to their needs. No true democratic society can exist, nor any true community of spiritual people, where an upper and middle class manage a lower class that does not have access to the same privileges. When the people closest to Earth—women, children, and the poor—are still not able to be heard, the spirit of democracy will not be reached. The true spirit of democracy lies in an awareness of community and must, therefore, be communal. This is very different from how communism has been practiced. This is the fundamental principle of the Council ways that are solely and primarily a way to heal the planet, encompassing the highest universal laws by including the most extreme forms of thinking, whether religious, political, or social, beyond dogmatic doctrines. The Council way offers a compatible way of being and thinking that includes all forms, by weaving circles of inner freedom. In the Council ways resides *a major call to consciousness*, displaying strong and ancient roots and even futuristic tendencies.

Communism, socialism, and capitalism have not sustained the complete answer to our human condition. With the downfall of socialism, the inevitable war between classes pictured by Marx's model resulted in division. In both communism and socialism, the laborers who rose up against the upper, securely established classes that controlled the capital of all the people were still not able to take control of the industry and justly administer their own capital. This revolution demonstrated the major pitfall in these unbalanced ways. "Having everyone share equally the wealth of the state is an impractical answer."[2] When the poor receive the wealth from the rich without having to work, this does not teach them to be autonomous, by developing their own skills and managing their own resources. To take the vast land holdings of aristocratic landowners and divide them into small farms for poor families will never create prosperity, for it is not based on a true, communal form of government. Moreover, it creates karma for the nation. The socialist reforms of

2 Eklal Kueshana, *The Ultimate Frontier* (Chicago: The Stelle Group, 1974), p. 128.

eliminating the corrupt privileges of the rich, as well as eliminating intellectuals, irremediably led to a dictatorship over the nation. In the end, this resulted in a form of capitalism advantaging the supreme state, practicing a form of total tyranny, and creating absolute paranoia among the citizens.

That the hard workers of the society received no more than the indolent or disabled citizens is more than a simple penalty. It builds tremendous frustration, as well as fostering a lowering of the standard of living that results in the simple retardation of the whole society. The work of the laborer becomes a real mortification meant to enrich the State. It is a disenchanting ideology, a form of slavery. When the hard-working poor know they will always remain poor, they become tremendously depressed and this cannot lead to any spiritual advancement. A society whose burdens create old people long before their time leaves no place for initiative or young entrepreneurs with new ideas. Money (though not in excess) foments creativity. It is absolutely necessary for the healthy gestures of life and a certain natural abundance is needed to keep honesty as a principal value. Always being poor and having to count every bit of money at all moments of life creates constant disillusionment. The spiritual evolution of a nation can only be based on a natural abundance of life and its rejoicing.

On the other hand, capitalism has stimulated incredible growth and technological development. It holds a great danger, however: that the people and the rulers will not be sufficiently spiritually developed to properly establish the true status of technology without becoming enslaved by it. The harm of capitalism lies in a mentality based on constant competition toward more productive efficiency and less manual labor. Only quantity is valued, to the detriment of quality. The true maturity of a society is observed through its standard of quality, not quantity. Thinking of more for less creates hungry people always striving toward materiality instead of sensible lasting values. The fierce competition of capitalism compels unscrupulous humans to do everything in a forceful and illegal manner in order to protect their investments and interests. This breeds pure corruption and even fascism. A good honest worker in an enterprise can immediately be displaced under the basic principle that capitalism is profit without mercy in the service of opportunity. The hungry ones, always seeking more material goods, behave as immature beings who are never satisfied. For example, they will seek the first cheap thing, instead of working hard and with patience to acquire a true article. The capitalist system reflects a total lack of maturity and self-discipline. This kind of capitalism instills values of making quick money, doing less for more. This leads to total indulgence, in which working becomes the worst thing someone may do. In the end, this mentality induces moral insanity and, of course, a very bad, national economy. The basic principles of capitalism and neo-liberalism, also practiced by governments in third-world countries, depicts a fierce jungle law, in which everyone may seek advantage over each other, imposing more and more damage, to the point that whole nations are sold (as Mexico) to the extended financial powers of the dominant culture. Inevitably, the rich become richer and the poor poorer. The poor class becomes miserable almost everywhere. The people are not given the possibility to develop and manage their own resources—those of the nation, as well as their local ones. The people in both first- and third-world societies only survive, frustrated, stressed, restrained, and full of resentment.

There is nothing wrong with the principle of profit within certain limits, as in capitalism. There is nothing wrong with the idea that wealth should be shared by a whole nation, as in communism. On the contrary, both these tendencies should become allies. In practice, a monopolized abundance for the sake of a few industrialists who run the government (supposedly elected from the people and by the people), deciding the fate of entire nations, most often through lies and the covert assassination of those who stand and resist, is a dead end. In modern societies, the people are no longer seen as humans, but exclusively as numbers and consumers in the large "mall" of the nation. When people and governments base the values of a society on creating positive and alternative ways of living, rather than on creating competition and violence, rather than always taking fiercely, when people are encouraged to do good work, to demonstrate solid initiatives and inventiveness of enterprise, when humility, gentleness, and courteousness are valued in the cultural education, rather than the search for a false of sense power, only then will the lodges of people flourish in health. As long as there is a handful of men, however, who seize all the capital of entire nations for themselves, whether in the name of socialism, capitalism or neo-liberalism, there will always be poverty and sick societies.

In the medicine wheel, the ways for the people to reorganize themselves in Councils is given to prevent and reform these terrible false models. These ways must be applied by everyone, starting on a small scale, in your neighborhood, at work. This allows you to create an energetic circle that will allow the true ways of living together to return. Once people *from below* are applying the ways of the councils in their daily lives, however, it will grow stronger and stronger and will be reflected as well in the form of governments. This is Earth law.

THE CENTRAL FIRE OF THE PEOPLE

A healthy society is not an unrealizable Utopia, but the only *real ideal* we should all have. It is indispensable to nourish practical ideals, at whatever level, to bring forth these tangible objectives for the good of all and toward a higher planetary equanimity and balance. It is imperative that the people acquire the capability to self-govern their communities. It is imperative that the representatives of the people stand as spiritual and wise leaders, owning an impeccable integrity, without fomenting personal interests, but concerned exclusively with the prosperity of civilians and the implantating of higher values. For this, the people must redeem their public responsibility and reclaim the power they have ceded to incompetent rulers.

In the majority of nations around the world, the voice of the people is not heard. Even less commonly are they given the opportunity to decide for themselves. This results in an oppressive separation. No one above should adjudge laws and the course of a nation without referendum on every decision. Laws must be issued with the full awareness of the Earth laws and must clearly be understood by the civil society—men, women, and children—before anything else. Laws are the foundation for our family, our community, and our world. Every law must thus spring from the heart of the Earth. Right now, in every country, the legal system is outrageously complicated. People have lost interest in it. Laws no longer articulate the truth of their communities. This results in a collective passivity toward choosing our destiny.

In the Council ways, the chiefs, both men and women, stand as the representatives of various clans of the community. They form and sit in the circle of the united lodges. They are the holders of the Council laws, with their respective attributions conferred by their role. The center of the Council is the Fire in the teepee or the Long House, the heart of the people, to which all the chiefs look and attend. The central fire of the Council is fundamental. Without it, there is no unity, no focus at which the chiefs and the people may gather their spirit. In the central fire of the community, people find the faith, regeneration, and power to stand together in one harmonized body. The central fire in the teepee, whether as the heart of the people or as the great central councils, symbolizes the council fire of the Earth, the great fire within her womb, at her very core, at the center of our mother planet. These fires are aligned in an indivisible link and, when the chiefs attune to the center fire of their teepee, they commune with the fire of the Earth core.

The council of chiefs, in accordance with the circle of the people, must consistently proceed as an organic circle, in which every rising challenge to the community's life must be examined. The ancient Council ways offer some guidelines, but these must be adapted with keen discernment. They can never become rigid to the point of creating separation. This violates the coalition of the confederacy. When a clan or an individual becomes inflexible to the point of refusing to understand another's point of view, it seriously endangers the unity within the council. People must, therefore, learn to be flexible and adaptable to the larger will.

In the larger council's gathering, there co-exists the council of women and the council of men within each clan. In order for this organic configuration to subsist, the foremost relationship within the community requires that every individual, with their assigned tasks, align toward their own spiritual learning and growth. Without this, the edification for personal and collective integration is not ensured and problems cannot be faced as a whole. Assuming your personal solitude is the passage by which to meet all your brothers and sisters. If you enter or form a council out of a fear of being alone, the council will consequently be built to revolve around everyone's personal inconsistencies. If individuals cannot face life for themselves, they will be unable to meet obstacles within a group, even if it offers healthy ground.

Every member of the council must owe great respect to the chiefs themselves. You should not, however, blindly give them your power to the point of no longer discerning for yourself. To understand and accept the leadership of a chief, man or woman, it is important that you place yourself in their moccasins. To achieve this, you must learn from your own chief within, or you will not easily accept the authority of a born chief. This is something I have observed in Western, individualistic societies, where many resist learning from a person of power, thinking that by doing this they will give up their own identity. Unfortunately they have lost track of true alignment to the Earth. A people cannot reach full maturity without a recognition and respect toward their true chiefs. Chiefs and natural leaders are absolutely essential to bring vision to the community as a central focus toward which everyone is working, toward the fulfillment of a purpose, as we must dream the medicine wheel's purpose. I have seen groups of people formed together because they share some spiritual interest, stating they have no need for spiritual guides. Without a true leader and guide to always bring back the interest on one aspect of the teachings, however, these groups irremediably start to indulge and often do not last long for they face a great emptiness.

The expression of these laws could be called parameters or guidelines, if you prefer, for the word law may seem very male and rigid. In the vast range of guidelines that the chiefs must hold, together with the people, there are a number of predetermined sets of laws that bind the community together: economic laws (for the subsistance of the people), laws for agriculture and work, basic social laws for the responsibility of people among the community, juridicial laws of how decisions will be handled in the council laws, laws for the behavior of the representative chiefs, legislative and executive laws, laws of environmental preservation (and restoration), war laws, peace laws, funeral laws, laws for the warriors who protect the people (or the laws of security), and laws of women and children (or laws of education). And let us not forget laws of independent sovereignty, as well as renewal laws. All of these laws are found within the four major aspects of a society that create strong foundations. These four aspects constitute the way to a balanced medicine council:

in the South, the social council;
in the North, the political council;
in the West, the economic council;
in the East, the spiritual council.

The laws of renewal require that the people, together with the chiefs, reconsider every law after a number of years to determine whether modification is needed. The renewal law states that no law can become rigid. When this happens, the laws, symbolized as wampum belts (or political belts), shell strings, or even arrows, are broken and returned into the waters. New ones are then created, in alignment with the growth of the community. This allows the community to adapt their ways to new forms of being. These symbols confer on the leaders the legal authority for their important deliberations and decisions.

If the majority agrees that a law is no longer suitable to the community's growth at some level, it is necessary to decree a law that ensures certain changes within the legal system. Law must be envisioned naturally as part of the greater harmony of the cosmic movements that govern us all. Because law is essentially *movement*. The omission of this fundamental understanding results in a rigidity of perspective and internal conflicts within the community. Regarding this, I can only agree with the Cayuga Bear Clan Mother of the Iroquois Nation:

> *In making any law, our chiefs must always consider three things: the effect of their decision on peace; the effect on the natural world; and the effect on seven generations in the future. We believe that all law makers should be required to think this way, that all constitutions should contain these rules. . . . We are the carriers of knowledge that the world needs today.*[3]

The principal of *natural justice,* based in the medicine wheel, is a way of discernment for the people. Trials are called peace councils and are held in the medicine wheel, where the clans and respective chiefs gather. The ancient principles of the medicine wheel state that, in the circle of men and in the circle of women, the lodges must meet as a whole to consider any dilemma placed in the middle of the central fire. An important chance is always given to the offenders, the benefit of the doubt, resulting in a much more natural way of dealing with problems. Everyone present is allowed to give their opinion from all their different perspectives around the wheel. The peace council's pur-

---

[3] Carol Jacobs, Cayuga Bear Clan Mother, 1995. Presented to the United Nations. Published in the *Akwesasne Notes,* New Series, Fall 1995, vol. 1, nos. 3 and 4, pp. 116–117.

pose is not to condemn, but to evince a true natural justice that is expressed essentially through conciliation and amending opposition. Corruption has no place in a peace council, although this is a predominant reality in most Western judicial systems today. Among the Iroquois, *Gai Eneshah Go' Nah*, or the Great Law of Peace, creates societies based on principles of equity, justice, and the "power of good minds." The condemnation based on God-fearing values that is at the core of many antiquated legal systems does not help release the reactive guilt of individuals, but, on the contrary foments more defiance and ignorance toward the same system. In his profound maxim, Benito Juarez, an important indigenous Mexican president of the last century stated: "Among the nations as among individuals, the respect to other's legitimacy is Peace."[4]

When a specific law is not respected by a member or a group, a council is called and those in question are first asked to explain the reason for their infringement. No law can be above anyone and no law can be imposed on anyone without a proper comprehension of its enactment. A law is essentially a model, not a dogmatic edict. In any litigation, therefore, an elementary debate becomes necessary in order to judge carefully if those who transgressed the law were in the right. Perhaps that particular law requires further improvement. If the transgressors (chiefs or individuals) do not present any solid justification for their disturbance among the community, their attention is called three times by the chiefs and their clans. Eviction from the circle can be their ultimate fate if, after three times, no improvement is shown.

In its decision-making, a community vote is considered valid when a margin of 66 percent, or a two-thirds majority exists. Fifty-one percent is not weighty enough to shift the balance on one side or another. In this case, the chiefs must help bring further understanding.

A distinct disinterested and unprejudiced judicial system of natural laws based on a cosmic understanding of its inherent principles becomes absolutely essential in expressing the consciousness of humanity. A guarantee of respectful and mutual cooperation of the people in the fulfillment of the universal principles is what ensures the

---

[4] Benito Juarez, "Manifest to the Nation," July 15, 1867, in *Historia De Mexico, Sexto Grado* (Subsecretaria de Educacion Basica y Normal, Col. Centro, Mexico DF, 1997), p. 43.

freedom of communities and allows each to exercise their rights and aspirations in accomplishing their tasks. This consolidates a true democracy within the genuine sense of community.

This consciousness entails an ability to hold, in a responsible way, our place within the council of our society. Speaking your truth in the council broadens clarity within the community of mind. Being apt to express your individual truth, you are, in like measure, apt to hear another's integrity without being disconcerted. The basic awareness of your truth, along with the space you must give to another's rightful expression, creates an inviting circle in which to grow into full consciousness, instead of being suppressed. Working toward these parameters within the community's context becomes the collective guide for impersonality beyond the emotive personality of ego.

The Council's Lodge manifests a mature place for bridging in fullness with your brothers and sisters. In the rainbow Lodge of nations, *the touching of the brothers and sisters* becomes a principal parameter. This is expressed as a capacity to open without any resistance, letting go of your personal concerns, your susceptibilities, frustrations, and feelings of having been offended. The circle must ostensibly expose a spirit place of *sharing strength*. Touching thus enriches the encounter within your unique learning, meeting together, ready to die like warriors in this moving experience. Because we all stand somewhere around the wheel, this meeting in the people's circle takes place at the central fire. This central fire is the empty zero, the spiraling void of the universe, and the emergence of the great mystery. As the meeting point, it is your responsibility to surmount the apprehension of emptiness, showing your capacity to lose yourself in the infinity of your true feeling. Only then, when everyone has acquired the strength to withstand the great void, can the circle be a most powerful one, in complete harmony with the great universal laws.

The role of mother chiefs is crucial, not only among their clan of women, but for the entire community. This cannot be forgotten. Every woman who sits in the council hoop represents the Earth spirit goddess, symbolized also as the great being in the central fire pit. Because women are the Earth, there is nothing more powerful on this planet then a circle of decided women. There is nothing, for instance, more powerful than a circle of pregnant women, because of the elemental forces residing within their wombs fostering life. When women hold hands in a true united manner, there is nothing on this planet that can rupture this circle, not even a group of resolute men. Generally speaking, this has been the fear of many men for thousands of years—that if women were to organize, communal ways would probably return and men's "plans" would be undermined. This fear has been induced in the people for centuries, expressed as a perverse intolerance toward the emancipation of women and the burning of witches, for example.

This principle that a circle of women is the most powerful hoop on this planet has revealed itself to be true, for I have seen this at work more than once. In 1990, the Council of Mohawk Mothers literally stopped an army from besieging Kahnawake on the Canadian Mohawk reservation. The native warriors clan of veterans, already in revolt, had decided to block the main bridges of Montreal, in an expression of solidarity for another Mohawk reservation, at Kanesatake, Oka, and as a protest against the government's possible takeover of Iroquois land at Oka, with the intent of making a golf course. The Canadian army, which had already encircled the protest a few days before, was approaching the reservation limits at Kahnawake to confront the armed warriors. The scene was quite tense and offensive. Then the "miracle" happened. A circle of mothers, from the League of Peace for the most part, resolved to intervene, standing together between the two armed groups, preventing the entrance of the army. The women held hands in a perfect circle, chanting and praying together. Confronted with this, the Canadian army had to stop their progress and withdraw definitively.

Another striking example of this inherent principle occurred more recently in Chiapas. In December 1997, at Acteal, Chiapas, forty-five pro-Zapatistas, unarmed native *campesinos*, were slaughtered by paramilitary groups armed by the federal government, primarily to destabilize the peace dialogue. Most of the dead were innocent women and children, shot in the back while praying in their temple. Shortly after the massacre, in response to international and civil pressure, and under the pretext of disarming the coercive paramilitary groups, the Federal army intruded upon various Zapatista communities to seize their weapons. Many civilians think that their primary intention was never to disarm the paramilitary, but rather to break the cease-fire agreements signed between the Zapatistas and the Mexican government in 1995. For the Zapatistas, who had not used their weapons since January 1994, thus respecting their part of the agreement, to remain armed signified their only guarantee against possible genocide and their only hope of ever asserting their claims. When the army made their entrance into many Indian communities of the jungle in December 1997 and Janaury 1998, they were met by unarmed women, with their babies on their backs, who kept the army and soldiers from proceeding further, waving their arms and shouting at them to go away. This forced the army to retreat from their villages, giving irrefutable great evidence that this principle, in action, is invincible.

THE CROW LODGE

The universal laws, principles of the Earth's plane, stream from the northwest door of sky and intelligence. The guardians of this door hold the universal laws represented in each direction. All the laws for the people enter through this gateway, from the cosmos into the Earth, resulting in the true marriage of the women's and the men's lodges. The guardians are called the crow chiefs, who are the primary educators of the ways of the Council.

Every council of people is assigned to a council of chiefs, to which they are deeply and directly connected. In the wheel of chiefs, there are eight seats, in accordance with each chief's potential and ability. It is the duty of every chief to learn from their role, thus consolidating their own place. Traditionally, the mother's council is composed of eight women, one for each of these eight position-directions. The men chief's lodge consists of seven men and one woman at the West.

When the two circles of Earth and Sky come together, each position is occupied by one man and one woman, except in the West, where two women sit. In some structures, these seats are filled by pairs, placing sixteen women in the Earth lodge and fourteen men and two women in the Sky Lodge. The presence of a woman in the Sky Lodge represents the entrance for the men into this Earth plane. Interestingly, I found this same council configuration among the Mongolians and the Northern Amerindians. The model exposed here is thus a synthesis.

The leaders, whether men chiefs or clan mothers, must hold a stimulating position toward the council. They are revered as men and women of vision. Depending on their personal power and respective

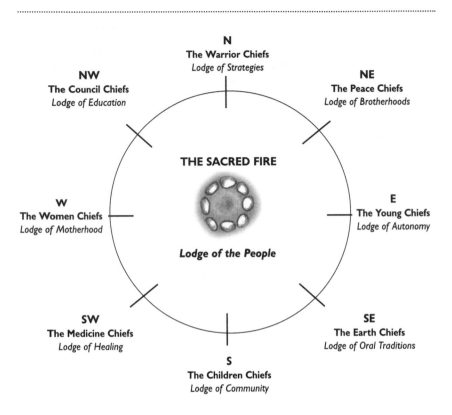

N
The Warrior Chiefs
Lodge of Strategies

NW
The Council Chiefs
Lodge of Education

NE
The Peace Chiefs
Lodge of Brotherhoods

THE SACRED FIRE

W
The Women Chiefs
Lodge of Motherhood

E
The Young Chiefs
Lodge of Autonomy

Lodge of the People

SW
The Medicine Chiefs
Lodge of Healing

SE
The Earth Chiefs
Lodge of Oral Traditions

S
The Children Chiefs
Lodge of Community

Figure 11. The Crow Lodge: Central Fire of the People.

talents, they are required to be convincing orators, lucid activists, always exposing the larger awareness to the people with explicit decisions based on sensitive information. They must never become involved personally, and are always expected to hold impersonality as their highest protocol. In this, they must teach people to emancipate their individual views and emotional involvements, so they may bring forward agreements that eventuate unity. They are expected to shake people when necessary, and furthermore, invariably to solicit reconciliation. They must listen and attend to their people's voice at any cost, and, in exchange, the people must respect their chiefs' integrity and validate their power of perception. When chiefs are not dedicated enough to their assignment with the clan, they must be called to attention three times, then, if necessary, asked to renounce their position.

Usually, a tribal leader is elected for a lifetime in order to bring forth his or her own vision. This maintains the possibility of making a true mark on this world with his or her people. Traditionally, the chiefs may change places within the wheel over the years, although it is rare and depends on their abilities. This allows them to bring their vision from another appropriate perspective.

1. In the South, the perspective of the children chiefs (always adults) consists of bringing the heart of the council (see figure 11). They must always open the gate for everybody to speak from their inner fire, their innocence. Here, the children chiefs stand as the teachers of the laws of equality for all, because this is the lodge of community. They represent the children. Their duty is to ensure that the laws are applied, thus respecting every voice.

2. In the Southwest, the place of shamans, the medicine chiefs own the lodge of healing for all the people. The shamans also teach the purpose laws within the community. In this very important aspect, they must inspire the people with an understanding of their medicines, sacred mission, and aspirations of all in the community.

3. In the West, the women chiefs represent the lodge of mothers and hold the last vote. It is the decision place of the Earth ways, the perspective of true reality where the principles of common sense must prevail. In the women's lodge and in the men's lodge, this place is always held by women.

4. The Northwest, the council chiefs stand at the crow place in the lodge of education. They are what we might call the politicians and activists of today. Their role as perfect arbitrators and educators resides in always opening the council with an understanding of natural justice and self-determination. They are not allowed to vote or to take any decision. Politicians should never make any decision, but only facilitate the exchange of discussion or conversation. The crow chiefs are the care keepers of the laws of natural justice.

5. In the North, the warrior chiefs must present directional aims to the people. They are the fighters and also the activists. They must protect the people, holding the war laws and arrows, exemplified as the laws of security. With their organizational skills, they also represent the

lodge of strategies. They must be in constant status quo, meaning they must never declare war, but must always be ready to fight if this is the people's decision.

6. At the Northeast sit the peace chiefs, keepers of the laws of the sacred and the ritualistic ceremonies. They are responsible for the unity of the brotherhoods and sisterhoods. They speak always for conciliation of opposition, and must never go to war. This is the lodge of brotherhoods, also called the lodge of mediation.

7. In the East, the young chiefs, or the fool chiefs, with their gift of clarity, teach humor of the spirit and unity of contradictions. They hold the principles of freedom and the laws of renewal within the souncil. They bring alternatives, always seeking new options. They encourage and advocate freedom of choice, liberty, and enlightenment of the collective vision. This is the lodge of autonomy of all the nations.

8. At the Southeast, the Earth chiefs are the storytellers, keepers of the lodge of oral traditions, preserving ancient traditions and the spirit of the ancestors' knowledge. They also stand as the keepers of human rights.

9. At the Center, no chief sits, but the people are represented at the central sacred fire of the nations. Here, the lodge of the people holds all the laws and no laws. Every chief must know how to recognize the spirit of the fire and must consult within its spiraling zero, the cosmic fire of the tree of life, the Underworlds and the Upperworlds, before pronouncing any statement. In this way, their minds must consider the heart of the Earth and heavens, together with the heart of the people.

Depending on the native traditions, the council is usually called by the northwest chief. The neutral crow chiefs should initiate by holding the talking stick, declaring the purpose of the meeting, and passing the talking stick in a clockwise manner, until it returns to the Northeast for a last allegation from the crow chiefs before the collective vote. In all types of councils, every chief's statement must be respected, as well as their ways of approaching the circle, as long as they show a high level of commitment. They are expected to be fully responsible for the place they hold.

Every chief has a voice in their respective clan and the council itself must also encounter its own voice in relation to the councils of other nations, especially if there is a central council representing the central fire within the nations. Traditionally, each particular council is assigned a cardinal direction and purpose, in the same way as a chief's position.

The crow chiefs, at the Northwest, have an interesting role. They represent the crow medicine, independent of their personal totem animals. Crows are excellent keepers of their tribe's nest, and are the main teacher of the councils traditional ways. Because crows are group-oriented animals, they have special ways of communicating among themselves within their specific clan. They show a great capacity for following specific, inherent laws within their flocks. Crows are territorial, thus the crow chiefs must develop a keen capacity for the protection of their council. They understand, more than others, the ways of relating to others in a community in an interdependent way, for their medicine symbolizes both female and male energies at the same time, expressing perfect balance. Therefore, the crow lodge represents the coming together of the men's and women's lodges in one. Another important aspect of the crow medicine is that they teach us about individual solitude, as well as about relating to the group. They are teachers of the necessity to keep one's particular essence and integrity within a community of people.

In every council, everyone in the circle stands equal to everyone else, always possessing the freedom of choice, the power of decision, which must be respected by all. No external person should oblige anyone to be part of the council. However, when you are part of a council, it is your choice to be responsible for your particular place. The day you are not adequate in relation to your responsibility, you must act conscientiously by conceding your position and leaving with honors. To pledge your participation in a council expresses your readiness to die as a warrior/ess and do everything possible for the purpose of the council. Another rule of action affirms that no council holds an obligation to keep an inactive and undependable member under its protection.

The major responsibility of every member is to acquire an awareness of how to hold the energy of the circle as a recipient of higher truth and wisdom, ensuring always its maximum incentive force. To attain this, every member must eliminate the tendency to focus solely on their own personal issues within the council, but must particularly center upon the larger collective vision of the circle.

The first motivation of every member, therefore, should reside in always holding unity as the primary objective within the council. In unity resides authentic individual and collective strength. How to maintain unity and restore it when endangered must be the major aim for all. Before conceiving your personal attainments, you must understand the aspiration of the whole. In this resides your realization as an individual. The vision that a warrior may receive for his or her life comes from the Earth and is, therefore, unavoidably linked to the dream of all other sisters and brothers. The expression of your personal vision can only exist as a manifestation within the larger council of the community. Doubting the council, your place, or the place of the others results in its debilitation and separation, and leads to major confusions. This does not mean that no one must question or propose possible improvements of the Council ways in light of their own position. This is not doubt, but enhancement toward genuine communion. And for this, *openness* is absolutely essential.

There are four major and absolute requirements for creating a strong circle of people, whatever the purpose and direction of your coming together might be.

SELF-RESPECT: To respect others you must learn true self-respect and integrity.

LOYALTY: This involves a deep commitment and understanding of the purpose of being together.

TRUTHFULNESS: This means not holding thoughts in the back of your mind that may create confusion or disturbing feelings in the long run. You must recognize your own mistakes, always, and express them in order to gain greater lessons of truthfulness.

DEEP LOVE FOR THE EARTH MOTHER: This is the most powerful and sacred obligation of all. The only major cause of internal dissension within a council comes when members start diverging from their collective purpose on Earth. If one of these four requirements is not met, by even one of the members, the council is doomed to dissolve or always to face internal conflicts. These precepts set the way for the true order required in every community. Order is not only external, it also encompasses divine order, the divine law of heaven and Earth, the very first law of the universe. Order begins within yourself. It is the power that allows you to create real changes. Order is located as a medicine center in your body at the crown center, where you receive the greater inflow from the Sky Lodge into the Earth in all the other centers within.

The concept of love among common people does not evoke the same understanding of love as it does for the rainbow warrior. True love must be disposed to reach far beyond the limitations of your self, even if you have to fight for this. This breakthrough consists of reaching beyond the ego. It is true love, having the courage to put your ego right in the middle of the central fire, to witness its beauty and its ugliness. This is *self-respect*–to differentiate between the false notions of your ego and the respect of your real spirit integrity. It is always preferable to provoke a fight out of love with someone who will not accept you or themselves. Most people are caught in an attempt to be too nice to others, unable to recognize when someone reaches out of love, even if it is in a brusque way. This shows that they are terrified of expressing their true feelings, of growing by exposing their selves. Being outwardly nice in a superficial (and often hypocritical) manner is not necessarily love. It may be pure cowardice. This is quite different from developing sound, courteous ways of relating to each other. The way in which it comes often expresses truth even straightforwardly. True love grants you the power to be prepared for everything, even the death of a friendship out of love, for only then is there no fear of fighting for the love of a friendship.

In a council, everybody has a responsibility to the circle of energy. Without making up any artificial goals, but by focusing on the predilection of coming together, your feeling of being in a circle must be experienced at an energetic level with the Earth. You will then naturally begin to journey to the true purpose of your council with all the others. This is envisioning the brotherhood and the sisterhood, *dreaming the Council ways,* where we have connected to each other in the womb of women and the being of men. The great quest for the council shield reveals itself to us and is made apparent to all. What is the true purpose of your particular council or community of people? Is it a healing council, a dreaming council, a teaching council, a justice council, a human rights council, a Moon or a Sun council? What is the council's vision that animates the purpose of coming together in a single united idea? Taking responsibility toward this vision must offer a place for enhanced growth. As an organic process, you must be moving along with its maturation. You have a responsibility toward growth. The Council ways require a clear understanding of where each individual stands on the wheel, the wall that is faced, your place of origin, what you have gained. All of this constitutes your uniqueness. If, at any point, a member restrains from growing, believing that he or she already knows it all, then the energetic circle is hindered. Once you dedicate to the Council ways and relate to the community, in whatever form, you are inevitably connected, even during your sleep, in a permanent awareness—especially when the true dreaming takes place.

In every organization, whether small or large, confrontation and challenges will always appear as incredible opportunities for true meeting. When there is confrontation, there is meeting, a possible coming together or a learning. When one or two sides decide to be enemies for the rest of their lives, they fall off the medicine wheel and no longer follow the path of life. It is a natural duty, therefore, to invite other people to the central fire where true meeting can occur, people from all other directions, from all differences. It is unrealistic, nevertheless, to expect other people to come all the way in your direction, to ask them to understand you, unless you will also walk to perceive their place. At the fire center, the true sharing of each one's perspective can take place on a neutral ground. When a member refuses to proceed to the center, the whole wheel is obstructed. The wheel, overweighted on one side, starts shifting, to the point that everybody may fall from it altogether! When there is a problem of communication between two people or two clans, it affects the whole circle. Of course, we are all interrelated, all of us, revealing one of the deepest laws of the universe.

When you remove yourself from the natural circle of life, the awesome forces of the universe may defeat you. When individuals or groups refuse to hear about other's learning or discover their specific perspective on the wheel, they enter into a direct fight. When they agree to share, to enlarge their minds, a larger representation, one not envisioned before, is conceived. In this resides dreaming together.

As we have seen, in your life you are right now, facing the specific challenges, walls, and obstacles of your particular position. Meeting with others at the center is, therefore, often difficult in the larger scheme of things. Only if you have encountered and opposed all the positions, challenges, and walls around the wheel and reached the center within, can you perceive the minds and hearts of everyone, as a true chief. "To touch within invulnerability" is what is necessary to meet others. A chief at the center of the wheel holds the power to bring everyone together in justice and clarity, by seeing the heart of each man, feeling the womb of each woman, and hearing the cry of each child, touching brothers and sisters beyond self-defensiveness. Usually people are, in fact, afraid to touch. They prefer to remain "untouched within their vulnerability," self-absorbed in the little problems of their daily lives.

The most transcendent principle within the Council laws is inclusiveness. This is opposite to individualism. Many people in the Western world carry a long tradition that has lost the understanding of how to live with community ways. To restore this sense of being in council, you must first be able to sit in silence and enjoy the presence of everyone in the circle. Genuine touching implies just being who you are, allowing yourself to cry, fight, laugh, and grow. Open, naked, and, above all, with a rooted sense of humor, in a council you must not fear being straightforward and taking a blow to your self-pride. It is simply to be human. It is to accept this in others, as well, in impersonal and unconditional love. How many live in permanent fear of being attacked, of saying something wrong, of being the target of unpleasantness, of what others may say? All of this masking, justifying, evading, and lying hinder the meeting and touching of others and it discourages creating a sane space for serene truthfulness.

An important Council law specifies that members cannot bring their personal issues within the council more than three times. They can be given advice that may be helpful, but if they raise the same issue three times, they are asked to resolve their issue, or leave, until they find resolution within. Sometimes resolution of a personal or collective problem may occur in the circle in the form of major breakthroughs, and, often, no other healing than this is required.

Breakthroughs always have to do with truthfulness, the first basic touching. If you hold yourself back from affirming your truth, you create unhealthiness in the long run, even if your "truth" is based on ego stuff. How will you ever differentiate the truth of your spirit from the truth of your ego if you do not express it? It is your exposed vulnerability that will confer on you invulnerability. In our ways, this concept of vulnerability is opposed to the general understanding that vulnerability is synonymous with disadvantage or weakness. An Earth council suggests the opposite, providing a safe space-womb in which to express your inner feelings. This is, in fact, a requirement for joining the Council wheel, to be open to this safe space.

Projections are frequently excellent mirrors to place in the center, for they are based on ego expectations. To deal with your projections alone may result in entering an unending labyrinth of complexities. It requires strong discernment in order to understand them, both for the subject and the object of the projections. In a Council context, however, the looking glass is magnified, enabling everyone to examine from various perspectives the prevailing misinterpretations that are leading to all sorts of internal distortions. The Council guideline, stating that everything must be discussed in the circle, prevents you from crossing the council hoop to personally confront your opponent. Rather you must seek understanding within the hoop. In this resides the great shield, as a neutral ground on which differences may meet.

Every conflict contains the seeds of an agreement that should finally prevail. In our native minds, we know that, even if the other brothers and sisters are not entirely aware of it, whatever we are living on a personal level may affect them. Immediately calling the council at any sign of an important problem that may involve the greater circle should therefore stand as your major motivation, based on the precept that the sense of community comes first.

For example, a woman may seek advice in her council of women about a serious conflict with her husband. If, after some personal attempts there has been no solution within the couple, then her man may be asked to meet her in the women's lodge. He must accept. If no resolution is reached in the women's lodge, then she must ask to meet him in the men's lodge, exposing her situation to the men. If there is still no resolution in light of the people's advice, separation may be inevitable, but only after this whole process has been completed. Separation is always an unfortunate resolution, but in it is much learning. It is more likely, however, that at some point during this extensive process, clarity, and reconciliation will come. These rules offer a healthy way to deal with any individual challenge, within a group context.

In a situation I recently witnessed a man who refused even to enter the lodge of his women. His unwillingness, being a mirror, meant that she constantly had to go into his lodge in their daily lives. This is clearly unjust. If a man accepts to enter the women's lodge, it does not mean he will unavoidably lose the "battle" in front of the other women. Surely, other women may stand up to defend him, if they feel he has been betrayed or is right. In the same way, a woman may receive thoughtful consideration from other men when she enters his lodge. This is a clear example of how the two foundation circles may serve a greater purpose in enlarging consciousness.

The great laws of the council emanate from the reflection of the larger cosmic circle of love also dwelling within humans. The circle of universe lives as an immense council of planets and star beings, with its micro-expression inside you, marrying one circle to another circle and mating in perfect synergy. In the Council form, this marriage must also occur inside and outside you, with others.

Whatever frustrations or difficulties you may have within the council, expressed as resistance or lack of openness, or difficulty hearing what the circle has to say, reflect a mirror to learn in the process of your relationship to the circle itself. When you have let go of all resistance, you can then truly meet, unaffected and independent of how others are. Through this internal aperture, your awareness of a situation, your apologies or pledging, renew the greater flow of harmony within the circle. This feeds the heart of every member. This feeds the heart of the council.

Chiefs and members in the council must assist each other in an interrelation of absolute determination that ensures a perfect strategy of organization. This is the responsibility of everyone. Everyone must fulfill their tasks at every level, thus creating an effective, organic infrastructure, synchronized in an impeccable equilibrium. The tremendous moral and spiritual support that a council provides manifests one of the highest and strongest protections you can own in life.

Finally, an understanding that touching, the ability to hear (with the ears of your spirit), is an essential ingredient to reach impersonality, to reach the first sense of relating to others, is the greatest lesson of the council. To sit and listen to others in the circle, without judging, comparing, interpreting, or interfering, to listen as plainly as that, requires true touching. This means that you are *inside* what you are listening to. *You touch.* Many cannot truly hear other people's problems, since they are so tired of hearing their own minds that nothing more can get in. In the Council way, you are naturally and gently compelled to consider each other by the circle itself. The importance of this respectful silence toward others lies in the awareness within that dwells at the root of truthfulness.

The last time I traveled to the United States, away from the extinguished volcano of "my" Third World, I was amazed to observe some Americans, apparently so much more "educated" than the Mexican Indians with whom I live, being so "noisy" as they talked. I was in a restaurant in Santa Fe, New Mexico, with a good friend of mine I had not seen for years. When we first sat down, we were practically alone and we started our conversation very quietly. At one point, an hour later, as the restaurant gradually became full, we realized that we were literally screaming in order to hear each other—screaming our profound thoughts of our very spirited conversation, because everyone around was talking so loudly. I was struck very clearly and quite abruptly by the contrast to public places in southern Mexico, where people talk quietly and mindfully when with others. After screaming like that for a while, we realized what we were doing, and just stopped, laughing at the ridiculousness of this boisterous situation! Apparently, no one else noticed how disturbing this was, each in his own little, loud world of thoughts, words, and chatter. The waitress came and, about to remove my plate (which I had not yet finished), shouted at me in a very straight, almost irritated, tone, "Ma'am, are you still working on that?" I was perplexed! On top of the cacophony, eating in this country is not about enjoyment at all, but is considered "work," reflecting yet another stressful disease of these modern societies. I am sure this is not the only restaurant in the United States that displays these "dissonant" characteristics, for it seems to be a widespread cultural phenomenon.

My modest story reflects how many people possess no awareness of the silence within. They are afraid of their *emptiness* (of their zero within), of their own internal empty space, because, when they are quiet, they feel awkward. The ego is restless, afraid of truly touching the peacefulness, in life, in death, in emptiness, in fullness, in impersonal love, in honoring the freedom and the space of others, in *stillness*. But silence is the most nourishing place in which to touch spirit and the awareness of the inner council of chiefs. Working, an important value of the American society, has unfortunately become a big national escape, not attuned to natural time (and even less to Indian time!). The "business" of many (disconnected from the real notion of work) reflects the irritability of the individuals in such a society. You cannot hear each other. You have to talk loudly to be heard. You can't feel each other, which leads you to be completely cut off from real feelings.

Another observation that strikes me each time I cross the border is that most people begin every other sentence with, "I feel this," or "I feel that." In a more traditional, earthy society, people do not express themselves this way. We just feel—that's it. We do not have a need to always refer to what we feel in our mind. This is a reflection of how hard it may be to feel in a society in which you have to scream to be heard, where people are compelled to live in their heads, with no time to truly feel, isolated from one another, where the guilt of experiencing the empty space within must be replaced by an appearance of working trepidation. On the other hand, Indians just feel, expressing thoughts in a most simple, quiet, impersonal, and practical manner, without forcing the moment. There is no need to talk of our feelings all the time. To feel them is enough, as the first touching toward self-respect. In any event, words will never thoroughly reveal the grandeur of sentiments. My "restaurant example" may be simple, but it exposes how the Council ways begin in the very trivial activities of our lives, that we can realize the circle of people within and without and develop mindfulness of energies everywhere. It starts there. The council of people is already around us.

Once you find inner quietness, you must challenge it in adversity, along with everything else. If you can maintain this sense of perfect silence anywhere, without having to go to the Himalayas, even in the worst conditions of life, then it is truly yours forever. Then can you realize your place within the great circle you form at every moment, even when sitting at square tables, in the square room of a restaurant.

THE COUNCIL OF ORIGINS

Here is the origin, when the creation of humans and what should penetrate in the flesh of man was ordered. So the Progenitors and the Creators, whose names were Tepeu and Gucumatz, said: "The times of dawning have come, the task must be finished and now must rise those who will sustain and nourish us, the illuminated sons, the civilized servants; now must emerge the existence of humanity on the surface of Earth."

So the Creators gathered and celebrated a Council in the obscurity of the night. Then they searched and discussed, they reflected and thought. This way they brought forth to the light their decisions and they found of what the flesh of humans should be made. This was just before the Sun, the Moon, the Stars appeared over the Creators and the Progenitors. From Paxil and Cayala, they called the yellow and white corncobs. The names of the animals who brought the food were: Yac, the Wild Cat, Utiu, the Coyote, Quel, the Parrot, Hoh, the Crow. These four animals gave the good news to the yellow and white cobs and they show them the way to Paxil.

So the Creators found the food which conceived the human flesh, the created man. This was his blood, from the cobs was made the blood of humans. This is how the corn entered in the work of the Ancestors.

And the Creators were filled with joy for they had found a beautiful land, filled with delights and abundant white and yellow corn, abundant in cacao and pataxte and countless tropical fruits of zapotes, jocotes, nances, matasanos and honey. There was a profusion of delicious aliments in the villages called Paxil and Cayala.

There was food of every kind, small plants and tall ones. The animals showed the way. Then grinding the yellow and white corncobs, Ixmucane, the grandmother goddess, prepared the nine sacred beverages and from these came the strength and the flesh of humans, and with these drinks, they created the muscles and vigor of humans.

Then the Progenitors discussed the creation and formation of our first mother and father. From yellow and white corn, their flesh was made. From a corn masa, their arms and legs were created. Exclusively of corn, the flesh of the first four men was given form.

The humans were then gifted with intelligence; they could see to the place their sight extended, they achieved the knowledge of all that there is in the world. When they contemplated, they could see all there is around them as well as in the Sky dome and the round face of Earth. They could see all that is occult as well as the whole world, even at a distance, without having to move. Their wisdom was so great and their sight reached the forests, the rocks and lakes, the seas, mountains and valleys. They were admirable men, Balam-Quitze, Balam-Acab, Mahucutah and Iqui-Balam, the four first men.

After they had seen it all in the world, they expressed gratitude and offered their praise to the Creators: "In truth, we thank you two and three times, you have given us a mouth and a face, we talk, we hear, think and walk; we feel perfectly and we know what is close and what is far away. We also see what is big and small in the Heavens and on Earth. We offer our thanks for having been created, and to have been given a being, oh, our grandmother, oh, our grandfather."

So the four men who knew it all, examined the four corners of the vault of the Sky and the face of Earth.

But the Creators didn't like what they heard from the four humans: "It is not good what our creatures said. They know everything, the big and the small."

So the Progenitors held Council again: "What will we do with them? Their view should only reach what is near, they should only see a bit of what is the face of Earth, not all. What they say is not good, should they also be Gods as we are? What if they do not procreate when the Sun rises? Should they equal us, we, their authors, we who can see at great distances, we who can encompass and know it all?"

This is what they said, the Heart of Heavens, Huracan, Chipi-Cuculha, Raxa-Caculha, Tepeu, Gucumatz, Ixpiyacoc, Ixmucane, the gods and goddesses, the Creators and the Progenitors. So they immediately proceeded to change the nature of their work and their creatures.

So the Heart of Heavens, Hurracán, placed a misty veil (one for each direction) on their eyes which became as clouded as when it blows on the mirroring surface of the Moon. Their eyes were veiled and they could only see what was close, only this was clear to them now.

This is how their wisdom and all the knowledge of the four men, the origin and principle of the human race was hidden. This is how they were formed and created by our grandfathers, from the Heart of Heavens and the Heart of the Earth.

Then, their wives existed. The creators made them very carefully. So in the Dream, their women arrived, absolutely beautiful, to the side of Balam-Quitze, Balam-Acab, Mahucutah and Iqui-Balam.

So when the four men awoke, the four women, principal ladies, were there and the hearts of men were filled with joy. Together, they engender the small council tribes and the large ones which is the origin of the red people. Many were created then and in obscurity they multiplied. The Sun and the light were not born when they engendered.

So together they waited with anxiety for the aurora. They elevated their pleas to the Heavens: "Hear us, do not leave us, you who are in the Heavens and in the Earth, Heart of Heavens and Heart of Earth. Give us our lineage, our descent. May the Sun walk and may there be light. Come, great aurora, arise. Give us good and straight paths. May the people have peace and be prosperous."

This is what they said while invoking the arising light, the coming of the dawn. At the same time they watched the sunrise, they contemplated the Morning Star, the Great Star precursor of the Sun, which shines in the vault of the Sky and on the surface of Earth, and which illuminates the steps of the created humans, so there may be order.[5]

---

[5] Inspired from a version of *Popol Vuh: The Mayan Book of Council* (Mexico City, DF: Fondo de Cultura Economica, 1952), pp. 103–110.

13
TOTALITY

THE RENAISSANCE OF THE
TRUE HUMANS

When I was a teenager, I rejected the brown color of my skin. I went to Europe for a couple of years and decided I would "educate" myself, which of course didn't really work in this Western sense, considering my strong roots. I found it was impossible for me to adapt anywhere and I just ended living with the Gypsies in southern France. There I was, in a transient home, in this vast civilized Europe. From there, I went to Asia for another cycle and then back home to Canada, in 1984, where I decided simply to return to the Mohawk people, to learn further from my native ways. Among many things, I observed, at the traditional Long House, how elders and children (now learning Mohawk at the boarding school) spoke together in the native language and that most of us adults, from two or three generations apart, didn't understand what they were saying. It is a great relief to know that our tongue is coming back and will not be lost. I decided then to start learning Mohawk, which of course was not easy. I found a Mohawk language book and by myself started to learn a few words. It happened that the very first word that I learned, the one that struck me the most, was *Ongwhe Onwhe,* which means the true humans, or the real people. This is not a word commonly used in conversations with Mohawks. It refers to the true people, the Indian people, the *Ongwhe Onwhe.* This word has stayed deep in my mind along my path since then, like an *Ashta,* a soft wind whispering within, in my times of spiritual despair.

Shortly after I started to learn Mohawk, the great spirit's signs sent me to Mexico, where I ended up among the Maya. I had no one with whom to practice the Mohawk tongue, but this word has followed me through all these years. It was as if I had started learning Mohawk primarily to find this word, *Ongwhe Onwhe.*

One day, in Chiapas, as I was hiking with my Maya companion in the mountains, we found two old books thrown away on the side of a path. This is something truly unusual here, because of the scarcity of books among natives, and because people don't usually throw such things away. These books were written both in Tzotzil (Maya dialect) and Spanish. The title of one of them was *Nichimal Vinik,* translated in Spanish as the "Flowering Man" or the "True Human." Needless to say, I became highly interested to read and compare the Mohawk concept with what the Maya envisioned as the "Real People."

So this notion, both from the Maya and the Mohawks, had become a big part of my life, representing a way to be true to myself, springing and thundering from very deep in my soul.

Six years later while I was reading the book, *Return of the Bird Tribes*, the word *Ongwhe Onwhe* appeared again, though this time not to my surprise. This word has a special resonance to my spirit. It is more than a word describing something. Its expression whispers in the winds the return of our Indian blood. It insinuates the return of the Red Lodge. Its sound moves as the spirit. It is as if, when I pronounce it, the entire soil vibrates within my very soul. *Ongwhe Onwhe* and *Nichimal Vinik* convey more than a concept. These words carry an entire way of being, a path of integrity, the purpose to fight to become true humans, true warriors, to take responsibility with the clearest mind and the strongest heart. These words tremble as a pure frequency linked to my ancestors, to all the native people, to the true humans. These words, the passwords to the soul, arise not only as an expression, but as a reality. Within them is heard the return of the Bird Tribes. *Ongwhe Onwhe* is murmuring, talking of dreaming the ancient Councils, whispering with strength not to forget and not to lose hope.

Years after this, in January 1994, this voice of the true men and true women, *los hombres y mujeres verdaderos*, reappeared right in front of my eyes, in a local Mexican newspaper of Chiapas called *Tiempo*, in the words of subcommander Marcos in his very first communiqués, with the exact same consonance of my own vision. It was the Red Voice rustling, as a spokesperson for the native Zapatistas, this time loudly enough for the whole world to hear.

> *"When the EZLN [Zapatista Army for National Liberation] was only a shadow crawling between mist and darkness of the mountain, when the words of Justice, Liberty and Democracy were only this: words. A scarce dream that the elders of our communities, true guardians of the voice (word) of our dead, have given us in the exact time in which the day leaves the passage to the night, when bitterness and death began to grow in our chests, when there was nothing else than despair.*
>
> *When the times repeated themselves, without any way out, without any doors, without any mornings, when everything was as unjust as*

it was, than spoke the True people, those without faces, those who walk in the night, those who are mountains, and they said:

"It is the reason and will of the good man and good woman to search and find a better way of governing the people and ourselves, what is good to others is good to all. But the voices of the smallest should not stay silent, but they must hold their place in waiting when the mind and the heart be shared in common and with the same will among all. This way the people of the true men and true women will grow internally and will become greater, and there is no external strength that can break them and take their steps toward other paths.

"It has always been our ways that the will of the majority be shared also in the hearts of the commanding men and women. It has always been with the will of the majority that the one who commands should follow in his or her path. If he or she would walk away from the reason of the people, the heart in command was to be changed for one that would obey. This is how our strength was born in the mountain, the one who governs must obey if he or she is truthful, the one who obeys must govern with the shared heart of the true men and true women. Another word came from the far away so this government could be named and this word was 'Democracy,' this path which is ours, the path walked much before the words walked."

Those who walk in the night talked: "And we see that the path of the governments is not the road for all, we see that it is a few that now govern and they command without obeying, they command commanding. And in between themselves, they pass on the power of governing without listening to the majority. And the word which comes from the far away said that they govern without democracy, without the people's voice and we see that this leads to the gate of our pain which is the cause for the sadness of our dead. And we see that those who govern commanding must go away so there can be again reason and truth in our soil. And we see what we must change and that those who command obeying should rule to name this government "democracy," what is good for all is also good for the few.

And the men without face continued to talk:

"This world is another world, the reason and the will of the true men and true women does not govern yet, few we are and forgotten we are, above us walk our dead, despised, we are small and our voice is subdued, it has been a long time that silence inhabits our homes,

but now the hour has come for us to talk our heart and other hearts, from the night and from the soil must come our dead, those without faces, those from the mountain, may they dress of warriors so their voice be heard, and may they become silent again and return to the night and to the Earth.

. . . . The men without faces talked this way, there was no fire in their hands and their words were clear and without duplicity. Before the day overcomes again the night, they left and their word stayed alone in the soil: "Ya Basta!" [that is enough!][1]

Dreaming the ancient ways of the Council is also the return of the voice of the ancient brotherhoods and sisterhoods that once inhabited this very continent thousands of years ago, when people lived in harmony, sharing the true knowledge, when the Red people of this turtle continent were *Ongwhe Onwhe,* when all the people would gather in the largest councils, often holding hundreds of people, when they formed the camp circles around the ways of the true chiefs. This is all in the Earth. The memory is there. The Earth remembers and wishes to talk. It is talking now. Do you hear it, in the Earth?

Energy cannot be destroyed and the prayers and ceremonies of the Red people in those times, before the war between Indians much before the Conquest, were very powerful, for everyone understood their meaning and everyone joined their spirits in the most powerful communities that have ever existed. These prayers are there and rising from the Earth now. This is why, everyday, there are more people seeking the native, or shamanic, ways. The pull is very strong. The sounds of the drums are everywhere in this America. They are chanting intensively their return. During the devastating conquest of the three Americas, prayers and pacts were made among natives to preserve these ways—powerful covenants, pledging that one day in future reincarnations and times, those native souls (as Bird Tribes) would return, remembering the Wheel ways and assisting others to recall. These pacts are now being fulfilled in the voices of this long turtle land, from north to south, in the uprising consciousness of the *Ongwhe Onwhe* and the

---

[1] Sub-commander Marcos, EZLN (Ejercito Zapatista de Liberacion Nacional–Zapatista Army for National Liberation), *Tiempo* (San Cristobal de Las Casas, Chiapas, Mexico), February 2, 1994, p. 1.

return of the plumed serpent, rising cosmic snake from the Earth in all Americas.

A few years ago at Summer Solstice, my Council organized a wheel connection ceremony through which four wheels in faraway places in the United States and Mexico, connected themselves to our central crystal wheel in Chiapas at the exact same time (for a total of five wheels). The ceremony took much preparation for all the five councils (natives and non-natives). It included a whole day of prayers, fasting, and sweat lodge ceremonies, at a distance, but all at the same time. The intent was to make an energy bridge between the various groups already attuned to these ways, and lines of energy supporting each other, both from below the Earth and from the rainbows of light through the sky. Above all, we sought to call peace, healing, and resolution for this beautiful, yet deeply wounded area of the world in which I live, Chiapas. Apparently, the ceremony felt very powerful to all the other councils, who shared their comments the next day with me through the World Wide Web (the other one). What was most interesting for me, however, was to observe the "course of action" of my central crystal cluster (measuring two-and-a-half feet in diameter) to which all the drumming and prayers of the other four councils were directed, through their own central wheel stone. At the time of the wheel connection, the focus down here was definitively very intense. The day after the ceremony, my central cluster, extremely clear until now, started creating a slight rusty color. This rusty effect increased continually for one whole month. When it first appeared, I was a bit concerned for my beautiful central cluster. Later in a "fit," I decided to scrub this rust out with a hard brush, bio-degradable detergent, and water. I went to enter my wheel, but was stopped in the act, when the cluster, real companion of my everyday life, started *talking* to me. It said that this newly created rust was an expression of tears, *tears of blood*, grieving and being released through this amazing cluster.

Through the awakening of our five wheels by and from the Earth, it had awakened ancient buried wheels from the passage of energy from Chiapas and New Mexico, all the way up to Maine. It uncovered ancient energy wheels lost in the times when many natives were forced to abandon their sweet ways. This "oxidation" was no more than a powerful healing for these buried wounds, now having a place to express their grief. Needless to say, I gladly desisted from my very bad idea of scrubbing the crystal, and learned to love the healing reddish-brown pain in my cluster—a pain that I have felt myself so many times in my own bones, all through my life. I was also told that the rust would fade away after a full solar year, which amazingly it did, once some of these ancient awakened pains had been released.

The ancient native ones are truly returning in these times, not only for the Red people, but for all those who can *hear* the Earth—all those whose nights are inspired by the true song of their lives. To those who might object to this, I say: Why is it that, since the late 1980s in various states in the US where, not long ago, it was forbidden by law for native people to play their drums and practice their religion (still considered as dark magic), there are today people of all colors, especially from White roots, telling me how they have become very excited at the prospect of a new drum they may buy or make, asking me to teach them native drumming? It is because, now, people sense this return, consciously or not. One must be really closed and ungrounded not to receive the flows of the Earth itself, to understand and be open to these truths.

Independent of your color, the great vision of true humans is dreaming your inner council, the one that lives within as your spiritual guide, the one that abides within and without you, the one that inspires your lucid dreams. These are the guides of your inner council who send you signs on your arduous path, those who induce in you these feelings of being unsatisfied with the world as it is, who make you feel this pressure in your heart, this universal sadness for the desecration of nature (to the point that you may not know why you are crying, but know that it is not for yourself). Your inner council of chiefs are those who allow you to climb the clouds with prayers, and to embrace the whole cosmos. This is the council that dwells within each one of us.

In this process of hearing the Earth, you will dream in the wheel of revelation, the sacred medicine wheel of the people, in all the four directions, starting first with the **South**, the place of children. You will reeducate the child within you as a spontaneous, growing self, heal the child within, and free it from all your wounds and traumas of the past, the resentment that most people carry all their lives. Then, the dark hole within you will be filled and there will be a place of light to regenerate vitality in your body, to pursue the spirit that requires the inner power of life. In most native societies, children are taught to play in silence and to be mindful of adults around them. We are not treated as children, but as little *Ongwhe Onwhe*, as small adults with a potential to dream the vision of our becoming. We are taught at a young age to know our place in the community of people and to respect it. The first step toward dreaming the council is thus education in sound principles of life and an understanding that the South magic is in the little, very ordinary movements of life. We must be mindful of these and observe them. This starts at home.

In the **West**, dreaming the council is where you meet the other Self, your counterpart, as a male or a female warrior. It is also the meeting of the universe, as sexual energy living within you, involving your most intimate being, intrinsically linked to the expression of your spirit. Sex should be considered sacred. It is a spiritual expression far beyond egoistic satisfaction. In the mating of *Ongwhe Onwhe*, of a man and a woman, there must be a true merging of spirits, of Earth and sky in freedom, total beauty, and perfect vision. The act of sex should journey the true warrior and warrioress to the depth of love in the womb of Earth and the heights of the light in the sky, at the same time. Most people "make love" without truth, without real power, out of fear of shadows. They don't make love to life itself. They will never meet in the act of love, one of the most spirited and profound gestures of life. Only the true humans discover that, in the act of love, life and death mate in perfect synergy.

In the **North**, you learn to dream the council in relation to the community. In the native traditions, this is symbolized as a rite of passage throughout life. The first rite of passage is the birth ceremony, as you leave your mother's womb to enter the life womb of the family. At age 8, the rite of passage is the ceremony of being weaned from the family, being presented now to the third womb, that of the community. At age 13, boys are usually sent for their Vision Quest and girls to the Moon Lodge. At 13, you leave the safe womb of the community to enter the fourth womb of the great mystery. This prepares the young, warrior adolescent to meet the tests of life. Without this, adolescents may undergo a major crisis, or even become lost under the Dark Mentalist's influences or dark forces, for they have not been prepared to meet fears in the solitude of the Vision Quest. The Vision Quest manifests to spirits and the universe that you are ready to receive the true vision of your life. One cannot be a true human without a true vision of inspiration given by the Earth as the root of life.

In the **East**, with the inspired vision, you meet the Sun lodge as a rainbow warrior, in the gathering of races of all colors and the unification of the different minds of people, and in your own community as well. This is called the killing of your true vision onto this world, making it come true. Rainbows are the myth of Earth. They are the visions of the future, enlightenment beyond false illusions. In simplicity, you eliminate from your life and your community what is not true to the collective Self. You fulfill the rainbow bridge toward a perfect society.

To create a true community of people, to become *Ongwhe Onwhe*, *Nichimal Vinik*, and *Nichimal Antze*, the flowering man and flowering woman, you must return to being a true human, one of tolerance, of clear purpose and powerful vision. The major aim is to find totality of being emerging with all that you are from all directions. Totality is the growth of your spirit in all its essence and the expression of your deepest divine intelligence stored within the most ancient memory of being a human. *Totality* is a medicine center located above your crown center at the eighth center, or the star. When activated, this center allows you to remember your Earth walk, the one that has been unfolding for eons. The road, when clear, guides you toward your purpose in the community.

Toward the fulfillment of this aim, it is imperative that you realize and conquer all the pitfalls and negative entities along your path to spiritual sanity. An *Ongwhe Onwhe* will encounter more than a dark spirit in the quest, wanting to keep you from growing in light. As we saw, these dark spirits, called the Dark Mentalists, have developed the power to subdue individuals with terror through the lowest frequency of human mind energy. Being of base frequency themselves, whether incarnated physically on this plane or not, they seek primarily to keep humanity from pursuing sensible self-growth. Under repression of fear, they maintain humans in the slavery of the Undwerworlds and the house of vices.

The Dark Mentalists, at whatever level they may be, will cause all sorts of forceful distractions, causing sincere seekers to desist from their spiritual path by creating a powerful internal struggle against the true self. Most well-intentioned seekers, as they start their true path, will irremediably confront themselves with a period of life in which they can seemingly never obtain a moment of quietness and tranquillity to meditate and develop themselves in a more spiritual plane. This occurs when their spiritual awakening is just beginning and, therefore, "crossing" the band of frequency of the Dark Mentalists in an attempt to reach another inward level. To grow spiritually, it is quite imperative that you go through their dark influences, learn what they are, and overcome them. This is what they have created, these dark spirits—a band of vicious frequency that maintains humanity in indifference and lethargy to the world's doom. It will be a hard struggle for those who wish the spiritual betterment of our living conditions. Even the most sincere seeker may even abandon the pursuit of something true. These dark forces have developed deceitful strategies, to the point of instilling in a seeker a sense of spiritual satisfaction that is antagonistic to the true spirit quest. Satisfaction and complacency is a major foe to the real *Ongwhe Onwhe*, because it is dissatisfaction that impels us to look for the true food of spirit.

Their targets are mostly people in power or positions of leadership who are able to reach a large number of people—those who wish to make true revolution—for these dark forces exploit the weakest part of the human character. This was how the high priest, Kukulcan, was defeated by the smoking obsidian mirror. This obsidian mirror also directs dark mental energy toward vulnerable teenagers. Sex, alcohol, drugs, violence, and pornography are induced subconsciously in them through a telepathic influence, keeping them from becoming true adults. And it is not only adolescents who are immersed in their influence. Unfortunately, dark spirits are everywhere on this planet.

Because their frequency is so low and heavy, they often seem more prevalent than the true beneficial and protective spirits, who can genuinely guide us without coercing us in any way. Because it seems easier to be drawn by the vices of humanity and personal weaknesses than to strive toward becoming true people, it takes much courage to withstand, at every corner of your life, the attacks of the Dark Mentalists. To keep the integrity of your pure soul and overcome their unenlightened appearances, despite irresistible people and dreadful situations on your path, is a major trial. They are seemingly invincible, with implacable psychic practices. One of their current practices consists of infiltrating some dream frequencies and using sexual energy to create illnesses and even kill the dreamer. Fortunately, their power is not omnipotent. Only the seeker who has made a strong and solid commitment to reach full spiritual sanity will be endowed with the capacity to traverse this dark field without harm. Beyond this, in the climbing of the upper branches, these dark lords will never affect you again, even if they attempt to target you with their terrible attacks. The difference resides in the fact that you have developed the inward means to overcome their aggression.

To overthrow this low frequency that is constantly seeking to suppress the spiritual awakening of humanity, you must learn from this enemy, its territory, its tactics. You cannot see the light without knowing the darkness. You cannot know what is truth, if you do not know what lying is. No one, therefore, can awaken spiritually and morally without a cognizance of these surrounding dark forces, the shadow side, planting terror at all levels of the society, seeking only to undermine all possibility of the true elevation of humanity. You must banish the ways of terror on this planet, at all levels at which these may express themselves. This is the only purpose of the *Ongwhe Onwhe*—to recognize and fight them by planting seeds of light in the world.

One of the major aims of the dark entities is to scare people in their guts. At the very moment you give in to dismay, they have won the war over you. Because their influences are so predominant, most people often choose not to walk toward a true life and make true changes in society, for fear of having to meet these negative and obscure beings. They prefer a boring contented life of comfortable routine, never asking too many questions about life, themselves, or the path of humanity. These obscure entities will not touch those who are indifferent to any spiritual advancement and those who are neutral to the eternal duality of good and bad, of balance and imbalance, for fear of being different and true. Allowing no place for spiritual anxiety, living in an apparent peace, but mostly in an unconscious state of being, many people are half-dead and half-alive. It requires a tremendous courage to fight these entities, to start asking the true questions. This is why any real seeker must eventually become a spiritual warrior. There is a need to fight, but not for love of war—only for the love of spirit.

Usually, a lack of proper spiritual education and moral guidance in a society is a powerful factor that allows the dark shadows easy entrace into clouded human hearts. Uneducated about these dangers, many people are induced with strong compulsive desires, expressed as ego-grasping tendencies that can even lead them to kill. When you awaken to the possibilities of the spirit, the dark widespread influence makes you feel as if you are inadequate and misadapted in the society, to the point that you may think you are losing your mind. Many go crazy, or may feel as if they are. If they ever surrender in the struggle with the dark forces, they become lost in despair, insanity, depression, and profound neurosis. On the other hand, a lot of people have an understanding of their influence, and may resist their induced immorality, but will be unable to render these dark forces ineffectual. Due to this, common people usually have a pretty confused spirituality, expressed as a normal life of deep frustration.

Many people, from all professions, are so cynical that they have given up the dream of a perfect society, alleging that history always repeats itself, endlessly, in an inevitable and irrevocable loop, that humanity is bound to wars and suffering and that nothing can be done about it. These people have no true vision. There are apparent liberals who never take real sides, forever arguing that concepts of good and evil are just relative. This is a confused state of mind disguised as open-mindedness. The intellectual fairness of liberals affirms that there can be no absolute laws, even positive ones. These people may eventually become dangerous fools, with their double-talk and their lack of a true sense of morality. For such people, total common sense does not exist, and they may go far out of their way to rationalize and justify even the worst transgression. This is an emotional imbalance and immaturity often seen in the media.

Your original nature, your essence, is genuinely good, for you are primarily a child of the universe. You must, at every moment, affirm your forces of life with a knowledge of your death. True awareness can only happen in listening, touching, dreaming, and opening to the connection of your spirit.

Generally speaking, the problems that face every society are bound to the dialectic of violence and liberty. Wherever prosperity exists without a true sense of natural measure, we will find all forms of violence, luxury, and a lack of true ethical, respectful behavior.

Wherever there are a few individuals who control the economy, there will exist desperate people in the lower classes. Wherever there is ideology at the root of a society, there will be politics, and politics, *per se,* are tremendously limited, unless understood as a spiritual incentive. Ideologies claim that they have an answer to human suffering, but they do not. They only present a system of ideas disconnected from true reality and promise theories bound to disintegration. No ideology can make true changes or true revolutions. Only the heart of the people can do that. Only the internal courage and discernment of true warriors can accomplish this. Although an ideology may apparently mend things for a while, this only lasts until the rotten apple surfaces again from below, *from the Earth,* and the discontentment of people.

The most "politicized" people I have ever met are Indian people, anywhere on this great continent, because of their innate communal sense. Politics is, for us, primarily spiritual. For most natives, everything was and is already lost, so the only thing left is, and has been for centuries, a deep communal sense, a relation to our brothers and sisters. Therefore, our understanding of the Council ways is straightforward, clear, and without double talk, for we know it is important to always speak our truth. We also know it is stupid to try to coerce another to our point of view. If politics has any meaning, it can only be based on a spiritual perception of these principles.

Ideologies are not based on true principles, because real principles are primarily rooted in the observation of the great universal laws. When you carefully observe, you find the same common factors, the same needs for a better life among everyone, whether in Asia, Africa, or America. These common factors extend beyond political parties or religious institutions; in this sense the shamanic ways, teaching true knowledge, go beyond ideas. *Ideologies* must not be confused with *ideals.* Humanity does not need ideologies, but sound human principles grounded on the deepest ideals emerging from the dreaming of the *Ongwhe Onwhe.*

The return of the Earth consciousness goes beyond ideologies. It is just a simple fact. Today, a regional problem or war is no longer the problem of the local people. It becomes an international problem for all to see. To embrace the inward responsibility of the world's problems within our womb, our being, is the only way we will repel the dark forces obtruding on humanity preventing freedom and the circles of people. It is a fine line, however. This responsibility should not be an excuse to interfere in foreign affairs without first being invited.

The way in which politics are applied in the world's cultures denotes a definite competition of young souls striving for places of superficial power. This is why most people are definitively not interested in the politics of their country. The way in which politics are practiced (and always have been) creates an accepted form of violence and remains a way to divide the people into different classes or parties, through distinct ideologies bound to structures and cultural modes that alienate those within and without the society. There have been approximately 28,000 wars in the last 7,000 years, all over the planet—big wars and small wars. This reflects only that the war is inside each one of us. Look inside your own negativity. Everyone is fighting internally against someone else most of the time, fighting for their ego interest and unfulfilled desires or beliefs. The only worthwhile war, however, is the one that fights off the biggest enemies of humankind: fear, terror, ignorance, and the stupidity that creates war. It is the only useful war to the *Ongwhe Onwhe*.

To discern between ideologies and communal, spiritual principles, a true people must have a lucid, precise, and clear mind that sees and understands, without any distortion, the Medicine Wheel of Revelation. To be free of distortion, one must be vulnerable and open, willing to learn, empty of too much intellectual knowledge, without giving up one's particular essence and experiences of life.

Today's actual societies still admit and foment competition, ambition, greed, and violence, without true consideration for the people. Such societies disguise themselves under false morality and dishonest respectability. There is no real order in these societies. What we must understand about human suffering, the hopes and the despairs of entire populations is that we are *all* responsible for the global human chaos inflicted upon the very sacred being of and on which we live. Whatever you do and think at the office, in your living room, in your deepest thoughts, affects the rest of humanity for good or for bad. Whatever fear you hold is translated as a contracting energy that irremediably attracts the fears of other people in your surroundings and contributes to the massive national and international entity of fear. This is the main entrance for the dark forces.

When every mind on this planet is psychically free from fear, we will see together the door to a perfect society. A perfect society does not imply one that is free from problems. Perfect means rather that there exist the spiritual means for every individual and the community to confront and challenge what the society needs for its growth. If the universal principles of the Council ways work in a smaller case, such as in a native tribal council of various nations as the Iroquois League of Peace or in thousands of Zapatista communities of the Maya jungle, if the universal principles of the Council ways also work in the larger Council stars of our cosmos, there is no reason why they could not be applied at the intermediary level of this global humanity. We must strive conjointly for this aim.

We can talk on and on about the New Age, the new order to come, and the inspiring prophecies I have shared. This can easily become just another bit of intellectual information to add to our collection. In the meanwhile, there are still millions of people who have no chance to read books or to undertake spiritual education of any sort, and who will never know anything of the wisdom I have shared through these pages. These people (the "lower" classes), with their own intelligence and means, try to survive and live on an everyday basis. They are also bound to the great cosmic influences, however, just as everyone of us is, if not more so. It is there, with them, that we must keep our feet on a firm ground. We must keep our perceptions with those "below," those who are closer to the Earth, who do not have access to all this information that affects the majority of humans on this great orb. Even if we are at the edge of a new dawn, expressed as an emerging awakening of the spiritual awareness of humanity, we still have to take a look at the chaos and the garbage we produce in such massive quantitites. This is our shadow side as humans. We can see ourselves as an autonomous humanity, taking responsibility for all aspects of life, only if we incarnate here, in our human body and soul. For no one else will take care of the garbage and the needs of everyone.

It is easier to place the responsibility on the great incognito, disguised "other." To be responsible for our thoughts is the first step in taking action for a true, inward revolution. You must feel responsible for everything happening in the world, without morose and pathetic mortification, but in full consciousness. Your own struggling thought, confused being, and competitive behavior create a dissonant energy that is, indirectly or directly, responsible for the disharmony in the field of the Earth, for the wars and the misery of millions of people. When each individual becomes aware of this simple truth, all our educational systems will truly undergo a massive transformation. If it is possible for someone to be spiritual, it can only be in this sense.

The majority of people do not care for this, because they do not love their children—not really. They do not love them for the sake of loving them, for who they are, beings of light, children of the universe. If they truly loved them, they would be moving mountains, effecting revolutions, internal and external, to create a new, organized culture and a different education for the seven generations to come and stop the violence on this great Mother Earth.

Generally speaking, most rich people only want to watch over their own interests, while lower and upper middle classes are essentially lethargic and disinterested, preferring to content themselves with the comfort level they may have reached. Those "below" are too busy trying to find something for their children to eat on a daily basis, not knowing if tomorrow there will be enough. At least these last have a true "excuse." Even in the midst of their great struggle, however, the real claim against abuse will often come from the poorest and most severely abandoned ones, for these are the ones that have "nothing" to lose.

Those below are those oppressed, and oppressed people have always existed in every culture, every country, everywhere around the globe, right now. When I talk of the pain of the Red people or the struggle of the Maya Zapatistas, I am likewise seeing and embracing the larger cultural memory of persecution and despotism of the dark forces that many of you, independent of your origins, may still carry within, as the same and unique voice that speaks into our human blood.

A MAJOR CALL TO LIFE

This was the giant call of the Zapatistas on January 1, 1994, in Chiapas, Mexico—*Ya Basta*! This is enough!—the call of the Maya people, one of the most ancient native people in the Americas, a call to manifest to the universe that they love their children. It is enough for them to watch their children and their people die of hunger and curable diseases of all sorts, abandoned by the authorities, in the poorest corner of rich North America. They thought: if we will die anyway, let's die with honor, with integrity, as true warriors, as *Nichimal Viniketic*, as *Ongwhe Onwhe*. Let's die, but at least let's die fighting for our human dignity.

As we awoke that morning of the New Year in Chiapas, January 1, 1994, as we were taking our morning coffee, local radio stations were taken over by "revolutionaries," reading the First Declaration of Principles of the Lacandoon Jungle, the war declaration of the Zapatistas against their national government, a declaration of war against the worst enemies of humankind: fear, greed, corruption, and ambition. The bombing of the federal army then started and lasted for twelve days. We learned to get to know who these "revolutionaries" really were. It was clear to me that this was, at last, the opening of the third eye of America, predicted at the Maya site of Palenque, Chiapas, where the Harmonic Convergence was celebrated in 1987 to announce the powerful signal of the Maya return. In Chiapas, the Zapatistas had declared their "liberated territory" of America, consisting of thirty-six autonomous municipalities that will not be under Mexican jurisdiction. This holds great meaning for all America, for the Red people, especially at the third eye. This was also clearly the return of the dead of the Red people in this area of America.

The strategic response of those in power who "badly govern" (as Marcos says) has been to break the cease-fire treaty and the San Andres Agreements (signed in August 1995 between the Mexican government and the EZLN). These agreements were supposed to support a respect for indigenous autonomy and the rights of the Indian culture. The Zapatistas are asking for land, food, education, roofs, work, healthcare, independence, democracy, justice and peace, women's equality, protection of the environment, culture, and the right to information and security. But the smoking obsidian mirror in "power" has, on the other hand, acquired more and more expensive war machinery from other richer countries. From the Zapatistas' perspective, this is with the intention of eventually eliminating them under the justification of an anti-drug war and the disarmament of the paramilitaries. Instead of spending money to buy food and medicine, pencils and tools, for these sincere men and women, the government daily spends money on 60,000 military troops in Chiapas and they unfortunately accuse the Mayas of being the "transgressors." Accused of what? Of making a major call to life? Of dying? The presence of an increasingly effective body of soldiers in the area since 1994 has brought alcoholism, prostitution, robbery, and drugs where there were none, not to mention the contamination of rivers and the grains of local farmers. This situation has represented a truly gross abomination at this end of an era, when, supposedly, we are about to reach a new order.

The call of *Ya Basta!* was the only cry of revolt heard at the signing of the NAFTA agreements between the United States, Canada, and Mexico in January, 1994. In Mexico, the NAFTA treaties represent a total sale of the national sovereignty, creating more misery and allowing, once more, a few monopolists and capitalists to enrich themselves. Their call in addition was against the abolition of Article 27 of the Mexican Constitution (under Salinas' rule) that protected communal lands from privatization, an article instituted by the revolutionary leader Emiliano Zapata, after the Mexican revolution of 1910. This abolition meant the end of that revolution and the end of the rights of natives as stated in this Article. The land belongs to those who work it, not to those who own it. The abolition of this article marked a major change in the deepest roots of this country, the decision of a few monopolists made without the consultation or a referendum of the people.

Chiapas, a natural paradise on Earth, is one of the most resource-rich states in Mexico and in all America, because of its timber, coffee, hydroelectric power, corn, cocoa, and oil reserves. But the systematic plundering and exploitation of indigenous communities by the "dinosaurs" in power—the big ranchers and their repressive armed guards—has created the critical conditions against which the Zapatistas organized themselves.

The response of the Zapatistas, after 1994, to the dialogue occurring in the civil society, was for the 20,000 natives, men and women, to hang white scarves on their rifles (often only wooden sticks) and pledge to respect the cease fire, which they have not broken to this day. These men and women are ready to die as warriors for their ideals, *their dreams of a true world,* and they will not compromise their basic principles, in spite of the fruitless negotiations with the government that, until now, has turned a deaf ear on their pleas. But the misery through which this most ancient people is living has suddenly become an awakening of their spirits. It is their hope—the only one they have held so highly since the conquest.

In the requests of the Zapatistas, I recognize their true native spirits. Every move they have made (even their mistakes) has been sound and aligned with the highest understanding of their Red blood. In an attempt to reach the whole world, they convoked many intercontinental meetings, forums for humanity against neo-liberalism. These were attended by thousands of people from the international community. Various national indigenous meetings also took place after 1994. One, in particular, was blessed, on the day of its inauguration, by a tremendous sign: six consecutive, full, and magnificent *rainbows* appeared, one after the other, all morning long.

We were driving northwest in the state that morning with some native companions and we all thought it was definitively a great sign. The rainbows talked to me of the return of the rainbow warriors from the East. We were a five-hour drive from where the convention was being held. Marcos, in his inauguration speech, also referred to the six rainbows they had seen much further south that morning. This was amazing to me, to know that such rainbows could be seen such a great distance apart. The seventh, and most important, rainbow, in his words, was this very native convention, this Red gathering of indigenous cultures.

The native Zapatistas have asserted very strongly they are not interested in becoming a political party, or a coalition of organizations. Nor are they seeking political power. They are far more than a local guerrilla group, however. They are a people who have taken arms to be heard because the "dinosaurs" of the world are so hearing-impaired that they have created the extreme situation and misery in which these Mayas live.

They have organized in such a way as to follow a perfect model of clear and direct democracy that allows every one of their people to have a voice, through a system of consensus of all members of these communities and council representatives. This is, in all ways, similar to the Iroquois League of Peace. The Zapatistas' internal laws must be submitted for approval by the majority. Every action they execute depends on a decision of the people, as in the old form of native councils and most important, of course, the voice of women.

Their intention to open a dialogue with the civil society (national and international) is extremely important. Not only does it make the international community their principal witness in preventing a possible genocide, but it also sounds a major call at all levels of society to fight alongside them, wherever and whoever we are, against all the dark oppressing forces. This is the uniqueness of this revolution. It is not only a peasant revolution for justice and land within a country. It is an invitation to a revolution for true changes everywhere, for spiritual and moral changes, for the sake of our children, and the future of our human world. The call of Ya Basta! is not only their clamor, but is a deep call to all of us to answer in our lives. It is a call to a revolution for human dignity, whether poor, middle-class, or rich, everywhere we are, to fight against the dark smoking mirror, wherever it is. It is beyond the fight of social class. It is to retaliate with human decency and it is given to anyone to feel how the Maya return unfolds within each one of us. This call, from one of the humblest and gentlest people on the planet, must not be forgotten, we must not forget and cease to seek the awakening of spiritual humanity.

> *Zapatismo is not a new political ideology or re-fried old ideologies. Zapatismo is not, it does not exist. It serves, only in the way bridges serve, to cross from one side to the other. As such, in Zapatismo everyone fits, all who want to cross from one side to the other. Each one has one or the other side. There are no recipes, lines, tactics, laws, regulations or universal slogans. There is only one desire: to construct a better world, that is, a new one.*[2]

In 1994, seven years after the Harmonic Convergence, a first signal and call arose that, in these great times, this war was not as others, not a war for particular interests, or a war fomented by divisions of ancient clans, or a war over religious differences, but a war by and from the true humans, for the love of all our children, our mothers, and for the hope of all humanity. This war concerns us all, this fight is the fight of all of us. If there is hope that one day we can become true *Ongwhe*

---

[2] Marcos, "Intercontinental Meeting for Humanity and Against Neo-Liberalism," *Tiempo* (San Cristobal de Las Casas, Chiapas, Mexico), June 9, 1996.

Onwhe, it is time for our true souls to break free and crack their shell (the zero shell), to open to light. All must join our prayers so the return of the plumed consciousness is not aborted.

For many natives, from the great cold north of Canada to the southern pampa of Chile, Marcos is not only the spokesperson for the Maya Zapatistas, but also for the Red cause against the same enemy—those who desecrate the Red Lodge on this very continent. When I read the Zapatista communiqués, the words of Marcos that stay with me are the words of the reality of the Maya children and of the Indians in the jungle. It was as if I had read of my own ancestors from my beloved Canada, of their suffering, their stories, their dreams, and the expression of their spirits.

> *The strong banner of the Maya will shine in the hands of all those*
> *who raise their spirits to the blue sky and claim their call to*
> *freedom.*
> *It will extend like a banner of seven colors which burns and salutes*
> *the hope of those who long waited.*
> *It will be the victory of those who had faith and fought with courage*
> *and purity.*
> *Land of the Maya, you will return one day*
> *but it will not be with false pride and arrogance that you will rise*
> *above the blood.*
> *Long has been the night of the Indian, but now from the East and*
> *the West,*
> *from the South to the North, the land is filled with signs and*
> *messages of coming light shining in the darkness.*[3]

UNBURYING THE RED SPIRIT

In the year that I awakened to another reality of myself, on a morning in 1985, in Canada, another me, another self, now a true self, knew as I read the potent sign on my road that I had to go to Mexico. As I was traveling in Mexico that fall, something was pulling me further and further south, until I stopped at the Mexican border with

---

[3] Inspired by Antonio Mediz Bolio, *Tierra del Faisan y del venado* (Merida, Yucatan, Mexico: Produccion Editorial Dante, S. A., 1989), pp. 150-152.

Guatemala. I could not go further south, so I stayed and began building a life here. Being the independent woman that I am, for many years, I resisted being here, in one of the most macho and corrupt countries of the world at all levels of life. I often felt lonely in the midst of a culture where women are resigned and distrusted, where many men do not understand women, and where local natives are not always aware that they are Indians themselves, part of the great Red tree (although now this is rapidly changing). It was certainly not easy. But something in the soil of Chiapas was aligning with something about my own essence that strongly made me stay, which since 1994 has become obvious. I remember in the first years in Chiapas, in the mid 1980s, I often caught myself saying to the native people with whom I worked that soon, in this most peaceful paradise, there was going to be a revolution, something big and profound. That in Chiapas, with the conditions of life and the constantly rising inflation strangling everyone, it was quite unavoidable. Many really didn't take my words seriously and most looked at me without reaction. People were so disillusioned and so used to the difficult conditions of life that they could not understand there was actually a need for a change, or that it was even conceivable that something could ever change. But I could hear the Earth talking to me.

In January 1994, nine years later, I had almost forgotten about "my" predicted revolution, when federal bombs started falling all around, creating without and within us, and for the whole world, a major commotion. I was then nine months pregnant, about to give birth—not without reason—to quite a little warrioress. Not until I started building a ceremonial medicine center in the early months of 1995, in Chiapas, could I clearly find a symbol for the returning of the Red consciousness from this very Earth, for the true meaning of this revolution. As we start digging the foundation of the octagonal building of my medicine center, the mason (and apprentice) said that the soil was very loose exactly under the west wall. He suggested we move the center a number of feet, for it did not seem to be a good place. I asked him, however, to continue digging. Obviously, there was a hole below. We made jokes, thinking we might find gold, because it was a custom of the rich to bury their jars of gold during the Mexican revolution at the beginning of the century. A few feet deeper, he dug out a broken piece of what felt to us like clay. After cleaning it, we found it was a piece of bone. We were digging up a grave. We then stopped, and I asked myself, in reverence, if we should continue to dig.

But it was clear. We felt so strongly pulled. It was the west wall, after all, the west passage being the death passage–quite an unequivocal sign. It was also clear that this spiritual center was right where it should be. With our native council members, and with the utmost respect and care, we dug for two long weeks, as "real" archeologists. We found seven extremely old skeletons, all piled up in disarray, bones eaten away. It was obvious the bones were not those of conquistadors, who would have received a more dignified burial. They were natives (men, women, and children) who had been killed and surely tortured in the early years of the conquest, almost 450 years ago, then dumped in this large hole with no belongings but their wounded bodies.

It was also clear to us all that the dead as well as the living Maya people were calling for justice. The bones of their ancestors were returning, crying *Ya Basta!*, rising up from their graves, asking for a dignified burial, bringing to light their story of injustice, to the Red Sun and new wind of that late afternoon just before dusk. During these two intense weeks, a significant number of vultures were soaring very low over the center. As the spirit animals of warriorship, new purification, and freedom for the ancient pre-Columbian people, they were watching the event.

The dead of the Red people are truly rising. After offering these bones a decent and sacred ceremony, we proceeded to construct the center. On the very last day of work, as we were completing the roof, a gathering of over 100 hawks appeared, circling from East to West and then to the East again, over the round center and our crystal wheel. We had never seen such a large *rainbow convention* of hawks together. It was Sunday, Easter day, the sign of another resurrection.

Where there exists no beginning, there is no end, but there is only another beginning . . . always . . .

Now it is time to wake up. . . . The storm is here. From the clash of these two winds, the storm will be born, its time has arrived, the hearth of history is aroused. Now the wind from above rules, but the wind from below is coming, the storm is arising. . . . It will be. . . . The prophecy is here. . . . When the storm calms, when rain and fire again leave the Earth in peace, the world will no longer be the world but something better.[4]

---

[4] Marcos, *Chiapas: The Southeast in Two Winds, A Storm and A Prophecy* (Mexico D. F.: Colección Problemas de Mexico, 1994), p. 66.

BIBLIOGRAPHY

Alvarez Quinones, Francisco. *Nichimal Vinik, el Hombre Florecido.* Chiapas: Publicacion Bilingüe de la Direccion de Fortalecimiento, 1985.

Argüelles, José. *The Mayan Factor: Path Beyond Technology.* Santa Fe, New Mexico: Bear & Co., 1987.

Basic Call to Consciousness, Akwesasne Notes. Summertown Tennesse: Book Publishing Company, 1978.

Beauvoir, Simone de. *Second Sex.* New York: Knopf, 1993.

Beck V. Peggy, and Anna L. Walters. *The Sacred: Ways of Knowledge, Sources of Life.* Tsaile (Navajo Nation), Arizona: Navajo Coomunity College, 1977.

Bruchac, Joseph. *The Native American Sweat Lodge.* Freedom, California: The Crossing Press, 1993.

Carey, Ken. *Return of the Bird Tribes.* San Francisco: HarperSanFrancisco, 1988.

Chiapas, vols. 1-2-3. Mexico: Instituto de Investigaciones Economicas. Ediciones Era, 1995.

Coe, Michael. D. *The Maya.* New York: Thames and Hudson Inc., 1987.

DeLoria, Vine, Jr. *We Talk, You Listen: New Tribes, New Turf.* New York: MacMillan, 1970.

_____. *American Indians, American Justice.* Austin: University of Texas Press, 1983.

Diaz Bolio, Jose. *The Rattlesnake School.* Merida, Yucatan: Area Maya.

EZLN: Documentos y comunicados, vols. 1, 2, 3. Mexico: Coleccion Problemas de Mexico, Ediciones Era, 1994.

Garza, Mercedes de la. *Libro de Chilam Balam de Chumayel.* Mexico City, Mexico: Secretaria de Educacion Publica, 1985.

Hancock, Graham. *Fingerprints of the Gods.* New York: Crown Trade Paperbacks, 1995.

Highwater, Jamake. *Ritual of the Wind.* New York: Alfred Van Der Marck Edtions, 1984.

Mander, Jerry. *In the Absence of the Sacred: The Failure of Technology and the Survival of Indian Nations.* San Francisco: Sierra Club Books, 1991.

McLuhan, T.C. *Touch the Earth: A Self-Portrait of Indian Existence.* New York: Promontory Press, 1971.

Mediz Bolio, Antonio. *La Tierra del Faisan y del venado.* Merida, Yucatan, Mexico: Produccion Editorial Dante, S.A., 1989.

Momaday, N. Scott. *With Eagle Glance.* New York: Museum of the American Indian, 1982.

Moscoso Patrana, Prudencio. *Las Cabezas Rodantes del Mal: Brujeria y Nahualismo en los Altos de Chiapas.* Mexico City,: Miguel Angel Porrua Grupo Editorial, 1990.

Popol Vuh. *The Mayan Book of Council.* Mexico City, Mexico: Fondo de Cultura Economica, 1952.

Storm, Hyemeyohsts. *Lightningbolt.* New York: One World Book, Ballantine Books, 1994.

Thompson, J. Eric. *Historia y Religion de los Mayas.* Mexico City, Mexico: Siglo Veintiuno, America Nuestra, 1975.

INDEX

OHKY SIMINE FOREST was born in Quebec, Canada to Mohawk and French parents. When she was a small baby, a fireball fell on their house, manifesting as a great sign to the medicine people who eventually taught her that she was to be initiated to the way of shaman. Forest pursued her spiritual journey by traveling to Europe and Asia where she intensively studied with Mongolian shamans. In 1984, she returned to the Mohawk people in Canada, and was admitted into the Wolf Clan at the traditional Long House of Kahnawake, part of the  League of Peace of the Iroquois Nations. In 1986, following the signs of her path, she traveled to Chiapas in southern Mexico, where she met her Maya companion and life partner, who initiated her into the world of the Maya shaman and medicine healer. Together they founded a non-profit organization aimed at helping indigenous Maya communities of Chiapas. In 1995, Ohky created the first Medicine Center in this part of the world. The center offers spiritual retreats, sweat lodges, medicine wheel ceremonies, vision quests, and earth burial healings. Ohky makes her home in Chiapas, and visits the United States several times a year, giving retreat seminars and conferences. Write for her schedule.